TABLE OF CONTENTS

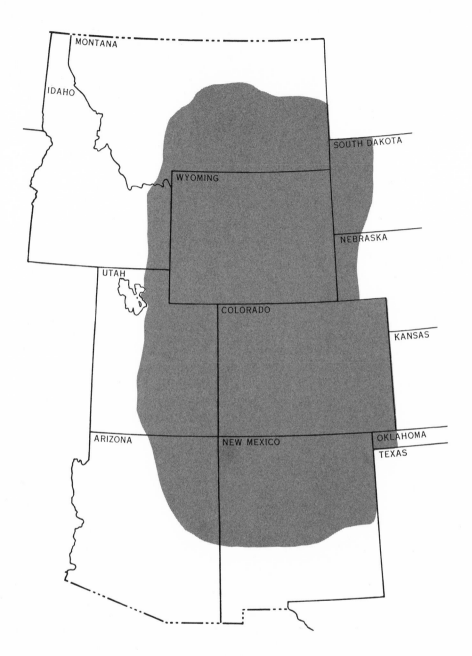

MAP OF ROCKY MOUNTAIN REGION

Chapter I: INTRODUCTION

THE STUDY of edible native plants has been of interest and concern to many people in the past; in fact such knowledge has sometimes been a matter of survival itself. Recently there has been a revival of this interest and a number of books and articles have appeared dealing with edible plants, usually treating those of a limited area. Since none of these publications deal particularly with the Rocky Mountain area, we have decided to record the result of a lifelong interest in the matter. This book covers the plants growing in an area bounded on the east by western Nebraska and Kansas, on the west by central Utah, and stretches south to central New Mexico, north to the Black Hills of South Dakota and central Montana (see the map). We have tried to write for botanists and nonbotanists alike. The plant descriptions are in nontechnical language, but we have tried to make them strictly accurate. The botanical names are given for those who may want them but may be ignored by the nonbotanists. These scientific names are the ones used in the various treatments covering the Rocky Mountain flora, especially Harrington's *Manual of the Plants of Colorado* (109). We have listed all the common names for each species that we have heard used in this area, but the reader may know the plant by one that we have never encountered. There is no law in the use of such names as we find in the case of botanical ones. This is discussed at some length in Chapter III of Harrington's *How to Identify Plants* (110). It follows that your own common names are just as "legal" as the ones used here.

The illustrations include not only a sketch of the mature plant in flower or fruit but also enlargements of those special parts that botanists consider to be diagnostic. This will allow the reader to become acquainted with the plant in the only stage when it can be identified with real accuracy, that is in flower and fruit.

Among the individuals or groups of people we hope will find this book of special interest will probably be the following:

1. Outdoor youth groups, such as Boy Scouts, Girl Scouts, etc.
2. Garden clubs.
3. Nature study groups.
4. Campers and hiking organizations.
5. Isolated families and groups located far away from food markets.
6. Anyone who must pack along all or part of their food rations.
7. Those interested in saving on the food budget.
8. Anyone who may be forced into periods of wilderness survival.
9. Those interested in trying new taste sensations.
10. In fact, anyone with an established or a potential hobby on the subject of edible native plants.

The information contained in this book was assembled in several different ways:

1. Actual personal experiments extending over a period of many years.
2. Information from numerous collaborators of the project. Among these investigators were Professor Y. Matsumura, Dr. N. Oshima, Dr. Mary Meserve, Dr. John Douglass, Margaret Douglass, Ben Gardner, Owen Smith, Angello Cuzetto, William Sears, Marilyn Colyer, Jack May, and Charles Bagdonas. All of whom remained in good health throughout the period of the experiment!
3. Specific information contributed by many interested people, this help acknowledged throughout the text in the appropriate place.
4. Information on the subject of useful wild plants found in various books and articles. Our own list of those consulted now runs well over 600 items; however, only a part of these are given in the bibliography at the end of this book. When we formally started this project in 1960, our colleague, Professor Claire Norton, and in addition Dr. Edward Castetter, who was formerly at the University of New Mexico, very generously turned over to us their extensive bibliographies on useful native plants. Among these items were many on the subject of ethnobotany, which deals with the use of plants by the Indians of the region. This

aspect of the matter is important in a study of this kind since the Indians in the past had learned to use many species of plants, particularly in times of extreme food shortage. Because of the change in lifeways of the modern Indians, much of this detailed knowledge may well be lost entirely unless someone puts it on record. The same thing can be said for the information on edible native plants once known to the white pioneers of the Rocky Mountain area. Some of this knowledge has been passed on to their descendants; much of it either has been or will be forgotten.

Some native plants are palatable and nutritious; unfortunately, others are bad tasting or actually poisonous. It follows that those people who wish to eat such food should know the species involved, just as they recognize the ones in their gardens. After all, when you go out to gather a mess of lettuce, you don't mistake it for ragweed that may be growing nearby. If you do you are certainly in for a surprisingly new taste sensation. The very best way to learn plants is to develop the ability to identify them in the technical floras and manuals covering the region. This skill is difficult to acquire, and few of us have the opportunity, the time, or the energy to master it. If you want to dine on native plants and do not wish to formally develop the technique of keying them out, then we suggest the following:

1. Fix in mind the appearance of some edible plant you already know (like *Typha*—ordinary cattail). Watch it throughout the growing season, from the time it pushes its shoots above the ground until it develops flowers and fruits. You may want to utilize it at various stages of its growth, even in winter, so you must be able to recognize it at any time. About 2000 years ago a famous herbalist, Dioscorides (Gunther, 104), pointed this out by reminding us: "Now it behooves anyone who desires to be a skillful herbalist, to be present when the plants first shoot out of the earth, when they are fully grown, and when they begin to fade." This initial acquaintance can be gained by having an edible plant pointed out to you by some knowledgeable friend. Also, you can often identify it yourself by comparing it carefully with a drawing, photograph, or description, such as one of those given in this book. When you have learned one plant in all its growth phases, you are ready to start in on others. Before long, you will have built up

quite a list of plants you know are good to eat. In any case, our advice is to go easy on each new trial and consume a small to moderate amount at first. It is possible that you may have actually mis-identified the plant and trustfully tackled a harmful one. Then again, perhaps you may have some special allergic reaction to some species that is harmless to most people. But once you are sure the plant is healthful for you, then you may proceed without fear. There is seldom a lack of such material in nature.

2. Learn the common poisonous plants of the area, particularly those that are likely to be mistaken for edible ones. For example, if you want to eat the bulbs of wild onion *(Allium)*, then you should know not only exactly what these onions look like but you should also be able to recognize death camas *(Zygadenus)*, which also bears bulbs and is apt to grow nearby. Stockmen, government agencies, county agricultural agents, etc., can help you learn these poisonous plants. You can also get some assistance from various books and state bulletins, which list and often provide drawings of such species. Our own common poisonous plants are illustrated and described in Chapter II of this treatment, and citations are made there to local books and bulletins.

When you wish to test out a likely looking edible species, in times of emergency for example, then the following rules are often given:

1. Place a small portion of the raw plant part in your mouth; chew, but do not swallow. Then remove it and wait for unfavorable reactions such as a burning, stinging or numbing sensation.

2. If all is well, chew up and swallow a small piece of the raw plant. Wait for at least an hour before you proceed.

3. Then cook some of the plant and swallow a small portion. If serious ill effects develop, induce vomiting.

4. Wait several hours, then eat a small to moderate amount of the raw or cooked portion. Do this several times over an interval of several hours.

5. If all goes well up to this point, it is safe to eat this new food in reasonable quantities.

6. If you have a limited amount of familiar food along, we suggest that you gradually work in the new food with the old. In any event, we advise that you do not gorge yourself on the un-

familiar food, at least for a time. Surely it is not the time to risk becoming physically sick when you are under survival conditions.

If the above rules are followed, then there is no reason for anyone to endure extreme hunger in any place in the Rocky Mountain area, even in the winter time. The inner bark of many trees can be peeled off and eaten either raw or cooked (AF Manual, 2; Stout 224). The algae and aquatic plants of rivers, ponds, and lakes can also be used to sustain life (Herter 120). Even the silt or mud at the bottom of such ponds and lakes can be cooked into a souplike mixture. Herter (120) claimed that Robert Beauchamp, Director of the East African Fisheries Research Organization, once fed himself and his family for a time on the mud from the bottom of Lake Victoria. This all seems a bit extreme; certainly more palatable sounding food is usually available if one knows where to look for it. In any event a number of experienced outdoor people have stated flatly, "If you starve to death in the wilderness, it is because you are just plain tired of living." This is probably an overstatement for the sake of emphasis, but it is true that the food is there, and it is your own fault if you don't utilize it.

The widespread practice that individuals or agencies have of spraying plants with various insecticides or weedicides (herbicides) has created a minor problem for anyone wishing to utilize edible native plants. Much of these chemical deposits can be removed by washing the plant parts thoroughly, and even those that are actually absorbed into the plant body are usually very low in toxicity in the amounts ordinarily present. However, we would not care to eat these sprayed plants ourselves, and advise you to secure your edible plant material well away from these treated areas. Such sprayed patches are usually in or around fields of cultivated crop plants, or along roadsides.

We wish to acknowledge the financial support of the United States Department of Health, Education and Welfare during the period from 1960 to 1963, support that allowed us to travel over the Rocky Mountain region in order to collect and try out many of the plants mentioned in this book. We now have records of many more food plants than are mentioned here; it is possible we have left out one of your favorite ones. We have had to be rather arbitrary in our selection of the ones to be included in order to keep the book to a practical size. We welcome any additional information you may be willing to contribute and will incorporate it, if possible, in some future edition.

No man could possibly write a firsthand treatment on edible native plants without a sympathetic, understanding and courageous wife. To Mrs. Edith J. Harrington must be given a large part of the credit for any merit contained in this book.

GENERAL KEY TO ABBREVIATIONS OF DRAWINGS

A—Annulus of Fungus
Ab—Abnormal Structure
Ac—*Allium cernuum*
Ag—*Allium geyeri*
Au—Auricle of Leaf
Aw—Awn
B—Bulb (or bulblike corm)
Bd—Bud
BL—Basal Leaf
BP—Base of Petiole of Leaf
Br—Bract
C—Calyx of Flower
Ca—"About"
CS—Cross-section
CFr—Cross-section Fruit
Cl—*Claytonia lanceolata*
Cm—*Claytonia megarrhiza*
Cg—*Calochortus gunnisonii*
Cn—*Calochortus nuttallii*
E—Enlarged Portion
E.S.—Earth Surface
F—Flower
FC—Fruit Cluster
Fe—Fertile Plant
FH—Fruit Head
Fr—Fruit
FrC—Fruit Cluster
Fs—Flower Stalk
FSp—Fruit Spike
G—Gill of Fungus
H—Habit of Plant
In—Inflorescence
K—Keel of Legume Flower
L—Leaf
Lb—Leaf Blade
Li—Ligule of Leaf
Ls—Leaf Sheath
LT—Leaf Tip

Nb—New Bud
O—Ovary of Flower
P—Perianth Part
Pa—Petal of Flower
Pb—*Polygonum bistortoides*
Pd—Petals-Dissected
Pe—Petiole of Leaf
Pi—Pistil of Flower
Ps—Perianth segment with Stamen
Pv—*Polygonum viviparum*
R—Root
Rh—Rhizome
RL—Reduced Leaf
Rs—Rootstock
S—Seed
Sa—Stigma of Flower Pistil
Sd—Standard of Legume Flower
SL—Submerged Leaf
Sn—Stamen of Flower
So—Sorus of Fern Leaf
Sp—Spike
Spl—Spikelet
Spp—Sporophore (bearing spores)
Sr—Sterile Plant
St—Stipule at base of Leaf
T—Tuber
Te—Tendril
Tr—Taproot
UL—Upper Leaf
V—Volva Cup of Fungus
W—Wing of Legume Flower
X—Times enlarged (x2 = twice
  natural size on original drawing)
YL—Young Leaf
♀ —Female or Pistillate
♂ —Male or Staminate
☿ —Hermaphroditic (Perfect or
  Bisexual Flowers)

Chapter II: POISONOUS PLANTS

EVER SINCE primitive man first tried eating the plants growing about him, he has been confronted with the bitter realization that while most of them are harmless, many of them are poisonous to some degree, and cause him discomfort, sickness, or even death. We like to think that nature is kind and benevolent, and usually it is. However, we know that sometimes it can be exceedingly cruel. In every pond, in every river, in every woodland, and on every mountain or prairie, there waits for us pillage, starvation, and death. There is a sad reality. As far as eating native plants is concerned, all nature asks of us, in order to escape her ill effects, is a certain amount of "knowledge." If you know the common poisonous species as you would recognize an acquaintance on the street, then you are as safe eating these native plants as if you were dining at home or in a modern restaurant. This chapter discusses and illustrates only the very common harmful ones of this area. Many states put out illustrated bulletins on species toxic to livestock; these are cited throughout this chapter. The most complete and up-to-date general treatment on this particular subject is the one by Kingsbury (141). A few general observations on poisonous plants are given below in the hope that they may prove to be of value to you:

1. There is no general test for poisonous plants, such as the presence or absence of milky juice. Many plants with this milky juice are edible (see *Taraxacum officinale,* the dandelion), and some of the most poisonous species lack it altogether.

2. The fact that wild animals eat the plant is no guarantee that it will not be poisonous to you. For example, just because birds often eat the berries and seeds of poison ivy is no indication that you can do the same with impunity.

3. Livestock usually do avoid poisonous plants if any others are available. However, when they are hungry for green foliage, as

when they have been closely confined for several days, or in the spring of the year, they often graze on poisonous plants they would ordinarily avoid.

4. Some plants produce their poisonous substances when wilted, such as the twigs of chokecherries.

5. The poisonous property may be concentrated or even confined to one part of the plant body.

6. In some cases cooking seems to destroy the poisonous substances, in whole or in part, but this is not a general rule.

7. Do not use any wild plant resembling parsley or wild carrot unless you are absolutely sure of your species.

8. Do not use white- or red-colored berries without being absolutely sure of the plant.

9. Eat blue or black berries but with caution; even here it is best to know the species tried.

10. Better avoid all fungi (mushrooms and toadstools) unless you know them to be safe.

11. Do not eat any plant from soils known to contain selenium, or that support plants known to be "indicators" of selenium (see *Astragalus bisulcatus*—Two-groove Milkvetch).

12. Be sure you know the plant in its very young stages, if this is the time it is used.

13. Never suppose a plant to be edible just because it bears some resemblance to a well-known edible species.

14. Always be cautious in trying out a new plant even though you are absolutely sure of its identity. Remember that the poisonous effects can be cumulative.

15. Read over the tests for edibility as given in Chapter I.

The best advice is to know and avoid the common poisonous plants of your locality.

Although we advise treating poisonous plants with the respect they deserve, we do not suggest that fear of them should prevent you from using any wild plant as food. With proper and reasonable precautions on your part they will not harm you. Where poisonous plants are concerned being reasonably certain isn't enough: be positive!

Plants more or less poisonous but illustrated or described under another chapter.

Allium cernuum IX.   *Pteridium aquilinum* IV.
Asclepias speciosa IV.   *Quercus* spp. VIII.
Berberis repens VII.   *Solanum nigrum* VII.
Caltha leptosepala III.   *Yucca glauca* VIII.
Equisetum arvense IV.

Aconitum columbianum (A. insigne, A. bakeri) MONKSHOOD, COLUMBIA MONKSHOOD, WESTERN MONKSHOOD

Description:
Herbaceous perennial plants about 2 to 5 feet tall; leaves parted with radiating lobes (palmately), the whole leaf about 2 to 6 inches wide; flowers usually blue, but not uncommonly pale blue to white, each very irregular with a forward projecting curved hood, this ½ to ¾ inch long.

Found in moist meadows and moist open woods up to timberline, from Montana to British Columbia in Canada, south to New Mexico, Arizona, and California. Present throughout our range.

Effects:
This plant is virulently poisonous to livestock and has occasionally caused death to human beings. It appears to be dangerous both before and after flowering, so it could well be hazardous when gathered as greens in the young stages. The roots might also be mistaken for certain edible fleshy roots. When chewed raw the plant parts may provoke a tingling sensation in the mouth (Kingsbury, 141). Fortunately, this plant causes little loss of livestock, possibly because it lacks palatability. It is so characteristic in appearance that it should be easy for human beings to give it the avoidance it deserves.

MONKSHOOD *(Aconitum columbianum)*

Related Species:
All the species of monkshood *(Aconitum)* should be avoided.

References (to numbers in the bibliography):
2, 5, 74, 138, 141, 167, 230.

Actaea arguta (A. rubra, A. eburnea, A. viridiflora) BANEBERRY, WESTERN BANEBERRY

Description:
Plants with rather stout stems about 1 to 3 feet tall; the leaves are few and much divided in "spray" fashion; flowers at first in a short cluster but this finally rather elongated, not very colorful or conspicuous; berries conspicuous, about ¼ to ⅜ inch long, beautifully red or white.

This species is found from South Dakota to Alberta and south to New Mexico and California. Consequently it can be expected in moist rich woods anywhere in the Rocky Mountains up to near timberline.

Effects:
Few of our berries are poisonous, but this is certainly an outstanding exception. The plant has caused illness and even death to people eating the rootstocks or the fruits. Children sometimes are attracted to the lovely red or white berries. A curious experimenter once ate 6 of these berries and became ill, with increased pulse rate, a feeling of dizziness and a burning sensation (Bacon, 11). It is too bad that these lovely berries should have to be poisonous. Perhaps a good rule would be to learn how to recognize the baneberry and avoid it. Then one could proceed, with due caution, to eat any other attractive fleshy berry or fruit of the area, providing it had a desirable taste.

Related Species:
Any of the various kinds of baneberries should be avoided. Botanists do not always agree on the correct names of the various kinds and it is possible that the one in the eastern United States is the same as ours.

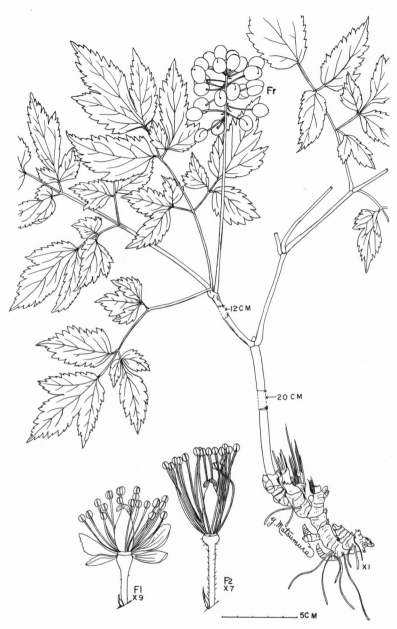

BANEBERRY *(Actaea arguta)*

References (to numbers in the bibliography):
2, 5, 40, 58, 84, 119, 167, 181, 230.

Amanita muscaria
Amanita, Fly Agaric, Deathcup

Because of their relatively low food value and the possibility of getting a poisonous species, we do not recommend eating fungi either as an emergency ration or as a casual hobby. However, the two species described below are the most poisonous ones and the main ones to be avoided. Eating fungi is a fascinating hobby but not one to be entered into lightly.

Description:

This fungi produces the familiar mushroom or toadstool-like structure, consisting of a central stalk and an umbrella-like terminal portion bearing radiating gills below, these bearing the small reproductive spores. The stalk bears a cup (volva) at the base and a veil (annulus) up the stem a way, marking the spot where the once-curled-in edges of the top broke away as it opens out. The general color is white but the top is often yellow but varies to red, with the surface flecked with white scales or spots. The gills are white in color, and are free from the extreme upper part of the stalk.

A related species, *A. phalloides,* sometimes called "Death Angel," has the same general structure, but the top is pale yellow to pure white. It is considered to be even more dangerous than *A. muscaria.*

Effects:

Both these fungi grow in wooded, shaded areas but may appear at the edges of clearings and might be mistaken by the novice for several commonly used edible species. It is stated that one or two of these "umbrellas" can cause death, even if mixed with harmless fungi (Kingsbury, 141).

The hobby of gathering fungi for food is both dangerous and interesting. The suggestions we would make would be:

1. Learn the poisonous species, not only by their general appearance but by their actual diagnostic characters. For example, any species of *Amanita* has the following characters:

    a. Presence of a basal cup (volva).

    b. Presence of a veil (annulus) on the stem.

    c. White colored gills and spores.

    d. Gills free from the upper part of the stem.

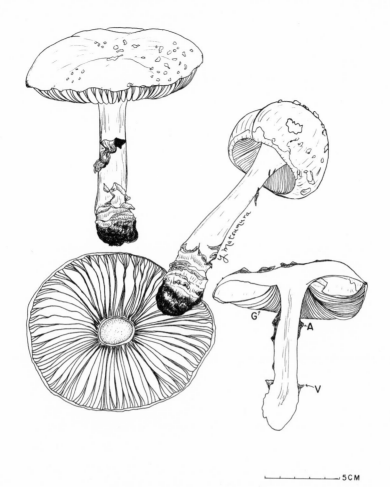

AMANITA *(Amanita muscaria)*

 — 5CM

There are other poisonous kinds of fungi but the Amanitas are the worst. If you avoid all fungi with the above four characteristics, there is a reasonably good chance you won't die from eating fungi!

2. Learn edible species one by one, by general appearance and by their diagnostic characters. Stick to these and if you must experiment with a new one, try only a small piece at first, then a larger one after an interval of an hour or two, etc. Unless you are willing to do all this, you had better leave the fungi alone.

References (to numbers in the bibliography):
   5, 58, 79, 141, 230, 240.

Apocynum cannabinum
DOGBANE, INDIAN HEMP, HEMP DOGBANE

Description:

Plants with milky rubbery juice when cut or broken; stems 1 to 3 feet tall, erect, somewhat branched; leaves opposite on the stems, 1 to 4 inches long, egg-to-lance-shaped, margins smooth; flowers in flattish or rounded clusters, each flower white in color, about ⅛ to ¼ inch long; pods becoming 5 to 9 inches long, bearing long-hairy seeds resembling those of milkweed.

This dogbane is found throughout the United States and the Rocky Mountain area usually below 8000-feet elevation. It is common along roadsides and in fields, and like all weeds may be abundant in certain spots.

Effects:

All the dogbanes are poisonous and have sometimes caused serious losses to livestock. Apparently the sticky, milky juice helps to render them unpalatable, since animals seldom eat the plants fresh, although they do sometimes consume them dry in hay. However, deaths to livestock from eating dogbane are rare. It is included here largely because it resembles, in some degree, the broad-leaved milkweed which is one of our favorite edible plants (see *Asclepias speciosa*). The leaves of the milkweed are wider, the stems less inclined to branch and the young shoots are usually more tender than those of the dogbane. Certainly dogbane should never be eaten, although Sweet (227) did mention that the seeds can be ground into a meal to make fried cakes. The milky juice hardens into a rubbery substance that has actually been used as chewing gum. Jaeger (132) and Anderson (5) pointed out that the stems produce silky fibers in the late season. The stems can be soaked in water for a time, which separates the outer bark and this can be rubbed off and the silky fibers rolled into a twine. This cord could be used in the wilderness to make snares or fish line in an emergency.

Related Species:

We have several kinds of dogbane in our area, but they all resemble the one illustrated. The leaves are all opposite and

Pi_{X20} F_{X15} S_{X3} Fr

.5CM

Dogbane *(Apocynum cannabinum)*

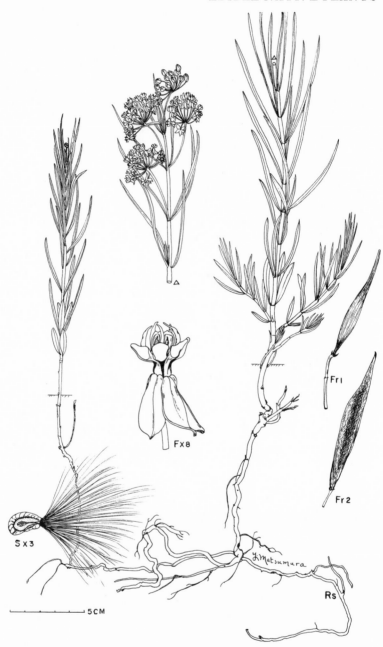

POISON MILKWEED *(Asclepias subverticillata)*

smooth-margined, the flowers are rather small and in clusters, but may be pink-rose instead of white in color. All of them should be avoided as food.

References (to numbers in the bibliography for all species): 5, 14, 58, 59, 74, 79, 84, 132, 138, 141, 167, 219, 227.

Asclepias subverticillata (A. galioides)
Poison Milkweed, Whorled Milkweed, Silkweed

Description:

Plants growing in patches from creeping rootstocks; stems 6 inches to 3⅓ feet tall; leaves usually arising 3 or more from one general place on the stem (whorled), narrow like a grass blade; flowers white to cream-colored, up to about ¼ inch long; pods 2 to 4 inches long.

The plant grows from Nebraska and Texas west to Idaho and Arizona, usually on plains or valleys. It is present all over the Rocky Mountain area, especially in the western part. It seldom grows above 8000 feet in the mountains and usually is found at lower elevations.

Effects:

This narrow-leaved milkweed has caused serious losses to livestock, especially to sheep. Fortunately, animals do not ordinarily like the taste of the plant and deaths usually occur in times of severe food shortages. This milkweed should be given a wide berth and we are lucky that it does not closely resemble the common edible species. Stevens (219) suggested that the poisonous principle is destroyed by boiling and claimed that the Indians used the plant for greens. Trying this has never appealed to us. The flower buds were reported to have been eaten by Indian children (Castetter, 43; Stevenson, 220).

Related Species:

A similar-looking, narrow-leaved milkweed comes into the eastern part of the Rocky Mountain area. It is *A. verticillata* and of course it should be avoided.

References (to numbers in the bibliography):
    74, 79, 138, 141, 167, 219.

Astragalus bisulcatus (Diholcos bisulcatus,
D. decalvans, Phaca bisulcata)
Two-grooved Milkvetch, Two-grooved Loco

Description:
    The stems of this species are 1 to 3 feet tall and are borne in clumps; the individual leaflets of the compound leaves are ⅜ to 1 inch long; the flowers are borne in rather narrow clusters, each flower about ½ to ⅝ inch long, of characteristic narrow sweetpea-like shape, usually purple in color but varies from rich reddish-purple to nearly white; the pods are around ½ inch long with two longitudinal grooves on the upperside.
    This species is fairly well limited to the Rocky Mountain area.

Effects:
    Many of the species of *Astragalus* and *Oxytropis* are poisonous to livestock, and are known as loco or milkvetch. The poisonous principle is variable among the different kinds, some types being poisonous on any soil, others (like this two-grooved one) cause trouble only when growing on ground containing the element selenium. Some kinds of plants will grow only on such soils, hence, they are known as "indicator plants" and their presence helps locate such formations (Beath, Gilbert & Epson, 19 and 20). Plants known to take up selenium should be avoided as human food unless the exact locations of seleniferous soils are known for sure. To complicate the problem, these plants take up the selenium from the soil and, by decay of their parts, return the material to the ground in a form that can be absorbed by any other plants. Hence, even common garden plants grown on such selenium soil can cause poisoning to human beings. It is better to avoid all locos and milkvetches, except perhaps the ones with fleshy plum-shaped fruit (see *Astragalus succulentus*).

Two-grooved Milkvetch *(Astragalus bisulcatus)*

Related Species:

The Rocky Mountain area has scores of species of *Astragalus* and *Oxytropis,* many of which are poisonous to livestock.

References (to numbers in the bibliography for this and related species):

2, 40, 43, 74, 79, 128, 138, 167, 219, 249, 254.

Cannabis sativa
HEMP, MARIJUANA, INDIAN HEMP

Description:

Stems simple to branched, 3 to 8 feet tall; leaves compound in "finger-like" fashion as shown, the individual leaflets 2 to 6 inches long; flowers small and not at all colorful, the pollen-bearing flowers and seed-producing flowers on separate plants (staminate and pistillate plants).

Waste places, along ditches and roadsides or along fields possibly as an escape from cultivation. This plant is common east of the Rocky Mountain area, but we seldom see it here since it is illegal.

Effects:

The seeds of hemp can be used as food and are said to be nutritious and even stimulating. They have been parched and mixed into a batter and fried into cakes. This could be done with caution in an emergency. Kephart (140) says that, in Belgium, the young shoots are used as a substitute for asparagus. However, the plant contains poisonous alkaloids and, as is well known, is smoked in various parts of the world for its narcotic effects. It would seem better to avoid using such a plant as food at all.

Related Species:

None.

References (to numbers in the bibliography):

59, 79, 84, 93, 117, 167, 202, 219, 240.

MARIJUANA *(Cannabis sativa)*

Cicuta douglasii (C. occidentalis)
WATER HEMLOCK, POISON WATER HEMLOCK, WESTERN WATER HEMLOCK, DOUGLAS WATER HEMLOCK

Description:

Perennial plants from thick rootstocks that develop cross-partitions in older plants about at ground level; stems 2 to 4 feet tall; leaflets 1 to 4 inches long with the lateral veins ending in the notches between the teeth (not in the tooth points as in some similar plants); petals white, small; fruits small, about 1/8 inch long.

Grows in swamps, ditches, along streams, and in wet meadows from the Rocky Mountains west to the Pacific. Our plant looks a great deal like the one present in the eastern half of the United States. We seldom see it growing above 8500 feet in our area.

Effects:

This plant (with its eastern relative) has gained the reputation of being the most poisonous plant in the North Temperate Zone. The poison is concentrated mostly in the lower part of the stems or roots. It often causes death to livestock, and it is sometimes stated that a piece the size of a walnut will cause the death of a cow. Human beings have sometimes been poisoned by water hemlock, eating the underground parts, having mistaken them for various edible roots like parsnips. Children will sometimes do this, often with fatal results. It is said that a piece the size of a marble can cause death to a man.

The poison is very virulent and causes violent convulsions. Vomiting should be induced at once and a strong cathartic administered. Everyone should become familiar with this poisonous plant whether or not they intend to eat edible plants. It would be best to avoid anything that even looks like it, and eradicate it if it grows near your home.

Related Species:

C. maculata is an eastern species with similar appearance and with similar poisonous properties.

Fr2

$F_{\times 20}$

Fr1
X10

R

5CM

Water Hemlock *(Cicuta douglasii)*

References (to numbers in the bibliography for this and related
    species):
2, 5, 40, 58, 59, 74, 79, 84, 131, 132, 138, 141, 167, 181, 202, 219,
230.

Conium maculatum
POISON HEMLOCK, EUROPEAN POISON HEMLOCK

Description:

Biennial plants from stout taproots, the lower part of the stem
or crown with few or no cross-partitions separating cavities (as in
Cicuta); stems 1½ to 10 feet tall, branching, spotted with brown
or reddish-brown dots; leaves filmy or fern-like, the whole compound leaf often as much as a foot long; flowers small, white in
color; fruits seedlike, small, each about ⅛ inch long.

Introduced into North America from other continents and now
widely distributed. We usually find it below 9000-feet elevation in
the Rocky Mountain area. It is often found in waste places, usually
in moist ground, in ditches or in valley bottoms.

Effects:

This is the famous poison plant said to have been used by the
Athenians to kill Socrates. It may be more poisonous at some seasons of the year, and some parts of the plant seem to be worse than
others. It has even been used as a food plant in the early spring.
We recommend avoiding it and also any plant that in any way
resembles it, unless you are absolutely familiar with everything
involved. The action of the poison does not cause convulsions as
in *Cicuta* but has a numbing, paralyzing effect. Livestock sometimes have been poisoned by eating the fresh plant. Human beings
have sometimes eaten the roots, mistaking them for those of parsnips or cow parsnips, with disastrous effects. The fruits have also
been mistaken for anise, especially since the poison hemlock often
grows around gardens, sometimes under the name of Queen Ann's
Lace (a name also applied to wild carrot). The seeds, especially
when partly developed, seem to be particularly poisonous and
were said to have been used by the Indians to poison their war

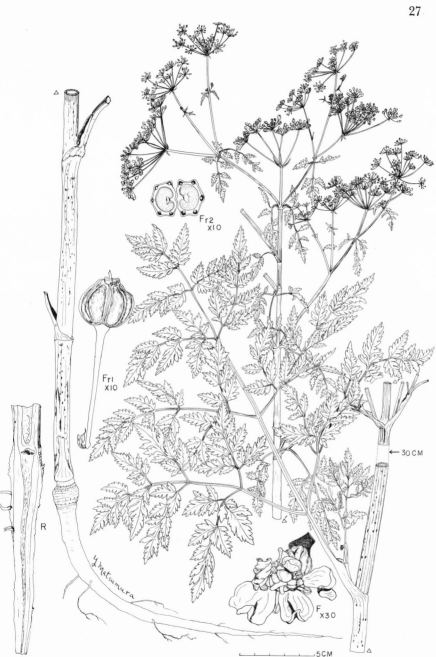

Fr2
x10

Fr1
x10

R

→ 30 CM

F
x30

5 CM

POISON HEMLOCK (*Conium maculatum*)

arrows. Children have been poisoned by blowing on whistles made from the hollow stems, but judging from our own experience, this is probably not a really great hazard. We have often had the plant sent in with the story that children have used it for whistles, but so far we have no reports of any serious effect. Everyone should learn this plant and attempt to eradicate it in their immediate area.

Related Species:

None. However, many edible plants belong to the same family and have a superficial resemblance to this poisonous plant.

References (to numbers in the bibliography):

58, 59, 79, 84, 117, 134, 138, 141, 167, 181, 202, 204, 219, 227, 230.

Datura meteloides (D. wrightii)
JIMSONWEED, THORN APPLE, TOLGUACHA, SACRED DATURA

Description:

Plants annual or perennial, but the roots usually rather thick; stems 1 to 3 feet tall; leaves large, about 4 to 8 inches long; flowers white to violet tinged, very large, 6 to 8 inches long.

Grows in valleys often along streams, on plains and hills. It ranges from western Texas and Mexico to southern California. In the Rocky Mountain area it is present in New Mexico, Arizona, southwestern Colorado, and southern Utah.

Effects:

All parts of this plant contain several poisonous alkaloids in rather high concentrations, particularly the seeds. People have been poisoned by using the young leaves as "greens" or the roots as food. Children are often affected by chewing the young fruit or the seeds. The long tubular corolla may have sweet tasting nectar at the base, and children may suck on the "trumpet," often with disastrous results.

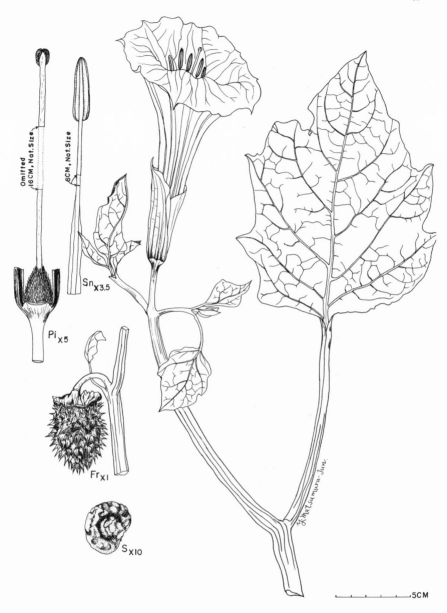

JIMSONWEED *(Datura meteloides)*

Jimsonweed has often been used in medicine and in various rituals, particularly by the Indians. The plant was mashed into a liquid or dried into a powder and when eaten, produced giddiness, dimness of sight, hallucinations, and stupefaction in general. It is easy to see how such a plant could come into use as a narcotic. In medicine, a decoction was used as a disinfectant or sometimes to deaden pain. Very often the use of the plant resulted in the death of the patient, probably because of an overdose. Recently we received a seedpod of jimsonweed from New Mexico, with an inquiry as to what it was, with the information that certain people in the vicinity were swallowing the seeds to cure arthritis! Probably the effect was to deaden the pain of the disease, but they were taking a terrific chance.

Apparently more human beings are poisoned than are animals, who either do not like the taste of the plant or have more sense than to eat it. Strangely enough, Castetter (43) recorded that the Navajo Indians ground up the fruits and by mixing them with clay were able to use them as food. Certainly, this is a good plant to leave strictly alone, as a medicine, a narcotic, or food supply, even in emergencies. Soldiers stationed at Jamestown in 1676 were poisoned by a species of *Datura* and named the plant Jamestown Weed; this finally by corruption became "Jimson Weed."

Related Species:

Datura metel (Hindu Datura) is a famous narcotic and poison producer in Eurasia (Stevens, 219). *D. stramonium* is widespread over North America. It has smaller flowers but is otherwise similar in appearance and properties to the one described and illustrated here (Core, Reitz & Gillespie, 59; Thomson & Sifton, 230; Saunders, 204; Stevens, 219; Palmer, 182; Jaeger, 132; Avery, 10; Muenscher, 167; Durrell, Jensen & Kinger, 79; Johnson, 134; Coon, 58; Palmer, 181; Fernald & Kinsey, 84); *D. discolor* of southern Arizona, southern California and Mexico is reported to have effects like our plant (Curtin, 66).

References (to numbers in the bibliography):

10, 14, 17, 77, 83, 97, 117, 138, 141, 183, 192, 195, 204, 220, 240, 249.

Delphinium geyeri
Larkspur, Geyer Larkspur

Description:

Root parts woody and fibrous; stems usually several together, 8 inches to 3 feet tall; flowers ⅜ to ⅝ inch long, not counting the backward projecting spur which is about 1½ times as long as the rest; pods ½ to ⅝ inch long.

Open plains, foothills, valleys of the lower mountains, often among bushes. Grows from Wyoming to western Nebraska and west to northeastern Utah.

Effects:

This is one of the very worst cattle-poisoning plants in the United States. The leaves, even in the mature plant, tend to cluster toward the base of the stem, and in the young stages form a luscious-looking tuft of green foliage which can be a tempting mouthful to a cow, especially in a dry spring when little else is available. Cattle seem more susceptible to the plant than sheep and horses. We know of no record of its effect on human beings, but it would be a poor risk to gather the young leaves for spring "greens" or to try eating the root as mentioned below.

Related Species:

Several to many species grow in our area, from the low plant of lower elevations to the tall larkspur of higher elevations in the mountains. Some of the short-stemmed ones like *Delphinium nelsoni* have a rather tender-textured, tuberous-like root that may look good to eat. The Hopi Indians were supposed to dry and grind the flowers to give their cornmeal a blue color. But all larkspurs should be avoided as any form of food.

References (to numbers in the bibliography for this and related species):
2, 74, 79, 138, 167, 219.

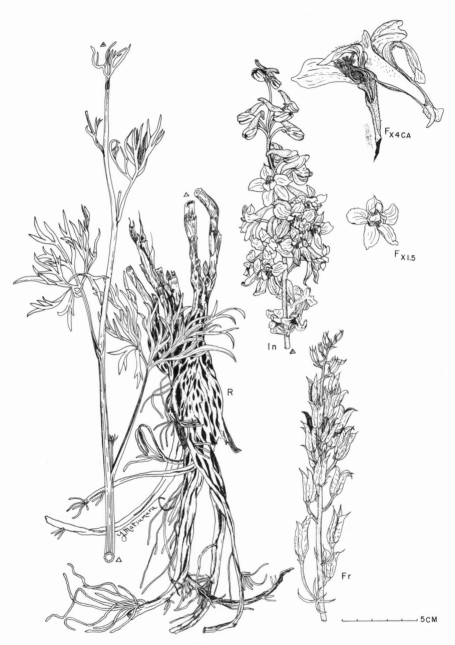

Labels on figure: F_{X4CA}, $F_{X1.5}$, In, R, Fr, 5CM

LARKSPUR *(Delphinium geyeri)*

ROCKY MOUNTAIN IRIS *(Iris missouriensis)*

Iris missouriensis (I. pelogonus)
ROCKY MOUNTAIN IRIS, WESTERN BLUEFLAG

Description:

This plant often grows in dense patches from thick rootstalks; stems about 8 inches to 2 feet tall; flowers somewhat smaller than most garden varieties of iris, the parts about 2½ to 3 inches long, usually pale blue-purple but varying to darker or paler.

Wet land of meadows, marshes and along streams. This iris grows from North Dakota to British Columbia south to New Mexico, Arizona, and California. One can expect to find it scattered over the entire Rocky Mountain area.

Effects:

Several of the native species of iris are definitely reported to cause poisoning to livestock, our own among them. The rootstocks are said to contain an acrid resinous substance, "irisin," and has caused trouble to animals, but fortunately the rootstocks have an acrid taste and are seldom eaten. One of our courageous collaborators (Douglass, 77A) tasted the raw rootstocks and found them rather sweet at first, but they soon became "terribly astringent, causing the mouth and throat to burn." Then some rootstocks were peeled and cooked. The odor and the first taste of this cooked product were pleasant, but soon produced the same burning, unpleasant, stringent effect.

Some of the kinds of iris (such as the Florentine) are said to be edible (Confar, 57), but we would not recommend that our species be tried at all.

Related Species:

The eastern iris, *Iris versicolor,* has been reported to be poisonous to livestock.

References (to numbers in the bibliography):

14, 57, 77A, 79, 84, 138, 167.

Lupinus spp.
LUPINE

There are many species of lupines in the Rocky Mountain area but at present they are poorly understood as to species by botanists. What we are presently calling *Lupinus argenteus* seems to be commonest. The following description fits all of them.

Description:

Annual or perennial nonwoody plants; leaves always compound, the leaflets 5 or more and connected at a common point (palmately compound), these leaflets usually narrow, the margins smooth; flowers of the sweetpea type but usually smaller, varying in color but commonly some shade of blue or purple with some parts usually white; fruit resembling a peapod.

Plains, hills, and open slopes. Lupines are scattered in the United States (the Blue Bonnet of Texas is one) but are more common in the western half.

Effects:

The lupines are a rather important group of poisonous plants, being especially dangerous to sheep. The fruits and seeds are considered to be the most dangerous parts, but the rest of the plant apparently may sometimes cause trouble. Fortunately, the poison is not cumulative and a lethal dose must be eaten at one time to cause death.

Sweet (227) and Lampman (143) mentioned that species of lupine were eaten by the Indians, who used the roasted roots and the boiled leaves. This seems like a dangerous practice to us, not to be tried in any emergency.

It is well known that a species of lupine, probably *Lupinus albus* or a closely related species, is raised in Europe, and we have seen it in cultivation around farm houses in Italy, undoubtedly raised for its edible seeds. These are canned and are sometimes exported to this country, often appearing on our local grocery store shelves. Because of this fact, some people assume they can use

LUPINE *(Lupinus argenteus)*

seeds of our native species as a kind of substitute for peas. Possibly the poison is dissipated by cooking, but we would not advise trying it. If a real emergency existed and it was necessary to eat lupine seeds to sustain life, than it would be wise to experiment with small amounts, especially at first. Since the raw seeds have killed sheep, we would not care to try them cooked. We advise you to avoid eating any part of the lupine plant.

Related Species:
Species too numerous to list.

References (to numbers in the bibliography):
2, 5, 40, 74, 79, 84, 93, 138, 143, 167, 227, 254.

Oxytropis spp. *(Aragallus* spp.)
CRAZYWEED, LOCOWEED

Description:
Plants usually not over 1½ feet tall and often much shorter; leaves usually clustered near the base of the plant, always with several to many segments (leaflets); flowers in rather long clusters with very short stalks to each flower; flowers sweetpea-shaped, white, cream-colored, pink, rose, or purple in color; fruit a pod.

The various species usually grow on the plains, slopes and hills, from lower to medium elevations in the Rocky Mountain area.

Effects:
This group of plants contain the "locoweeds" so famous in the history of the West. Its effect on horses is rather well known. All parts of the plant are poisonous, but in order to be lethal, the animal must eat large amounts over a long period of time. Some horses are said to form the habit of eating the plant; these are the so-called "locoed" horses so well known in Western stories. All animals can probably be poisoned by this group of plants.

We have no record of the effect of these plants when eaten by human beings. However, some species form a luscious-looking tuft of green leaves in the spring and might be tempting to try as a

LOCOWEED *(Oxytropis sericea)*

potherb. The roots are thick enough that they could be eaten by the unwary, particularly since locos belong to the same family as some famous producers of edible roots *(Psoralea* spp.). Also the young pods or seeds may appear to be possible food in an emergency. It is possible that in moderate amounts these could be eaten without serious effects, but we ourselves wouldn't try them under any conditions. This is a famous poison plant group to be avoided.

Related Species:

The white flowered loco *(O. sericea)* and the purple flowered species *(O. lambertii)* are the two species that have caused the most trouble to the livestock industry.

References (to numbers in the bibliography):
79, 138, 249, 254.

Ranunculus sceleratus (R. eremogenes)
BLISTER BUTTERCUP, CURSED CROWFOOT

Description:

Plants perennial with a cluster of rather thickish roots; stems 6 to 24 inches tall, erect or nearly so, rather stout and fleshy; leaves 1 to 4 inches wide; each petal about 1/8 inch long, yellow in color; fruits many, seedlike (achenes), borne together in a rather elongated cluster.

This plant grows in moist or wet soil often at the borders of ponds, lakes or streams. Widespread in Canada and the United States; of course widespread in the Rocky Mountain area, sometimes up to 10,000 feet.

Effects:

As the common names suggest, the plant has an acrid juice that may blister the skin on contact, especially with certain people. We have never noted such an action on ourselves or to anyone that happened to be with us. This buttercup contains a narcotic called "anemonal" that affects all classes of livestock, especially cattle, when grazed in fresh condition. Drying the plant as one would in

F x6

B P X15

5CM

BLISTER BUTTERCUP *(Ranunculus sceleratus)*

making hay, apparently renders it harmless. Apparently cooking also drives off the toxic property because the plant has often been used as emergency food for human beings in various parts of the world. The young tops and roots are boiled like spinach, the poison-bearing water being carefully poured off. Considering the various characteristics of this buttercup, it appears to us that it should be left alone, except perhaps in acute emergencies. Even then it would be wise to handle it carefully and taste it very cautiously at first trial.

Related Species:

Several buttercups have been known to produce this blistering effect. We have a rather large number of species in the Rocky Mountains and it would be advisable to avoid all of them under ordinary conditions.

References (to numbers in the bibliography for this and related
   species):
   2, 49, 74, 79, 84, 93, 102, 117, 132, 138, 140, 167, 217, 230.

Rhus radicans (R. rydbergii, R. toxicodendron, Toxicodendron rydbergii)
POISON IVY, POISON OAK

Description:

Shrubs or vinelike plants, often with aerial rootlets; leaves with 3 divisions (leaflets), the stalk to the middle division longer than the ones on the lateral ones; leaflets about 1¼ to 8 inches long; flowers small, the petals about ⅛ inch long, yellowish-white in color; fruit rather dry but berry-like, globe-shaped, about ¼ inch wide, yellowish-white in color.

Hillsides, plains and woods. The various varieties are found throughout North America. Widespread in the Rocky Mountain region, often found in valleys along streams, especially near picnic areas!

Effects:

The Rocky Mountain form of the species is usually a rather low shrub. Poison ivy contains a nonvolatile oil in all or in practically all of its parts, an oil which is poisonous to most people when it comes in contact with the skin. Some believe that about 2 or 3 out of 4 people are sensitive to it in varying degrees. The self-styled "immune" people may be surprised to find themselves some

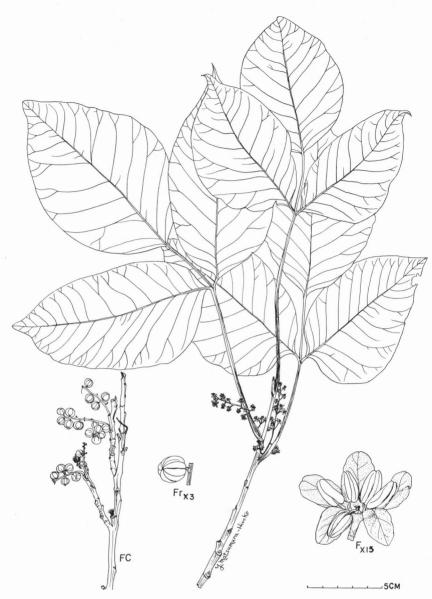

POISON IVY *(Rhus radicans)*

day down with a severe attack of poison ivy. Apparently the degree of contact, the growth stage of the plant, even the toxicity of the individual ivy plant you chance to meet, possibly your own physical condition at the time, all affect the degree of resistance. We once saw a youth, who handled poison ivy safely all summer, develop a severe case of poisoning in late summer. This plant should be recognized and avoided by everyone. This is difficult to do since inanimate objects such as tool handles, rope, shoes and clothing can be contaminated by the poison and cause trouble for many months afterwards. Some people swear they get attacks of the rash by merely being near the plant. This appears doubtful from experiments that have been made, although dust and smoke have been known to transport the oil through the atmosphere. Remember, the oil is nonvolatile and does not diffuse out through the air. The toxic substance has been called "urushoil" and causes the characteristic burning, rash, itching and blisters that almost everyone has experienced or observed in others. We have heard scores of remedies, preventives and cures for poison ivy. The commonest preventive suggestion is to wash the affected parts soon after exposure with a strong nonoily laundry soap. Preventive creams and injections have not had uniform success (Morton, 166). In light cases, the following measures have been suggested—the application of baking soda or Epsom salts, one or 2 teaspoonfuls to a cup of water, a fluid extract of *Grindelia* diluted with about 8 parts of water, a 5 percent solution of potassium permanganate or wet compresses of boric acid solution. In moderate or severe cases, it is wise to consult a doctor, especially if the parts affected are near the eyes. Deaths have been reported in extreme cases of poison-ivy poisoning.

Cases are on record where the leaves or the attractive looking whitish berries have been eaten, usually by children, with poisonous effect on the lining of the digestive tract. Birds eat the berries apparently without harm, and the plant is occasionally grazed by livestock or game animals without much effect. However, as indicated before, this is a good plant for all human beings to avoid.

Related Species:

All the various forms and varieties of common poison ivy should be on the suspected list. In addition, the related eastern poison sumac *(Rhus vernix)* is poisonous to many people (Coon, 58; Jaeger, 132) but fortunately for us, is not found in our area.

References (to numbers in the bibliography):

14, 40, 58, 59, 74, 79, 102, 132, 138, 141, 166, 167, 216.

In x 10

Fr

F2 X35CA

F1 X35CA

POISON SUCKLEYA (*Suckleya suckleyana*)

5 CM

Suckleya suckleyana
POISON SUCKLEYA

Description:

Annual, rather succulent plants; stems 4 to 12 inches long, much-branched, prostrate; leaves about 3/8 to 1 1/4 inches long; flowers very inconspicuous; fruit seedlike, about 1/8 inch long, enclosed in a pair of longer bracts.

In moist sinkholes, around the borders of lakes and reservoirs or along dry streams. From Montana south to eastern Colorado.

Effects:

This plant is fairly abundant in moist areas and in periods of drought may be the most conspicuous lush-green plant in the area. It contains a cyanogenetic substance that develops hydrocyanic or prussic acid when it reaches the stomach of a grazing animal. This has caused cattle poisoning in the plains area of Colorado.

We are including the plant here because the succulent green growth might tempt someone to try it as a salad or as a potherb. Also, poison suckleya has a superficial similarity to several widely used edible plants such as species of *Chenopodium* or *Amaranthus*, and it might be gathered by mistake with serious results. Fortunately, its geographical distribution is rather limited and, even within its range, it seldom if ever grows as a weed. The similar appearing *Chenopodium* (lamb's quarters) or *Amaranthus* (pig-weeds) are apt to be found in abundance, often being weedy.

Related Species:
Fortunately none.

References (to numbers in the bibliography):
79, 167, 231.

Triglochin maritima
ARROWGRASS, PODGRASS, SEASIDE ARROWGRASS, SHORE PODGRASS

Description:

Perennial plants with stout rootstocks; leaves grasslike, crowded toward the base of the plant; flowers always in a narrow spikelike cluster; individual flowers small and inconspicuous; fruit a dry podlike capsule.

Often grows in dense patches, in alkaline meadows, marshes or borders of lakes. Widely distributed in the United States except in the southeastern portion. Found throughout the Rocky Mountain area.

Effects:

Although this plant does not belong to the true grass family, it does have a general resemblance to a grass. It is a well-known poisonous plant particularly affecting cattle and sheep. Hydrocyanic acid is produced by both the fresh and the dried plant parts; hence it is both dangerous when grazed or when fed in the form of hay. Fortunately, the poison is not cumulative, but since the action of hydrocyanic acid is so rapid, many animals die from its effects, these deaths resulting from the failure of the respiratory system to function properly.

In spite of this poisonous record, the arrowgrasses have been used as food for human beings. The seeds were used by the Indians, parched and eaten, or used as a substitute for coffee. Possibly the seeds do not contain the poisonous principle, or this is dissipated in the roasting process. Moreover, Snow (212) and Uphof (240) stated that the leaves are used as a salad or cooked as a potherb in some localities. We have never tried the plant as food nor do we advise doing so even in an emergency.

Related Species:

A smaller species, *Triglochin palustris,* is in our area and apparently has similar toxic properties but is not as abundant as the one described above.

5CM

ARROWGRASS *(Triglochin maritima)*

References (to numbers in the bibliography):
26, 40, 65, 74, 79, 84, 138, 167, 212, 240.

Veratrum californicum (V. speciosum)
FALSE HELLEBORE, SKUNK CABBAGE

Description:

Plants perennial from thick rootstocks; stems thickened at base, 1½ to 6½ feet tall; leaves 8 to 10 inches long, strongly veined; flower clusters large, up to 20 inches long; flowers ¼ to ⅝ inch long, greenish-white; fruit a dry podlike capsule with 3 inner compartments.

Moist meadows and along streams. Montana to New Mexico west to Washington and California.

Effects:

This is a poisonous species that sometimes affects grazing animals, especially in the plant's young stages. Apparently it is seldom eaten, possibly because of a reported burning taste to the animals (they don't say how they know that), but sometimes young horses or sheep have grazed on the young growth, often with fatal results. The poisonous substance seems to be concentrated in the underground parts and in the developing shoots, for cattle will sometimes graze on the mature plant without ill effects. The flowers are said to have caused poisoning to honeybees working on them, while the seeds of a related species have been known to have poisoned chickens.

One might be tempted to dig up the thick rootstocks for use as emergency food, or to utilize the young shoots as one would asparagus. This, of course, might have fatal results, although fortunately, one of the effects of the poisonous substance is to cause vomiting. The Indians were said to have used the plant as a medicine, but they certainly understood its possible lethal effects since they also used it as a means of committing suicide. This is a plant to be avoided entirely as food for human beings.

Related Species:

Veratrum veride, often called American Hellebore or White Hellebore, is a related plant of the eastern part of the United States. It, too, has a record of poisoning livestock and human beings (Sargent, 202; Core, Reitz & Gillespie, 59; Coon, 58).

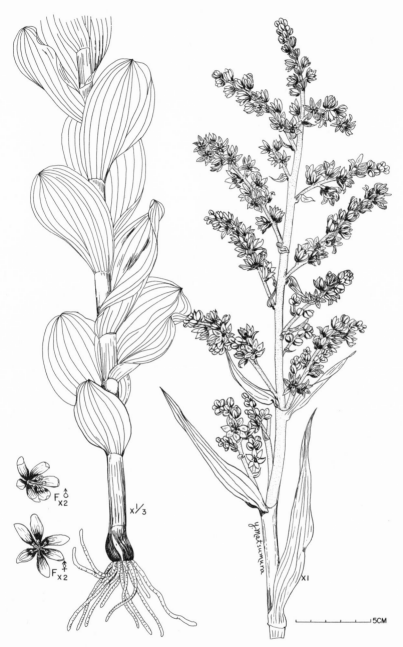

SKUNK CABBAGE *(Veratrum californicum)*

References (to numbers in the bibliography):
2, 5, 74, 79, 98, 138, 167, 254.

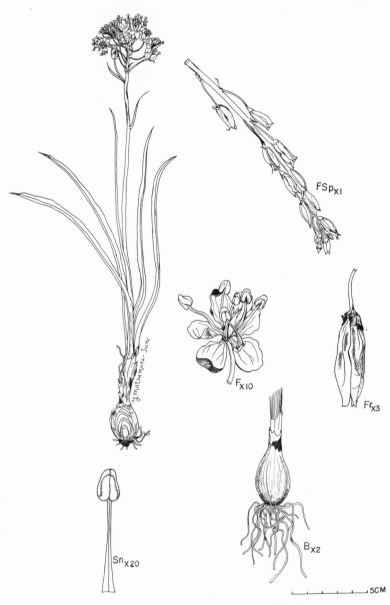

Death Camas (*Zygadenus gramineus*)

Zygadenus spp. *(Zigadenus)*
DEATH CAMAS, ZYGADENE

Description:

Plants perennial from bulbs; leaves narrow and grasslike, crowded near the base of the stems; flowers in rather short to elongated clusters, each flower with segments ⅛ to ⅜ inch long, greenish-white to yellowish-white in color; fruit a dry pod (capsule) with 3 inner compartments, these with several to many seeds.

Meadows, plains and open slopes. From Canada south to Florida, Texas, New Mexico, Arizona and California.

Effects:

All the different species of *Zygadenus* are poisonous to a greater or lesser degree and should be avoided by everyone. All parts of the plant are toxic, including the bulbs, leaves, flowers and seeds. The various kinds of death camas cause serious losses to livestock in the Rocky Mountain area, particularly affecting sheep. In a dry spring, the leaves of these plants may develop vigorously by obtaining moisture from the bulbs; often these green shoots are the only succulent growth in sight. The hungry animals will sometimes graze on the plants, especially if they have been penned up for awhile, when under more normal conditions they might avoid them completely. Cattle and horses seem to be less affected, probably because of their grazing habits. Even chickens have been poisoned, but seldom hogs, since they have the habit of vomiting and thus getting rid of some of the poisonous material.

The bulbs are the most dangerous parts to human beings, since they may be easily gathered by mistake for those of the wild onion, mariposa (or sego) lily or camass. We have actually observed people in this locality indiscriminately gathering wild onion and death camas bulbs to be used as food! The Indians apparently had this same problem because it is reported that they sometimes gathered these bulbs, mistaking them for edible ones, with disastrous results. To make it worse, even the dried bulbs kept their toxic effect, so the danger to the Indians could extend well into the winter. Children at play have been poisoned by eating the bulbs.

Certainly anyone utilizing such thickened underground structures for food in this area should learn to recognize death camas and, in addition, learn to distinguish the plant from other bulb-bearing species that are edible. (see *Allium* spp., *Camassia* sp. and *Calochortus* spp.)

The symptoms of poisoning by death camas are salivation, weakness; finally, lowering of the body temperature, coma, and nausea with a tendency for the animal to vomit. If you suspect that this plant has been eaten by someone, then by all means encourage free vomiting and get the sick person to a doctor as soon as possible. If this cannot be done, we can only recommend keeping the victim as quiet as possible and administering orally a water solution of common baking soda. This could certainly do no great harm and would be worth trying in cases where human beings have been poisoned by death camas.

There may be several poisonous substances present, but the primary one seems to be an alkaloid called "Zygadenine." Anderson (4) claimed that the toxic effect may be twice as potent as that from strychnine.

Related Species:

The poisonous effects seem to vary considerably among the different kinds. At least three species have been listed for our area, *Zygadenus elegans, Z. paniculatus,* and *Z. gramineus.* The last one is reported to be the most toxic, the first one the least. In addition *Z. nuttallii* is near the southwestern part of our region, *Z. virescens* may come in from the south, while *Z. intermedius* and *Z. venenosus* may be in the western edge of the Rocky Mountain area.

References (to numbers in the bibliography for all species):

2, 5, 14, 40, 52, 74, 79, 84, 119, 132, 138, 141, 152, 153, 154, 155, 167, 217, 219, 230.

Chapter III: POTHERBS (like Spinach)

The young tender leaves or the juvenile shoots of many wild plants are often used as "potherbs" or "greens." The practical problem is how to be absolutely certain as to the identification of the plant in this young condition, for many edible plants in this stage have a superficial resemblance to harmful ones. You may have watched certain of these juvenile plants in previous years grow into mature familiar forms, and can then proceed with assurance. If you can't do this then try gathering and pressing some of the plants at the early, eating stage, and then waiting until the others mature into flowers and fruit. These older, pressed plants can usually be readily identified by yourself or by someone else. Both the mature and the young pressed plants may then be mounted together to make permanent specimens. You are then ready for the following spring, and can proceed with much more certainty than if you had to trust to memory alone. Sometimes a few precocious individual plants flower early and these can be checked. Then the slower maturing ones of the same kind can be utilized with safety.

Here are some general suggestions made as a result of our own experience:

1. If at all possible use only the young tender parts. Of course, the age and tenderness will affect the cooking time. Remember that your elevation above sea level will do the same; boil them longer at high altitudes. The best advice we can give is to experiment a bit, using common sense in the matter. **Never overcook** is a good rule.

2. Usually springtime is the season for gathering greens, but remember our summer rains will often germinate the seeds of annual plants or cause a perennial one to push out its young shoots. One of the best bunches of greens we have ever eaten was gathered on November 20 (See *Atriplex patula*).

3. Some species have a rather sharp or bitter taste that is objectionable to some people, especially when it is first experienced. You can overcome this to some degree by changing the water two to several times during the boiling process. Also, many of us like to mix these piquant plants with others having a bland taste.

4. The rule is to use as little water as possible and change it as seldom as possible. This water can be saved to drink or it can be used in cooking other foods. Some of the minerals and vitamins may be lost if you pour the water away. Of course, in times of acute water shortage this cooking liquid may be very valuable.

5. Large root parts of many plants can be brought in to the cellar and buried in soil. Such structures can provide a supply of fresh greens at intervals throughout the winter.

6. Patches of growing plants can be covered from several days to several weeks with burlap, thick paper boxes, or tubs. The lack of light causes rapid elongation of the stems, the parts become yellowish or whitish (blanched), more tender, usually less bitter. This is what is done commercially to several garden plants, such as celery.

7. Some wildland greens are rather lacking in pronounced flavor and taste. If you find them so, then doctor them up with diced bacon, salt pork, or hard boiled eggs, using your favorite recipe for spinach. Gordon (99) and Sopher (212A) gave some mouthwatering ways to prepare these plants in novel fashion.

Potherbs properly cooked are considered to be relatively high in vitamins. They are rather seasonable, but when available are usually so in very large quantities. They do seem to be relatively low in actual nutriments. It is possible to can, freeze, or dehydrate greens and keep them for rather long periods, but the possibilities in this respect seem to us to be somewhat limited. Many of them are high in flavor and palatability (at least to some of us), much more so than their cultivated counterparts.

Plants used as potherbs, but illustrated or described in another chapter.

Arctium minus VI.   *Oxyria digyna* V.
Calochortus spp. VI.   *Ranunculus sceleratus* II.

Campanula rapunculoides VI.
Chenopodium capitatum VII.
Cichorium intybus IX.
Claytonia megarrhiza VI.
Cymopterus spp. VI.
Descurainia spp. VIII.
Erodium cicutarium V.
Erythronium grandiflorum VI.
Heracleum lanatum V.
Lactuca scariola V.
Malva neglecta VIII.

Rorippa nasturtium-aquaticum V.
Rumex acetosella V.
Sedum spp. V.
Solanum nigrum VII.
Sonchus spp. V.
Tragopogon porrifolius VI.
Typha latifolia VI.
Veronica americana V.
Viola spp. V.

Amaranthus graecizans (A. blitoides)
PROSTRATE PIGWEED, PROSTRATE AMARANTH

(Note to Botanists: A species of Amaranth with stems forming a rounded "tumbleweed" used to be known incorrectly as *A. graecizans*. It is now called *A. albus* in recent books.)

Description:

Stems 6 inches to 2 feet long, rather stout and branched, prostrate on the ground; leaves oval and widest at the middle or above the middle, not lobed or toothed; flowers inconspicuous in small clusters in the leaf axils; seeds about 1/25 to 1/20 inch in diameter, lens-shaped, black and shining.

This usually is a weed of roadsides and waste places where the soil is disturbed. It is common in the western part of the United States and has now spread all over this and other continents.

Use:

This is a widely distributed, often abundant plant and was much utilized by both the Indians and the early settlers in this area. The small black seeds can be gathered by picking the mature plants and letting them dry out, so that the seeds will shatter out on the surface of a rock, pavement, or blanket. This process can be accelerated if the plants are disturbed or handled roughly. The seeds are small but numerous, and a surprisingly large quantity can be

PROSTRATE PIGWEED *(Amaranthus graecizans)*

obtained with a little patience. They can be eaten raw or parched, or they can be ground into a flour or meal. The Indians often mixed the meal with that from corn and used it to make cakes or gruel. Such seeds were called "pinole." The writer has never tried the seeds of this plant (never having been patient enough or hungry enough), but they sound nutritious and palatable, to judge from the descriptions. They would surely make an excellent emergency ration.

The young plants have always been popular as greens. We have gathered them in the spring when they are young and tender; the roots were then cut away. The plants were cooked like spinach in an open kettle, or 2 minutes in a pressure cooker usually was sufficient. They are good served with salt and butter or salt and vinegar, but they can be enhanced with pieces of bacon or boiled egg. The taste is palatable and mild, with no strong or objectionable effect. Since the greens are mild and bland many people like to mix them with other plants such as purslane or mustard, which have a more pronounced flavor.

Related Species:
See *A. retroflexus.*

References (to numbers in the bibliography):
2, 26, 42, 49, 57, 65, 83, 84, 85, 92, 93, 138, 151, 158, 160, 220, 239, 240, 242, 249, 254, 259.

Amaranthus retroflexus (A. powellii)
AMARANTH, PIGWEED, REDROOT, CARELESS WEED

Description:
Annual plant with a red taproot; stems erect, 1 to 5 feet tall, sometimes branched; leaves egg-shaped (ovate) to lance-shaped (lanceolate); flowers inconspicuous in narrow clusters, these rather bristly in appearance; seeds black and shining, lens-shaped, about 1/24 inch wide.

This is a common weedy plant, often growing in crops, along roadsides, or on disturbed ground. It is widely distributed over North America and now is at home in several other continents. One can expect to find it in our area at elevations of below 9,000 feet, often in abundance.

Use:
This plant has always been a favorite among the Indians and was actually cultivated or at least encouraged by them to grow nearby (Hedrick, 117; Medsger, 158). They used the small black

seeds which are borne in surprising numbers. The mature plant can be stacked up on canvas or rock and allowed to dry, then the material shaken and beaten to shatter out the seeds. Colyer (56) placed the tops of these plants upside down in a large paper sack and let them dry for a week. Then the plants were shaken and beaten, the seeds and chaff remaining in the sack. The seeds were then separated using a sieve, and winnowed by the aid of a good breeze. The Indians parched the seeds and ate them whole, but they are so small it is difficult to chew up each one. They were also ground into a meal, often mixed with cornmeal and used in making bread, cakes, mush, or gruel. Soaking the seeds (or the meal) overnight in water may be a good idea according to our experience. The taste is somewhat "weedy" to some people but pleasant enough even if the resulting product is rather blackish in color. However, a dark-colored pancake, bread, or mush might taste about as good as a light colored one to a hungry person. Certainly the seeds can be an emergency food of great importance. We have seen people shake out the seeds in their hands, throw them in their mouth and eat them raw.

The young shoots and stems have long been considered favorite material for greens by the Indians, the early white settlers, and by interested parties to recent times. They are cooked like spinach. We cooked them 2 minutes at 15-lbs. pressure in a pressure saucepan or boiled them for 12 minutes in salted water (at 5000 ft. elevation). We have eaten them with pepper and butter or with vinegar, bacon, or hard boiled eggs. The flavor is rather mild but very pleasant and justifies the popularity of this plant for greens. Some prefer to mix these greens with those from plants having a more pronounced flavor. The young plants may also be served raw as a salad.

Related Species:

Several similar-looking, related plants have been extensively used and probably would be just as good. *A. hybridus* (Morton, 166; Kephart, 140; Medsger, 158; Uphof, 240) has been popular among Indians and other inhabitants especially in the southern part of its range. Some people have written to me referring to

AMARANTH *(Amaranthus retroflexus)*

it as "Careless weed" or "Keerless weed." It has been used as a salad, for greens, or the seeds ground into a meal. *A. palmeri* (Medsger, 158; Curtin, 66; Stratton, 225; Elmore, 83) was also used in the same way, as was *A. torreyi* (Fewkes, 85).

All these related species have been suspected of causing poisoning to livestock when eaten in large amounts, the danger being either from bloat or nitrate poisoning (Kingsbury, 141; Durrell, Jensen & Klinger, 79). There has never been a suggestion that they would cause disorders in human beings, at least when eaten in ordinary amounts.

References (to numbers in the bibliography):
  A. For this species only—12, 13, 31, 43, 52, 83, 99, 117, 158, 181, 194, 195, 218, 221, 225, 239, 240, 259.
  B. For all species of *Amaranthus*—2, 11A, 42, 49, 57, 84, 92, 93, 138, 151, 160, 254.

Atriplex patula (A. carnosa, A. hastata, A. lepathifolia)
ORACHE, SPEARSCALE, SALTBRUSH

Description:
  Annual plants; stems 6 inches to 3½ feet long, erect or sprawling, simple or branched; leaves variable in size, usually about ⅞ to 3 inches long; flowers small and inconspicuous, lacking colorful petals; fruits one-seeded, borne between 2 triangular bracts, these about ⅛ to ½ inch long.

Found throughout North America. In the Rocky Mountain area growing on salt or alkaline soils, seldom above 8000 feet in elevation.

Use:
  We have two types of *Atriplex*, one group forming woody shrubs, the other annual, nonwoody plants. Both types have been used as food, our plant of course belonging to the second group. The seeds of these plants can be collected in quantity if one has the patience to do so. The young shoots of the annual kinds have long been a favorite for "greens" and we have often seen them being gathered

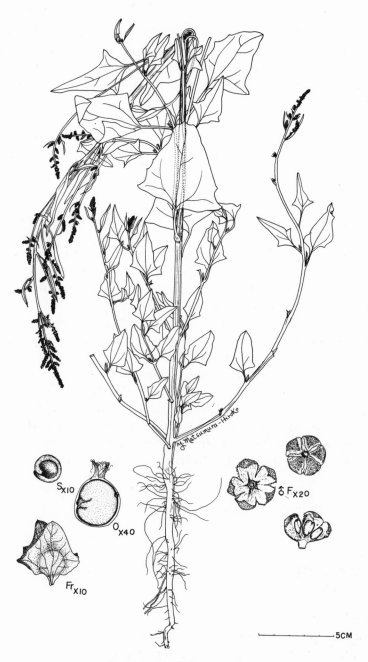

ORACHE *(Atriplex patula)*

for that purpose in this area. They are rather juicy and impregnated with salt which gives them a different, often a more desirable taste to some people. We have tried them when the plants were a little old, with rather unfavorable results. But taken at the right stage they can be delicious. Strangely enough, the best mess we have ever eaten was collected on November 20 from young plants that had sprouted from seeds due to some favorable fall rains. The water was not changed and the salty taste was not pronounced.

Other Species:

All the annual species can be used as described above. The most common one is *Atriplex hortensis*. This is a famous food plant and goes under the name of Mountain Spinach or Arrach as well as Orach (Muenscher & Rice, 168; Grieve, 102; Hedrick, 117; Uphof, 240; Clarkson, 53; Mal'Tsew, 151). Another species used is *Atriplex argentea* (Fewkes, 85; Hough, 128).

The shrubby species are often called "saltbushes" and often have the leaves so impregnated with salt that ground up pieces can be used to flavor other food. From our experience the different kinds of shrubby saltbushes vary somewhat in the amount of salt in the leaves. The seeds have been gathered and pounded or ground to make meal. The Indians are reported to have used the ashes of the burned plant to color their cornmeal, perhaps for ceremonial purposes. (Palmer, 183; Fewkes, 85; Castetter, 43; Whiting, 249; Jaeger, 132; Kearney & Peebles, 138; Colyer, 56)

References (to numbers in the bibliography for *A. patula*):
    18, 58, 84, 93, 107, 158, 228.

Brassica nigra
MUSTARD

Description:

Annual plants; stems erect, branching, 1⅓ to 6 feet tall; leaves varying from lobeless at least on the upper part of the plant, to deeply lobed as shown in the drawing; flowers in clusters; petals

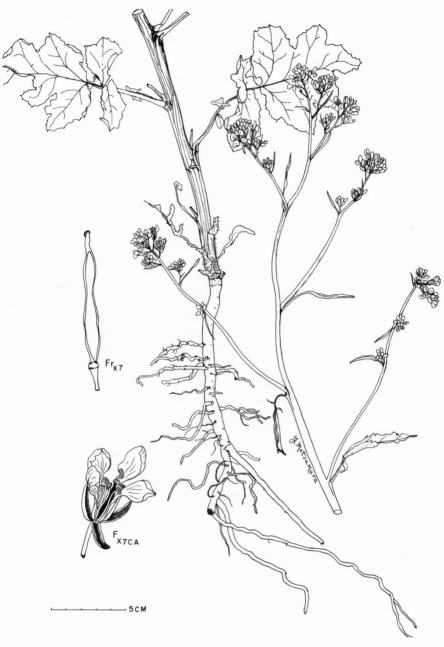

MUSTARD *(Brassica nigra)*

bright yellow, about ⅓ inch long; pods about ½ to 1 inch long and very narrow, erect on the main fruit stalk.

This mustard is now widely distributed in the United States, and is found as a weed in fields and waste places in our area, especially at lower elevations.

Use:

These plants, as well as related species, have long been used— the seeds to make the familiar mustard of the hamburger stands and the young shoots as the "mustard greens" often sold in vegetable markets. The plants contain a characteristic sharp taste and flavor; the seeds and fruits have been known to poison livestock (Kingsbury, 141; Core, Reitz & Gillespie, 59; Thomson & Sifton, 230), at least when consumed in excessive amounts.

The ripening pods can be gathered, spread on a cloth or plastic sheet and allowed to dry. Then one can beat out the seeds and add them to stews, meats, or greens for flavoring. These seeds can also. be ground into powder or meal and used as you would mustard powder. Also, this powder can be mixed with flour, vinegar, and water to make mustard paste, which may prove to be an acceptable substitute for the supermarket variety. Gibbons (92) suggested mixing this paste with soy sauce (1 tablespoon of mustard to ½ cup soy sauce) to give a sauce for Chinese food. We have never tried it, but it sounds good. This mustard paste may taste a little different from commercial mustard which probably is a blend from several plants, but will give the same effect to foods in general.

The mustard greens are prepared in about the same fashion as spinach but may take longer cooking, about 30 minutes boiling time being a good average, depending on the tenderness of the product. Since mustard greens may have a slight biting or pungent taste, many people like to use them to mix with other plants which have a blander taste, like *Amaranthus retroflexus* or *Chenopodium* spp. This can also be done when using the uncooked young leaves and shoots in salads.

Related Species:

All the similar species of *Brassica* can be used to make mustard paste or used as a potherb. Plants of our area that have been used are *B. juncea, B. kaber (B. arvensis), B. hirta (B. alba)* and *B. campestris.* (Uphof, 240; Bartlett, 18; Gordon, 99; Kephart, 140; Stratton, 225; Bale, 13; Harris, 112; Chestnut, 52; Stone, 221; Coville, 62; Muenscher, 167).

References (to numbers in the bibliography):
   31, 42, 57, 62, 84, 92, 93, 117, 134, 138, 158, 225, 240, 243, 251.

Caltha leptosepala (C. rotundifolia)
MARSH MARIGOLD

Perennial plants with stems short and bearing 1 or 2 flowers; leaves all basal, broadly egg-shaped with smooth to toothed margins; flower parts about 3/8 to 3/4 inch long, whitish to somewhat blue, especially on the outside.

Swamps and marshy meadows, often under the edge of snow banks. Rocky Mountains and northwest, usually above 8000 feet elevation and extending to above timberline.

Use:

This plant is locally abundant at higher elevations where other emergency material may be scarce. Several authorities warn against eating any part in raw condition and a sister species, *Caltha palustris,* has been reported to have caused livestock losses. However, Kingsbury (141) had no record of this occurring in the United States. Certainly, we have often eaten the flower buds and young leaves of our plant in a mixture with lettuce as a salad without ill effects. Colyer (56) concluded they add crispness and have a mild flavor.

The young leaves make an excellent potherb and are good until the flowers emerge; some writers say they are acceptable throughout most of the summer. We found them rather tough from the middle of June until fall. Care should be taken to wash the leaves thoroughly since the plant grows under marshy conditions and various small organisms may cling to the surfaces. We boiled the greens 10-60 minutes, depending on their relative tenderness. Some people prefer them in a cream sauce.

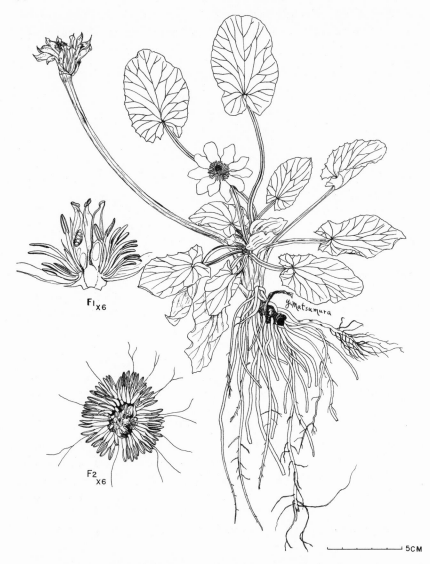

MARSH MARIGOLD *(Caltha leptosepala)*

The buds of the eastern yellow-flowered relative of our plant have been pickled and used as a substitute for capers. The roots are listed as being edible when boiled and are said to resemble sauerkraut in general appearance.

Related Species:
Caltha palustris is a yellow-flowered species growing east of our range.

References (to numbers in the bibliography):
    8, 29, 56, 57, 77A, 84, 93, 112, 117, 119, 158, 167, 168, 181, 198, 221.

Capsella bursa-pastoris (Bursa bursa-pastoris)
SHEPHERD'S PURSE

Description:
    Annual (or winter annual) plants; stems erect or nearly so, 4 inches to over a foot long in favorable sites; leaves tending to cluster near the base of the plants, at least in the young stages; petals white and small, only about 1/24 inch long; pod of characteristic triangular shape, $\frac{1}{4}$ to $\frac{3}{8}$ inch long.
    A weed in waste places, gardens, lawns, and fields, now widely distributed throughout the United States. Like all weeds it can be locally very abundant.

Use:
    This plant has a variety of uses and has appeared for sale on the markets in the eastern part of the United States. The ripening fruits were sometimes gathered, dried, and the seeds beaten out. These were ground into a meal by the Indians, but it would require a bit of patience to secure an adequate amount. The pods and seeds can be used to flavor other foods such as vegetable soup, and can be dried and stored for fall and winter (Harris, 112).
    The young leaves may be eaten raw in salads, especially if they are blanched. This can be done by covering a patch of the plants with straw, boards or canvas for a week or more. The fresh or dried roots have been utilized as a substitute for ginger, and have been candied by boiling in a rich sugar syrup (Coon, 58). However, the widest use of shepherd's purse is as a potherb. We boiled the young leaves for 20 minutes and changed the water once. This change, however, may not be necessary. We ate the plant with a

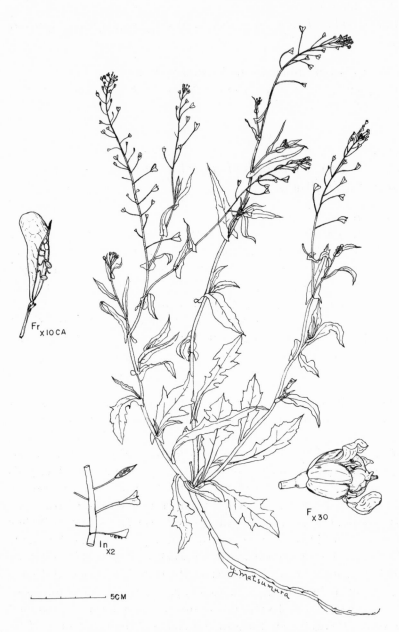

Fr ₓ₁₀CA

In ₓ₂

F ₓ₃₀

5CM

y.matsumura

SHEPHERD'S PURSE *(Capsella bursa-pastoris)*

little salt and vinegar and found it somewhat stronger than spinach but with none of the bitter peppery taste reported by some people. In fact, we rated it better than spinach with a background taste of cabbage or Brussels sprouts. The Boy Scouts of the area rate it second only to dandelion as a food plant.

This is a plant easy to identify and easy to collect in reasonable quantities. It might well be tried in moderate quantities at first or mixed with other plants in salads or greens until one is sure it will be relished alone.

Related Species:
None

References (to numbers in the bibliography):
11A, 14, 38, 42, 52, 56, 57, 58, 60, 77A, 84, 93, 99, 102, 107, 121, 140, 158, 181, 194, 206, 225, 227, 228, 229, 243.

Chenopodium berlandieri
LAMBS QUARTERS, PITSEED GOOSEFOOT, PIGWEED

This species is very similar to the common goosefoot (*C. album*) so well known in the eastern half of the United States. It differs from it in having its seeds roughened with minute pits, but this takes a good lens to observe. Both species are present in the Rocky Mountains, but the pitseed goosefoot appears to be more common. The following description and uses apply to both plants.

Description:
Annual plants, whitish green in color as if the leaves and stems were sprinkled with small flakes of white powder; stems becoming 1 to 5 feet tall; leaves 5/8 to 2 inches long; flowers very inconspicuous, lacking petals; fruit small and one-seeded, borne in clusters, often very many to a plant.

Waste ground and fields as a common weed. This species is found from Kansas west to the Pacific.

Use:
The seeds were commonly used by the Indians as a source of

PIGWEED *(Chenopodium berlandieri)*

meal for bread or gruel. They can be gathered in large quantities in various ways; for example, by placing them in large paper or cloth sacks, or by beating them out on rocks or canvas. The seeds are small and smooth so it may be necessary to boil them, mash them, and then dry the material before grinding. The flour is dark colored from the blackish seed coats, but bakes up into a nice tasting and surely a nutritious product. Some people describe the taste as somewhat "mousey" or "weedy" but pleasant withal. The seeds can be parched and eaten partly raw, but the taste may not be to your liking, and we have found that the seeds are so small they are hard to chew.

The young leaves and tender shoots have long been used in salads. However, the plant is most popular as a potherb cooked and served like spinach. It is one of our favorites and we find very few people who do not enjoy it, once they have overcome any prejudice they may have for eating "weeds." They cook down surprisingly in bulk, so gather plenty of material and use only the young growth. Boil them a bit longer than spinach, say 30-40 minutes (or 5 minutes at 15-lbs. pressure in a cooker). Several writers advise changing the water once, but we have never found this necessary.

Related Species:

Several similar species have been used as described above. These include *C. album, C. incanum, C. leptophyllum, C. fremontii, C. gigantospermum* and *C. cornutum.* Several species of *Chenopodium* have their parts spotted with small resin dots or sticky hairs that give a rank taste and odor. Two of these in our area are *C. ambrosioides* and *C. botrys* and they have been suspected of poisoning grazing animals. It would be best to avoid them, but a strong aromatic tea has been brewed from them and relished by some people. (Fernald & Kinsey, 84; Uphof, 240; Hedrick, 117; Muenscher, 167).

References (to numbers in the bibliography):

8, 11A, 12, 13, 17, 18, 26, 31, 37, 42, 43, 52, 56, 57, 58, 62, 65, 66, 67, 77A, 83, 84, 85, 92, 93, 95, 99, 102, 107, 112, 117, 119, 127, 128, 132, 134, 138, 140, 146, 151, 158, 162, 163, 168, 173, 182, 192, 194, 206, 208, 220, 221, 222, 225, 227, 228, 239, 240, 242, 243, 249, 254, 259.

Cleome serrulata (C. inornata, Peritoma serrulatum)
ROCKY MOUNTAIN BEEPLANT, SPIDERFLOWER, CLAMMY WEED

Description:

Annual plants with stems 1 to 3½ feet tall, freely branching above; leaves with 3 leaflets, these slightly toothed, ⅞ to 2 inches long; petals pink, rose or whitish, each about ⅜ to ½ inch long; pod 1 to 2 inches long, on a slender secondary stalk ⅜ to ⅞ inch long (in addition to the primary stalk).

Prairies, waste places, often on sandy ground from Kansas west to the Pacific. Widespread in the Rocky Mountain area, seldom above 8000 feet elevation.

Use:

This was an important food plant of the Western Indians and if it was not actually cultivated it was, in any event, encouraged to grow around their dwelling places. The most important value of the plant was as a potherb: the young tender shoots and leaves were used. The plant has a definite unpleasant odor, especially in age, and the cooking water should be changed 2 or 3 times. The Indians often boiled the plant for a long time, finally pulled out the stems and continued the boiling until a blackish, thick residue was left. This was often used as a paint or dye, but was sometimes left to dry in sheets, and then stored as a future source of food. The boiled shoots were sometimes rolled into balls which were allowed to dry for storage, to be soaked up and used later on.

The seeds were sometimes gathered and ground into a meal for gruel or bread. Young (259) said that the Navajos mixed 2 large ears of Indian Corn with ¾ cup of beeplant seeds. The shelled corn and the weed seeds were finely ground and molded into cakes which were then baked in hot ashes or in an oven.

This plant is locally abundant, often *very* abundant, and is certainly worth a trial as a food plant.

Related Species:

Cleome lutea is often very abundant in the western part of the Rocky Mountain area and was used by the Indians in much the same way. As the name suggests, the flowers are yellow, and the leaflets are usually 5 in number (Young, 259).

Rocky Mountain Beeplant *(Cleome serrulata)*

References (to numbers in the bibliography):
18, 35, 41, 43, 83, 85, 98, 128, 178, 195, 218, 220, 239, 248, 249, 259.

Epilobium angustifolium (Chamaenerion angustifolium, C. spicatum)
FIREWEED, WILLOW HERB

Description:

Perennial plants with erect, mostly unbranched stems 1½ to 8½ feet tall; leaves 2 to 6 inches long; petals ⅜ to ¾ inch long, lilac-purple to rose in color; pods 2 to 4 inches long, finally splitting in 4 narrow segments releasing the hairy-tufted seeds.

Open, often fairly moist ground or sometimes at the edges of woods, commonly coming in after fires (hence the name fireweed). Widely distributed in the United States and the Rocky Mountains where it seems most abundant in the mountainous area from 6000 feet to timberline.

Use:

This widely distributed plant has many uses. The young shoots can be cooked like asparagus, or the tender leaves can be stripped off and treated as a potherb. We found them very palatable, but inclined to develop a bitterness when they became too old. These young leaves made an acceptable salad, especially when mixed with other ingredients like lettuce. We also tried the flower stalks when the flowers were still in the bud stage, and used them in combination with other plants as a salad. They can also be cooked. If you cook the plants you might well vary the time according to the age and tenderness of the part used, but try 9-15 minutes (at 5000 feet elevation) for a starter.

If the leaves and shoots are too old the plant can still be used. Try drying the mature leaves and using them for tea. Some people advise mixing the leaves with conventional tea leaves, this would be worth doing in case your supply of the commercial product was running low.

The mature plants can be gathered and the bark peeled away from the central pith. This core is slightly sweet, tender, and pleasant to the taste when eaten raw. We found the stems difficult to peel and the remaining pith disappointingly narrow. Our conclusion was that it makes a chewy morsel but it would be difficult indeed to secure a satisfying meal. This pith has been used by

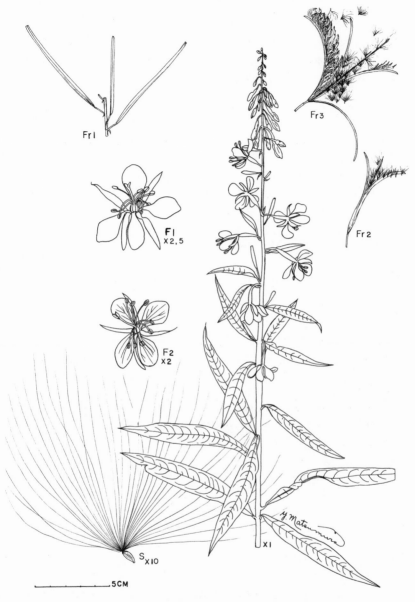

Fr1

F1
×2,5

F2
×2

Fr3

Fr2

S
×10

×1

M. Matsumura

5CM

FIREWEED *(Epilobium angustifolium)*

some to flavor and thicken stews and soups. Possibly you may find the stems easier to peel in the earlier stages of the plant's growth.

This plant can be very abundant and because it has such a wide range of seasonal use it must be considered very good both as a general and as an emergency food.

Related Species:

The dwarf or broadleaved fireweed *(Epilobium latifolium)* is less common in our area but is used like the common species, and preferred to it by some people. (Heller, 119; Hedrick, 117; Fernald & Kinsey, 84; Szczawinski & Hardy, 228). We have tried some of the smaller species of *Epilobium* and found them acceptable (Douglass, 77A).

References (to numbers in the bibliography):

4, 8, 13, 57, 77A, 84, 93, 99, 107, 117, 119, 134, 138, 151, 158, 176, 181, 187, 194, 214, 217, 227, 228, 229, 240, 243.

Galinsoga parviflora
Quickweed, Galinsoga, Little Flower Quickweed

Description:

Annual plants; stems usually sprawling as they mature, 4 inches to 3 feet long; flowers individually small, in small heads consisting of white marginal flowers and yellow central ones.

This species is found in flower borders, gardens, and waste places, often in partial shade and often acting as a weed. It has spread from South and Central America into most of the United States and can be expected anywhere in settled areas of the Rocky Mountain area. It seems to be only locally abundant.

Use:

This plant has been used extensively in other countries as a potherb. We selected young tender plants, removed the roots and boiled the tops for about 25 minutes (at 5000 ft. elevation). We served them with salt, pepper, butter, and vinegar. We found they made very acceptable greens, with no hint of bitterness. Quickweed is often very abundant, as any weed is apt to be, and certainly is worth a trial as food. It would be especially good in a

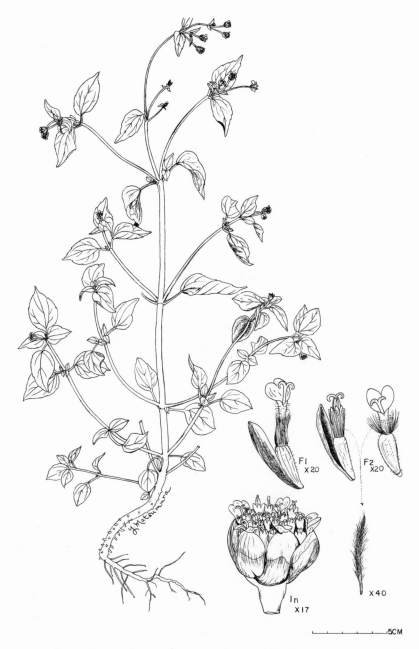

F1
X20

F2
X20

X40

In
X17

5CM

QUICKWEED *(Galinsoga parviflora)*

mixture with some other plant of more pronounced flavor, because of the bland taste of the plant. Since it grows in cultivated or settled areas it would not be particularly valuable as a survival species.

Related Species:

Galinsoga ciliata (G. aristulata) is a similar-appearing species found in the same places as the above one. We have not tried it, but others say it also makes a good potherb.

References (to numbers in the bibliography):
84, 93.

Hemerocallis fulva
DAYLILY, COMMON ORANGE DAYLILY

Description:

Perennial plants, often growing in dense patches spreading by scaly rootstalks and thickened tuberous roots; stems about 1½ to 5 feet tall; flowers 3 to 5 inches long, orange-red, or tawny-orange, deeper colored in the center.

This plant has been introduced into cultivation from Eurasia. It rather commonly spreads to roadsides and ditches, especially in the eastern part of the United States; this occurs sometimes in the Rocky Mountain area.

Use:

In the Orient the flowers of daylilies are picked in the bud, or when somewhat withered and closed after flowering. These are cooked in various ways, somewhat as green beans are prepared, or they are dried in the sun. These dry flowers are stored and used later on in various ways, often as a condiment. In fact, these dried flowers have been commercially imported into this country from China. We have tried the buds, boiling them for 10 minutes in salt water, and serving them with butter. They were tender although rather crisp, with a taste somewhat like that of green beans, but with a pleasant individual flavor. Professor Matsumura, our il-

DAYLILY *(Hemerocallis fulva)*

lustrator, told us that the young shoots are often used in Japan, somewhat as we would use asparagus or celery in this country.

The tuberous-like roots are used as food in many parts of the world. We tried them in July, boiling them for 40 minutes in salty water. The young tubers were tender and pleasant tasting. The older roots had a fibrous peeling that needed to be removed, but the taste of the inner portion was acceptable. The young tuberous roots are said to be excellent when used raw in salad mixtures.

This is an attractive cultivated flower that grows vigorously, so much so that the patch may need to be thinned out anyway. These plants, with those from patches running wild, should provide a large amount of palatable food.

Related Species:

A daylily with yellow flowers *(Hemerocallis flava)* is also commonly cultivated and may likewise escape to ditches and thickets. We have not tried the tuberous roots of this one but they are undoubtedly edible. The buds taste as good to us as those of the orange-flowered species and can be cooked in the same manner, that is, boiled and eaten with butter, or scrambled with eggs.

References (to numbers in the bibliography):
    84, 92, 93, 117, 184, 223, 240.

Monolepis nuttalliana
Nuttall Monolepis, Poverty Weed, Patata

Description:

Annual plants with prostrate or sprawling stems 4 to 12 inches long; leaves from ⅜ to about 3 inches long; flowers inconspicuous.

Waste places, edges of lawns and gardens, often on alkaline or salty ground. Canada south to Texas, Mexico, and California.

Use:

This plant makes a very good potherb. Select young and tender plants; we advise removing the roots, especially if they appear to

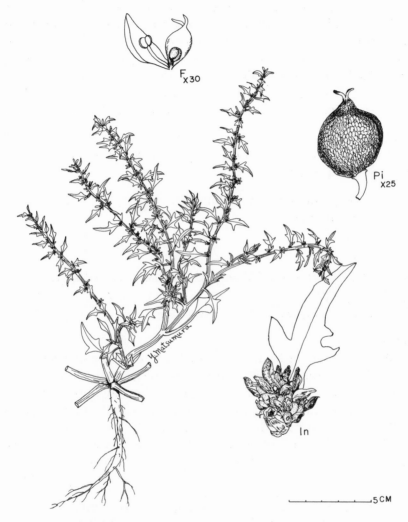

NUTTALL MONOLEPIS *(Monolepis nuttalliana)*

be tough and fibrous. We boiled the shoots for about 20-30 minutes, changing the water once. We liked this plant about as well as any we have tried. The taste was pleasant and mild so that we suspect the cooking water would not really need to be changed. The Indians were reported to have used the roots for food. We tried them, boiling them for 30 minutes and frying them in butter. They were acceptable but some of the older ones were a bit tough. Also, it is difficult to secure a satisfactory amount since the annual roots are so small. This potherb is often present in large quantities, but it sometimes takes a little patience in order to secure a large amount. The Indians were said to use the small seeds as "pinole," but even more patience would be needed to secure a sufficient quantity of them for that.

Related Species:

A far western species, *Monolepis pusilla,* comes into the western part of our area and would be worth a trial.

References (to numbers in the bibliography):
    43, 138, 225, 240.

Oenothera strigosa (Onagra strigosa, Oenothera biennis var. *hirsutissima)*
EVENING PRIMROSE, SUNDROPS

Description:

Plants forming a basal cluster of leaves only the first year, the second year flowering (biennial); stems erect, usually unbranched, 1 to 3⅓ feet tall; lower leaves 1¼ to 4 inches long, upper shorter; petals yellow but often fading to whitish or pink, ½ to ¾ inch long; pods 1 to 1⅜ inches long, narrow.

Valley and plains, often on roadsides where the soil is sandy. Minnesota to Kansas and west to the Pacific Coast.

Use:

This plant was at one time so popular that forms of it were cultivated in Europe, perhaps even to the present time. The young leaves and shoots were used as a salad. They probably would be better blanched, using straw, canvas, or an inverted basket to cover the plants. These shoots can also be used as a potherb, but we would advise changing the water at least once, to try to get rid of a distinctly bitter taste. This unpleasant taste may be more noticeable at certain seasons and perhaps is stronger in some local races of the plants.

Evening Primrose *(Oenothera strigosa)*

The roots are rather thickened, and can be collected and boiled like parsnips. We advise using the roots of the first year's plants, but even the older roots have an inner core that is edible in case of need. Again, we suggest changing the water in the process, but a lingering bitterness may persist even then. Perhaps the cultivated forms have larger, more tender, and less bitter roots, but from our own experience we concluded that this evening primrose has food value only in an emergency.

Related Species:

We would guess that all the related species of this large group of plants would stand a trial; as far as we know none are poisonous. In our area *Oenothera hookeri,* a large yellow-flowered plant, comes into the southern part of our range. It has been tried by us and appeared to be of about the same value as the species described above. A white-flowered annual species, *O. albicaulis,* has podlike fruits that were eaten by the Indians (Castetter & Opler, 45). We have tried eating the cooked young pods of several species of evening primrose and found them acceptable. Even the older (but still unripe) pods, although rather tough, can be cooked and eaten.

References (to numbers in the bibliography):

42, 57, 84, 93, 99, 102, 112, 117, 132, 134, 138, 140, 158, 181, 219, 225, 243.

Plantago major
PLANTAIN, INDIAN WHEAT

Description:

Perennial plants with a cluster of roots (as shown); leaves 2 to 14 inches long; flowers small and inconspicuous, borne in a spike.

A weed in waste places, fields, gardens, and lawns throughout most of North America.

Use:

This plant is often abundant in disturbed areas. The young leaves are often used as a potherb in various parts of the world.

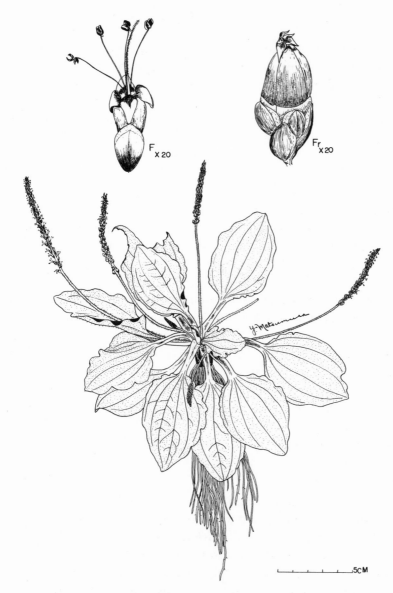

$F_{x 20}$

$Fr_{x 20}$

5CM

PLANTAIN *(Plantago major)*

They should be boiled from 15-35 minutes depending on their age, and can be used in any of the ways you would serve spinach. We suggest trying them as follows:

Select only the leaf blades, discarding the leaf stalks. Wash the leaves and dip them into a batter of milk, egg, and cracker crumbs or flour. Fry these leaves over a low heat for about half an hour, salting them during the cooking process. These coated fried leaves may remind you in many ways of potato chips and can be eaten warm or cold in lunches. Boorman (29) gave a recipe called "Sweet and Sour Plantain" using bacon, vinegar, sugar, hard boiled egg, salt, and pepper. The sweet-and-sour sauce was poured over the boiled plantain leaves.

The very young leaves have been used as a salad, or in a salad mixture. It would be advisble to try blanching some plants by excluding the light in some manner, especially if you use them as a salad. Plantain is said to make an acceptable tea when the dried leaves are boiled for an appropriate time and "plantain leaf tea" is for sale in various places. This is also one of the cure-all herbs, fancied or real, used to cure or prevent infections from cuts or blisters. The bruised fresh leaves are placed on the wound, or the boiled leaf mass is sometimes used, held in place with a bandage or adhesive tape. One of us has tried it several times and is inclined to think that it actually helped (Bagdonas, 11A). The bruised leaf can be wrapped around a cut finger and tied in place with a fiber or piece of string. At least it makes a primitive bandage. The plantain is often very abundant and is certainly worth trying, especially in a food emergency.

Related Species:

The narrow-leaved plantain *(Plantago lanceolata)* has been recommended as an emergency food (Uphof, 240). The seeds of certain species (such as *P. purshii)* are sometimes gathered (Kearney & Peebles, 138) to be used as substitutes for the "psyllium" seed of commerce *(Plantago psyllium)* which is sold as a laxative. Another broad-leaved species *P. rugelii* has been used as a potherb (Oswald, 179).

References (to numbers in the bibliography):

8, 11A, 13, 29, 42, 43, 56, 57, 84, 99, 107, 117, 132, 140, 146, 158, 181, 205, 221, 222, 225, 228, 243.

Portulaca oleracea
COMMON PURSLANE, COMMON PORTULACA

Description:

Annual plants with fleshy succulent stems and leaves; stems prostrate or sprawling, up to one foot long; leaves flat but still thick, up to ¼ inch long; petals about ⅛ inch long, yellow in color; podlike fruits ⅛ to ⅜ inch long; seeds very small, up to 1/16 inch wide.

Waste places, fields, gardens, often as a weed but sometimes well away from cultivated areas. Widespread in the United States and in the Rocky Mountain area at low to medium elevations.

Use:

This is a fleshy plant well known to gardeners as a weed that is hard to dry out and kill once it is pulled up. It has been widely used as food, and forms of it are actually cultivated in several parts of the world. The young shoots are used raw as a salad, often mixed with other plants because of the somewhat sour taste. We were once served a mixed salad at a restaurant in this area, and found that it contained leaves of purslane, but this may have been accidental! Because of the high water content (listed at 92.61 percent by Storer, 222), they can be eaten raw to quench the thirst. The succulent young stems and leaves can be pickled in vinegar and sugar, following any pickle recipe.

Purslane has long been a favorite when used for greens. The seeds have a way of germinating following summer rains, so that young growth may be available continuously up to late fall. Also, a single patch can be harvested all summer by picking off the young shoots as needed, and allowing the new ones to grow out for future use. We select young plants, wash them, remove the roots, and boil them for about 15 minutes (at 5000 ft.), sometimes changing the water once. We have tried them in the ways that one would cook spinach, and found them to be excellent. They have a rather mild taste with a somewhat mucilaginous texture but this does not detract from their pleasant, slightly sour flavor. If the fatty feeling bothers you, try mixing the greens with those

COMMON PURSLANE (*Portulaca oleracea*)

from other plants such as mustard. Gibbons (92) and Fernald and Kinsey (84) suggested disguising this slippery texture by mixing the purslane shoots with bread crumbs and beaten eggs, baking the mixture in the oven until done. Because of their mucilaginous quality, the young stems have long been popular for thickening soup.

The Indians and Mexicans at one time dried large quantities of this plant by spreading the young stems out in the hot sun on the roofs. This dried material was found to be fairly high in albuminoids (30.25%) and carbohydrates (34.73%) by Storer (222). It could then be soaked up later and boiled as a potherb.

The seeds of purslane, although very small, have been used as food, particularly by the Indians. A pile of these plants in fruiting condition can be placed on a flat rock or canvas and left to dry in the sun. Or they can be placed in a sack of paper or cloth to dry. In any case, the seeds will fall to the bottom, can be gathered, winnowed or sifted, and ground into a meal or flour. These seeds can be used in various ways, but we thought them rather tasteless when tried by themselves.

This is an excellent salad plant or potherb, often available in quantities, and is relatively easy to identify. Since it sometimes grows abundantly in isolated areas it has value as an emergency food.

Related Species:

A closely related species, *Portulaca retusa,* grows in the southern part of our area, from Texas to Arizona, extending north to southern Utah and possibly southern Colorado. It has been utilized in the same way as our species in the area where it grows, especially by the Indians. (Fewkes, 85; Uphof, 240; Elmore, 83; Robbins et al., 195).

References (to numbers in the bibliography):

2, 13, 18, 33, 42, 43, 56, 57, 58, 69, 83, 84, 92, 93, 98, 99, 112, 117, 124, 127, 132, 138, 140, 141, 146, 149, 151, 158, 160, 162, 165, 168, 181, 182, 183, 194, 195, 204, 205, 219, 221, 222, 225, 240, 243, 244, 249.

Rumex crispus
Curly Dock, Sour Dock

Description:

Perennial plants growing from taproots; stems 1 to 3½ feet tall; leaves 4 to 12 inches long, the margins distinctly wavy; flowers small and inconspicuous; fruit seedlike, with 3 wings, the whole ⅛ to ¼ inch long.

Cultivated or disturbed ground, waste places, and roadsides as a weed. Widespread in North America and common at lower and middle elevations in the Rocky Mountain area.

Use:

There are over a dozen plants of this area that resemble the above, and all are called "docks." All of them are edible to some degree, although some of them are not very pleasant tasting. They contain oxalates in varying amounts, and a few have caused losses to livestock when they are grazed upon them to excess (Durrell, Jensen & Klinger, 79; Kingsbury, 141). There has never been any difficulty reported with human beings; in fact, the docks have always been famous food producers. Many people consider the curly dock to be the best of all the docks, and that is our own opinion at the present time.

We gathered the leaves in the spring while they were tender and free from insect holes. It was rather easy to secure abundant material, and this lost less bulk in cooking than would be expected. The large coarse leaves, upon cooking, became surprisingly tender. We have been told that a second crop of young leaves may be produced in the fall, particularly after a rain. We boiled these young leaves for 10 minutes in limited liquid without changing water at all. Served with salt, pepper, and vinegar or lemon juice, like spinach, they proved to be very good. We have never noticed any rank, bitter taste to the plant, but this is sometimes described in the literature, with the advice to change the cooking water several times. You can find this out by experiment. Many of the docks have a sour taste that led one Indian woman to observe "It

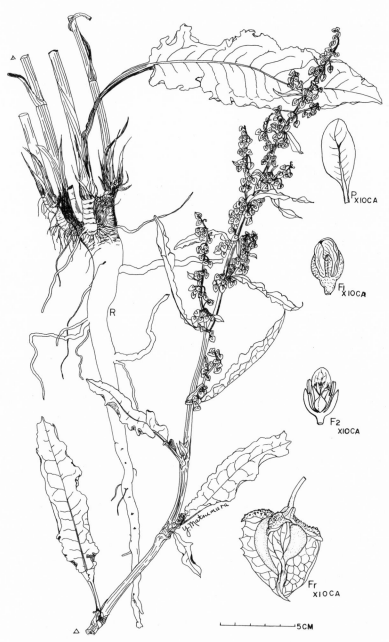

R

P XIOCA

F₁ XIOCA

F₂ XIOCA

Fr XIOCA

y.Matsumura

5CM

CURLY DOCK *(Rumex crispus)*

already has the vinegar in it." We consider the greens "bland" tasting and rather like them in mixtures with some others of a more pronounced taste, such as some of the mustards.

The tender leaves have been eaten raw in salads. Many people in this area have used the seed as a substitute for tobacco or in a mixture with it; in fact this dock is often called "Indian tobacco." We have tried it and it does seem to be a reasonably good substitute. In addition the Indians gathered these ripe seeds of the docks and ground them into a meal that they used to make bread and mush.

The curly dock is abundant, the leaves are bulky and palatable, making this plant an excellent survival source. The brown, conspicuous, seedlike fruits may protrude above a snow cover, and not only provide food for winter birds but are also available as food for some hungry human being.

Related Species:

Several similar docks have been favorite food producers including *Rumex mexicanus* (Uphof, 240), *R. altissimus* (Stevens, 219), *R. occidentalis* (Carver, 42), *R. obtusifolius* (Medsger, 158; Stratton, 225), *R. salicifolius* (Coville, 65), *R. patienta* (Medsger, 158; Stratton, 225; Hedrick, 117) and *R. hymenosepalus* (Curtin, 66; Budrow, 36; Medsger, 158; Hedrick, 117; Stratton, 225; Elmore, 83; Kearney & Peebles, 138; Uphof, 240; Castetter, 43; Bartlett, 18; Russell, 199; Saunders, 204; Yanovsky & Kingsbury, 256; Dodge, 76; Balls, 14). The last one *(R. hymenosepalus)* is famous as a source of greens; we have noticed a strong sour taste to it, so much so that we pour off at least one water in cooking. This is the species with so much tannin in its roots that it has often been used to tan hides. The Indians reportedly used *R. venosus* (Castetter, 43), but we found it unpleasant tasting. *R. densiflorus* leaves proved to be very good when cooked like spinach, but the large root was too bitter for us to enjoy eating it.

References (to numbers in the bibliography:

2, 11A, 13, 26, 31, 42, 43, 52, 56, 57, 58, 62, 66, 84, 93, 95, 99, 112, 117, 132, 138, 140, 158, 181, 182, 219, 221, 225, 227, 240.

Salsola kali (S. pestifer)
Russian Thistle, Tumbleweed, Saltwort

Description:

Annual, much-branched plants, forming roundish masses 1 to 3 feet or more in diameter that act as "tumbleweeds"; leaves 1 to 2½ inches long, becoming spiny-pointed at maturity; flowers inconspicuous; fruit seedlike, bearing horizontal, papery wings.

Dry plains, fields, roadsides, and waste places, often acting as a weed. This plant has been introduced from Eurasia in various parts of the United States, especially the western half. It is common in the Rocky Mountain area at low to medium elevations, seldom occurring above 8500 feet in the mountains.

Use:

The young, rapidly growing shoots around 2 to 5 inches tall make a very good potherb. We clipped off the roots, and boiled the tops for 12-15 minutes without a change of water. Served like spinach with salt, pepper, and butter; or with the addition of vinegar or lemon juice, we found Russian thistle plants mild, pleasant, and crisp tasting, making them one of the very best potherbs we have ever eaten. They can be dressed up with fried bacon strips or hard boiled egg slices as you would serve spinach, but are also good stirred into a cream sauce and served over toast. Because of the bland taste they can be mixed to good advantage with other more "tangy" plants such as mustard.

We try to collect the young plants soon after a good rain, when the parts are tender and succulent. In most years they are not available for a very long period of the year, although there may be several of these young stages during some seasons depending on the rainfall pattern. Russian thistle is remarkably resistant to drought and a light rain may bring up the young plants, which can quickly mature in dry periods. These young plants have been mowed and used as an emergency hay crop for livestock in this area. Russian thistle is available in almost unlimited quantities during its limited tender period; it certainly should be utilized

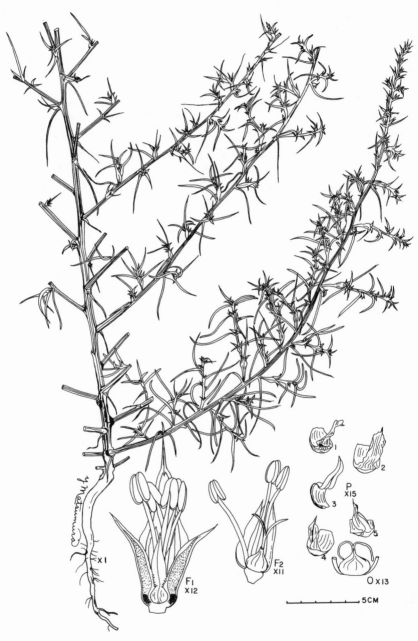

TUMBLEWEED *(Salsola kali)*

more often by the people of this area. The seeds are abundant and might be collected, ground into a meal, and eaten in an emergency. They might be rather hard to secure in quantity since the mature plant is so spiny. Carpenter and Steggerda (41) found the seeds contained 3.9 calories per gram.

Related Species:
A closely related species, *Salsola collina,* has been reported in our area and should be just as edible, especially since it is less spiny at maturity.

References (to numbers in the bibliography):
31, 158, 225, 240.

Sisymbrium spp.
TUMBLEMUSTARD, HEDGE MUSTARD

Description:
Annual or possibly biennial plants (producing a cluster of leaves the first year, elongating and flowering the next); stems up to 3 or 4 feet tall; leaves lobed, or in some kinds lacking lobes; petals 4, usually yellow but sometimes white or purple; fruit, a long slender pod.

Various species widespread over North America, some of them very weedy.

Use:
These plants have often been used as potherbs when the leaves and shoots are young and tender. It is reported that they have been eaten raw as a salad, but if you try them it would be wise to mix them with other plants. The foliage has been found to be poisonous to livestock, when eaten in quantity, according to Thomson & Sifton (230), so it would be wise to go slowly at first when eating the leaves.

The Indians used to gather the small seeds of these mustards. The plants were dried over a cloth and then shaken out, or the clusters of fruit were picked, placed in a bag, and allowed to dry.

F₁
×10

5CM

F₂
×10

TUMBLEMUSTARD *(Sisymbrium altissimum)*

In any event, the seeds secured were ground into a meal and used for such things as flavoring soup, or in making gruel. Since the plant is so abundant in places, it is worth remembering in a food emergency.

Related Species:
The two commonest weedy species, both widespread in the United States, are *Sisymbrium altissimum* and *S. officinalis.* However, other ones are present and should be tried.

References (to numbers in the bibliography):
83, 84, 93, 117, 167, 218, 230, 239.

Stellaria media (Alsine media)
CHICKWEED, COMMON CHICKWEED

Description:
Annual plants; stems 4 to 16 inches long, often prostrate; leaves about ½ to 1½ inches long; flowers small, the white petals about ⅛ to ¼ inch long, each 2 lobed at the apex; fruit a dry podlike capsule.

Waste places and cultivated grounds especially in shaded areas in lawns. Widely distributed in temperate North America and the Rocky Mountain area.

Use:
This chickweed is much used in Europe, and we in this country who have tried it agree that is certainly is a good edible plant. Although it is listed as an annual, it seems to sprout up all during the growing season, even staying green throughout part of the winter. The young shoots are used, since the parts toughen with age and often acquire a rather strong taste. You may consider it somewhat tedious to secure an adequate supply, but the plant is often very abundant. We enjoy it most in the spring, but it can be used the year round, even sometimes throughout the winter.

We have used these young shoots as a salad or as a garnish, often mixed with other plants. The taste was that of an ordinary green leaf, not very pronounced, but certainly not displeasing.

F
X10

X1

5 CM

CHICKWEED *(Stellaria media)*

The common chickweed is famous as a potherb, when cooked
and treated in any of the ways you would spinach. We boiled the
shoots in a rather small amount of salted water for about 20-30
minutes, and served them with vinegar or with butter. The taste
was definite, but not strong, very pleasing and, to us, certainly
superior to spinach. Some people claim they do not notice any

special distinctive taste and accordingly recommend mixing chick-weed with other "tangy" plants like some of the mustards. How-ever, we have always enjoyed them alone. Chickweed-leaf tea is for sale in a grocery store in this area.

This may not be an exceptionally good survival plant, but only because it is seldom found out in the wilds where you may desper-ately need it. However, it is an excellent general source of material for salads and greens, since it is apt to be growing in abundance close at hand.

Related Species:
See *Stellaria jamesiana.*

References (to numbers in the bibliography):
11A, 13, 42, 57, 84, 93, 99, 102, 112, 117, 127, 134, 140, 158, 179, 194, 219, 225, 229.

Taraxacum officinale
COMMON DANDELION

Description:
Plants perennial from taproots; the fresh parts exuding a milky juice when cut or broken; true stems very short, the leaves all clustered at about ground level; leaves lobed in from their sides; the leafless flower stalks hollow in the center, varying in height depending on where the plant grows and the age of the flower, usually about 2 to 12 inches long; flowers crowded in a head, one to a stalk, yellow in color, the head, when open, about 1/2 to 2 inches wide; fruits small and seedlike, pale gray to olive-green in color, each one bearing a parachute of hairs at the apex.

Almost throughout the world and widespread in North Amer-ica. In the Rocky Mountain area it is a common weed, especially in lawns and pastures. It may be abundant in meadows, even above 10,000 feet.

Use:
The common dandelion is a plant of many uses in many cor-ners of the globe. The seeds have often been deliberately carried

from place to place for cultivation. This accounts, at least in part, for its wide distribution. The seedlike fruits can be carried long distances on air currents since each one bears a very efficient parachute of hairs. Many people consider (or pretend to consider) that the bright yellow dandelion flowers are attractive on their lawn, and they may be right. However, the effect is marred later on when they form their globular heads of gray or white fruits which are quickly elevated above the surrounding grass. Other people wage a constant battle against them and use every method they can think of to clear them off the place. Some use various chemical preparations, like 2-4D, to spray on the plants. It is wise to avoid such sprayed dandelions in collecting them for food. It has been observed by many people that the prevailing winds always blow from a lawn well spotted with the yellow and gray dandelion heads toward a lawn where such a constant eradication battle is being waged!

The young dandelion leaves are fancied by many in a salad. As they age they not only toughen but take on a decidedly bitter taste that is displeasing to many people. We always look around for plants in the shade or for those that have been covered with sand or litter. Such plants may be naturally blanched and the yellow or whitish leaves are then at their best. If you wish, you can blanch the plants yourself by covering them with cans, pots, straw, or canvas. A clever arrangement is to dig up a supply of the roots and put them in earth in flower pots or boxes. These can be carried into the basement and later on, often during the winter, will supply you with an amazing amount of blanched leaves. Try the young, preferably blanched leaves, in a salad with onions, radishes, parsley, and a little sugar. We also like them tossed with diced hard-boiled eggs, with vinegar and oil. Some people find it easier to slice off the top of the crown with its attached leaves when collecting material. This crown top may be left on if you wish.

The young leaves are a favorite food when boiled as a potherb. When the leaves are tender or blanched you may not have to change the water in the process, but we have found that 2 or 3 changes are usually necessary to eliminate or cut down the bitter taste. In general, dandelion greens can be used as you would spin-

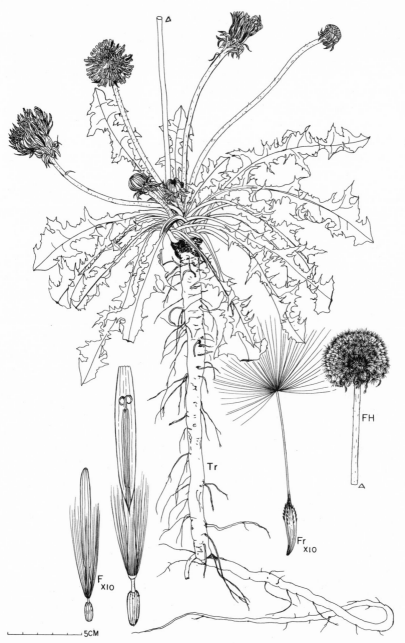

COMMON DANDELION *(Taraxacum officinale)*

ach, dressed up with crisp fried bacon or hard boiled eggs, creamed, in soups, scalloped or baked with meats, etc. If you find them strong tasting, try mixing them with other blander greens (see *Amaranthus* species). We boil them for 10-20 minutes depending on the age of the leaves.

The roots are said to be sliced and used in salads by some people. They are also roasted, fried or when dried and ground, made into a coffee-like beverage much as chicory is used. We have tried them and decided they have a distinctive taste that might take a bit of getting used to before becoming pleasurable. We have heard that the dried leaves can be used to make a kind of "tea" but have never tried it, although we have seen dandelion tea for sale in a local grocery store.

You might try the blossoms with pancakes. Use the young heads and drop them on the top of the pancake batter. When the pancake is turned over the heads are cooked and may add variety, and color to your camp breakfast. The blossoms are famous for wine making and several recipes for making it have been published. We give a representative one below:

DANDELION WINE

1 gallon dandelion petals	4 lbs. sugar
1 gallon boiling water	1 yeast cake (compressed)
4 oranges	1 lb. chopped raisins
1 lemon	1 slice toast

Pick the flowers from the heads, throwing away the hollow stalks and the denuded heads. Place them in a crock or jar and pour the boiling water over them.

Cover and leave for about 5 days, stirring several times during that period if you wish.

Strain out the liquid and add the sugar to it. Peel the oranges and lemon and drop in the peel, then add the juices of these fruits and the chopped raisins. Boil all this for 20 minutes in a preserving kettle and return it to the crock. Cool, place the yeast on the piece of toast and put it in. Cover and leave for about 3 days. Then decant the liquid into jars or bottles. Some say that the wine should be aged for at least one year before using.

A final use of dandelions was given to us by Bagdonas (11A). He stated that the Boy Scouts of this area eat the seedlike fruits raw as an emergency food. The plumelike hairs are grasped by the fingers and the fruits are readily broken off and eaten. Sometimes these have a slight bitter taste, but not enough to make them distasteful in times of acute food shortage. This plant is certainly a valuable edible plant, and since it is abundant at all elevations, it is a valuable all around source of food. It is said to be very high in vitamins A and C.

Related Species:

The red-fruited dandelion *(Taraxacum erythrospermum)* is similar in appearance and found in about the same places as the common dandelion. It can be used in the same way. In addition we have several, less common, native species of dandelion in this area that should be tried for their edible qualities.

References (to numbers in the bibliography):

4, 8, 11A, 13, 18, 29, 31, 38, 42, 43, 49, 56, 57, 58, 62, 68A, 74, 84, 92, 93, 99, 102, 107, 112, 117, 119, 121, 124, 129, 132, 134, 138, 140, 146, 151, 158, 162, 163, 168, 182, 187, 195, 196, 205, 206, 212A, 214, 219, 221, 222, 225, 228, 240, 242, 243, 244, 256.

Thlaspi arvense
FIELD PENNYCRESS

Description:

Annual plants; stems 6 to 20 inches tall, often branched above; flowers small, each of the four petals about $\frac{1}{8}$ inch long, white in color; fruit a flattened, roundish pod about $\frac{3}{8}$ to $\frac{5}{8}$ inch wide.

Waste places, roadsides, fields, and gardens, often acting as a weed. Widely distributed in North America. In our area from low elevations to as high as 10,000 feet.

Use:

This plant is a popular food plant in various parts of the world, often being cultivated in Europe. It is used when the shoots are

Fr

F×10

⌞_____⌟ 5 CM

FIELD PENNYCRESS (*Thlaspi arvense*)

young and tender, utilized raw as a salad, or cooked as a potherb
like spinach. Rexford (194) stated that it is high in the vitamins
C and G and contains a relatively large amount of sulfur. If so, it
may have the health effect of the old favorite, sulfur and molasses.

The plant belongs to the mustard family and the leaves have the characteristic mustard "bite." We boiled the shoots for 15-25 minutes and changed the water once or twice. Even then a slight bitterness is present, so we often mix the greens with those from some blander tasting plant like one of the pigweeds. (See *Amaranthus* species.)

We found the young leaves tender, when used in a salad, but rather bitter tasting, so we either mixed them with those from other plants or used a strong flavored salad dressing. All in all, field pennycress is not one of our favorite edible plants.

We have heard that the seeds and fruits have been used to flavor other food, but we cannot recommend doing so since they have caused illness when fed to cattle in hay. (Thomson & Sifton, 230; Kingsbury, 141). We have never cared to experiment in the matter and would rather have people say in cases like this, "He is a coward," rather than, "He was a brave man."

Related Species:

We have some native species related to field pennycress, but they are smaller plants and would be difficult to gather in sufficient quantity. *(Thlaspi alpestre).*

References (to numbers in the bibliography):
84, 93, 117, 158, 167, 194, 219, 225.

Urtica dioica (U. gracilis, U. viridis, U. procera)
NETTLE, STINGING NETTLE

Description:

Perennial plants from creeping underground rootstocks; stems 1⅔ to 6 feet tall, bearing stinging hairs at least below; leaf stalks about ⅜ to 2 inches long; flowers greenish colored and inconspicuous; fruit small and seedlike.

Along streams, canyons, and ditches or in waste places where the ground is somewhat moist. Widely distributed in North America and found throughout the Rocky Mountain area as a narrow-leafed form called, var. *procera.*

Use:

The nettle has always been popular as a food in other parts of the world. The French are said to make at least seven kinds of dishes from it; in Scotland it is as popular a potherb as it is in many other countries of Europe. The only drawback to its use is the presence of stinging hairs which make gathering it a problem. These stiff hairs are sharp but brittle at the ends and hollow in the center, this cavity leads down to a bulbous base that is filled with a stinging fluid, which is said to contain formic acid. If the tip of the hair is allowed to penetrate the skin, especially under pressure, the liquid is injected as if from a hypodermic needle.

We use gloves, preferably leather ones, when gathering nettles, or if we have forgotten the gloves we handle the young shoots carefully with the thumb and first two fingers to avoid letting them touch the tender skin of the hands. Even if we do get a few stings they are not serious (at least to us) and the effects soon pass away. Of course this sting is inactivated completely on cooking the plants.

The commonest use of nettle is as a potherb, cooked and used like spinach. We selected tender shoots about 6 to 8 inches tall. If these are pulled or dug up one finds a length of pink underground stem connecting them with the lower rootstock. These portions are tender and can be included with the tops. We boiled them for about 15 minutes with just enough water to cover the herb. They can be used to flavor or augment many other foods; we like them best when served with butter or vinegar. They have the bland taste of spinach and for that reason are often mixed with stronger tasting plants like sorrel or mustard. Cameron (38) suggested the following recipe for soup.

NETTLE SOUP

Wash and boil the nettle shoots, then rub the parts through a sieve. Melt a little butter, sprinkle in an ounce of flour, add the nettles, and (a little at a time) sufficient milk to make a soup of the desired thickness. Bring to a boil, simmer for a few minutes, and season.

NETTLE *(Urtica dioica)*

108

Nettle rootstocks can be dug in the fall, placed in a tub or box, and brought into the cellar. During the winter these will usually produce a supply of blanched tender shoots. Of course, during the growing season, the plants outside can be blanched by excluding the light in some manner from the developing shoots.

Nettles are said to be high in vitamin C and have been found by Storer (222) to contain about 5.5% of albuminoids and about 7.8% of carbohydrates. They can be used to make a kind of "tea," the directions usually given are to use 5 handfuls of nettle to 1 quart of water. We have seen nettle tea for sale in this area. Nettles have also been used as a substitute for rennet, to coagulate milk.

A beer or wine may be made from nettles, using, in addition, dandelion flowers, lemon juice, ginger root, brown sugar, and yeast. We have not tried this out, but it is said to be good. Finally, the fibers of the mature stems can be retted out and spun into a durable cloth. Thomas Campbell, the British poet once said, "In Scotland I have eaten nettle, I have slept in nettle sheets, I have dined off a nettle tablecloth."

This is an excellent edible plant and makes an acceptable substitute for spinach. It has the advantage of being easy to identify—even in the dark!

Related Species:
All kinds of nettles are worth a cautious trial. *Urtica gracilenta* is found in the southern part of the Rocky Mountain area and surely would be edible as the one described above.

References (to numbers in the bibliography):
8, 26, 31, 38, 56, 57, 58, 59, 84, 93, 99, 102, 112, 117, 119, 122, 132, 134, 151, 158, 167, 168, 204, 219, 221, 222, 227, 228, 229, 240, 243.

CHAPTER IV: YOUNG SHOOTS (like Asparagus)

THE PARTICULAR uses of the young shoots of edible plants are closely related to the ones discussed in Chapter III as potherbs. In fact, many plants can easily be shifted back and forth from potherbs to young shoots. You encounter about the same problem here as when you use wild plants for greens or potherbs, namely that you must use them in young condition when the characteristic, diagnostic flowers are not present. This poses a problem in how to be certain about their identification. The young shoots can be pressed; then the mature plant can be similarly treated later on. After identification these two stages, pressed and dried, can be mounted together and used the succeeding year to check out material gathered as food.

These shoots are often very abundant; they may also be available for several weeks, providing one keeps them cut off from an individual patch of plants. Even then they must be considered to be rather seasonable, being available mostly in the spring or early summer. Although such food may be rather low in actual number of calories, the mineral and vitamin content seems to be relatively high. They can be readily preserved by canning or freezing. Some people have taken asparagus shoots, boiled them slightly, split them longitudinally and allowed them to dry in the sun for future use. Probably many wild plants could be preserved in some similar way, especially in times of emergency. The Indians formerly dried the stems and leaves of the Rocky Mountain beeplant (*Cleome serrulata*) for use during the winter time. Professor Matsumura tells me that in Japan the shoots of bracken ferns (*Pteridium aquilinum*) are often dehydrated and stored for future use.

These young shoots can be tied into bundles for ease in handling during the cooking process. The time of boiling varies with the elevation above sea level and also with the tenderness of the product. These shoots can be dressed up with various sauces as you would asparagus, and prepared for the table in the various ways you utilize that vegetable.

Plants sometimes used for the young shoots but illustrated or described under another chapter.

Arctium minus VI.
Hemerocallis fulva III.
Heracleum lanatum V.
Opuntia spp. VII
Rubus parviflorus VII.

Rubus strigosus VII.
Tragopogon porrifolius VI.
Typha latifolia VI.
Yucca baccata VIII.

Agave utahensis
AGAVE, CENTURY PLANT, MESCAL

Description:

Plants with short vertical stems or rootstocks, on which are crowded the many basal leaves; leaves evergreen, thick, about 4 to 12 inches long and ¾ to 2 inches wide; flower stalks arising from the center of the rosette of leaves, 4½ to 8½ feet tall; flowers in a narrow elongated cluster, in groups of 2 to 6, yellow in color, each about 1½ to 2 inches long, the swollen ovary borne below the floral segments (ovary inferior); fruit a dry capsule about ¾ to 1¼ inches long. The plant resembles certain species of yucca, especially *Yucca baccata* (see p. 332), but is spiny instead of fibrous on the leaf margins, and the ovary is below the flower segments (inferior) instead of above (superior) as in yucca.

This agave is found from southern Utah and northern Arizona to California. It is particularly abundant in our area in the vicinity of the Grand Canyon in Arizona.

Use:

The smaller agaves and the larger southern ones were at one time extensively utilized by the Indians for food and drink. They were used at any time, but especially when the flower stalks were

Fr

F×2

In

5CM

AGAVE *(Agave utahensis)*

just arising from the leaf clusters. The centers of the plants were
dug out by using a pry-shaped piece of wood. These centers contained the buds, short stalks, and some of the leaf bases; the
whole structure in the larger species of agave was said to be up
to 2 feet in diameter. These were placed in circular pits about 6
to 20 feet in diameter and 1 to 2 feet deep. Stones were placed in
the pit and a fire was laid upon them. The mescal butts were then
placed in the pit, covered with grass or weeds, and finally with
dirt. The plants were roasted in this way for 1 to 3 days. The
product had a pleasantly sweet taste but contained fibers that had
to be spit out when chewed. It could be pounded flat and dried in
the sun in thin sheets and transported long distances as a future
food supply. The roasted material could be soaked in water and
a drink prepared by fermentation of the liquid. Also the large
southern species could be treated by boring a cavity in the center
of the plant and taking the sap out. This was fermented and often
distilled, the resulting product being called "mescal, pulque, or
tequila." The Mescalero Apaches owe their name to their use of
this plant; the presence of the old roasting pits throughout New
Mexico and Arizona testify as to the past importance of agave in
the diet of the Indians.

This plant can be a possible emergency food since it can be
used at any time. The bud or center of the plant can readily be
pried out by anyone, and roasted in pits or in the ashes of a fire.
The resulting product can then be dried, if necessary, and used as
sustenance on the journey to safety. Digging out the bud does not
necessarily kill the plant as it may reproduce by offsets clustered
around the parent. Of course, the presence of the flower stalk indicates that the primary leaf cluster producing it will soon die anyway. However, it seems better to us to consider this plant as an
emergency food only.

The leaves of many species of agave contain a fiber that can be
utilized in making twine or rope, and some kinds are cultivated
for that purpose in parts of Mexico. The seeds have been ground
up and used as food. Several writers, (Bourke, 30; Castetter &
Opler, 45; Kearney & Peebles, 138; Kingsbury, 141; Hedrick, 117;
Jaeger, 132; Merrill, 160; Morton, 164), suggested that at least
some species of agave contain laxative or irritants, especially when

eaten in too large amounts, so it would be well to try this food product with reasonable care at first.

Related Species:

Apparently any species of agave can be used with caution as an emergency food. In addition to *Agave utahensis,* the following have been reported in northern Arizona, *A. kaibabensis* and *A. deserti.*

References (to numbers in the bibliography):

2, 14, 17, 18, 25, 30, 43, 44, 45, 66, 67, 76, 117, 123, 132, 138, 141, 158, 160, 166, 182, 183, 192, 198, 199, 204, 215, 216, 224, 241, 249, 254.

Asclepias speciosa
MILKWEED, SHOWY MILKWEED, SILKWEED

Description:

Plants in patches from thick creeping rootstocks; stems erect and stout, 1⅓ to 5 feet tall; leaves opposite, oblong to narrowly egg-shaped, with characteristic veins as shown, rather thick; flowers in clusters (umbels); individual flowers up to ½ inch long or more, pink to light rose in color; pods about 3 to 5 inches long, often with soft finger-like processes on the surfaces.

Rather common at low to medium elevations from Kansas and Arizona north into Canada.

Use:

This milkweed has been listed as causing poisoning to livestock, but animals certainly seldom eat it (Muensher, 167; Kingsbury, 141; Anderson, 5). For this reason, we do not recommend this plant to be used raw in salad preparations. But properly prepared this is one of our most enjoyable and versatile edible species, and is one of our own favorite foods. The very young shoots can be prepared and cooked like those of asparagus. They are best gathered when they are about 4 to 8 inches above the ground level. We boiled them for about 15-20 minutes, changing the water one or two times. This is a good procedure in cooking any part of the milkweed plant as it helps get rid of the bitter taste of the milky juice. The shoots can be eaten like asparagus, creamed or with butter; we think that they are very tender and palatable. They taste as good or even better than asparagus to most palates, and have the advantage of being much more abundant in most localities. Sometimes they may not be very tender and may require longer cooking than given above.

If the shoots get too far along, the tender tops can be collected or, in any event, the younger leaves near the expanding terminal bud. These can be cooked like spinach, changing the water as mentioned before but probably boiling for a longer period because the milkweed parts are a bit tougher than the garden vegetable. If you miss them in this stage, the flower buds can be gathered before they open and boiled for about 12-15 minutes with several changes of water. We have tried them with salt, pepper and butter and found them delicious. The taste is somewhat like peas or asparagus but with a flavor all its own. We have heard that the flower clusters are so full of sugar that they can be boiled down to make a thick syrup.

If you come along too late for the flowers, you can use the young pods when they are about 1 to 1½ inches long. They may remind you of okra, but when boiled make an appetizing dish. Norton (176), suggested cooking them with rice and appropriate seasonings.

The Indians often cooked parts of the milkweed with meat with the idea that a substance in the plant had a tenderizing effect. (Bartlett, 18; Kearney & Peebles, 138). It is too bad that certain related milkweeds cause serious poisoning to livestock (see *Asclepias subverticillata*), but fortunately these narrow-leaved species are not too hard to tell from the edible ones. The broad-leaved milkweed is almost a "pantry in the wild," and surely no one should go hungry while it is in the earlier stages of its growth. Even after the pods mature the downy seeds can be gathered and used to stuff sacks that serve as pillows or mattresses. Surely this is one of our most useful plants. (Bartlett, 18; Kearney & Peebles, 138; Anderson, 5; Muenscher, 167; Castetter, 43; Uphof, 240; Blankinship, 26; Brown, 31; Fewkes, 85; Grinnell, 103; Szczawinski and Hardy, 228).

MILKWEED *(Asclepias speciosa)*

Related Species:

Asclepias syriaca: This is an eastern broad-leaved milkweed similar to the one figured. It has been widely used in similar ways. (Gaertner, 90; Carver, 42; Vestal & Schultes, 242; Harris, 112; Gibbons, 92; Gilmore, 94; Gilmore, 96; Gilmore, 95; Uphof, 240; Densmore, 75; Hedrick, 117; Gordon, 99; Gillespie, 93; Fremont, 89; Coon, 58; Medsger, 158; Muenscher & Rice, 168; Stratton, 225; Bale, 13).

A. incarnata: This is a narrower leaved species found in the Rocky Mountains usually in moist places. It can be used like the broad-leaved species, but we did not like it quite so well. (Gillespie, 93; Jaeger, 132; Smith, 210; Stratton, 225; Uphof, 240).

A. tuberosa: This is a brilliant orange-flowered species that is found rather sparingly in the Rocky Mountain area. It is used like the others, but in addition, has swollen tuberous roots (as the name suggests) which have been much used in medicine. However, the Indians boiled or baked them for food. (Palmer, 182; Uphof, 240; Kephart, 140; Grieve, 102; Stevens, 219; Core, Reitz & Gillespie, 59; Yanovsky & Kingsbury, 256; Medsger, 158; Jaeger, 132.)

References (to numbers in the bibliography for milkweeds in general):

11A, 14, 29, 57, 83, 84, 99, 124, 132, 138, 164, 176, 195, 205, 239, 241.

Asparagus officinalis
ASPARAGUS, GOLDEN ASPARAGUS

Description:

This plant is too well known to need a detailed description. The roots are thick and fleshy and store the food supply that is later used to send up the succulent shoots so familiar to everyone. These shoots, if not gathered, grow into bushy branched tops that may be over 6 feet tall in favorable spots. These bear many thread-like branchlets resembling leaves. The flowers are rather greenish and about 1/4 inch long, often followed by red berries.

The plant was introduced from the Old World and is much

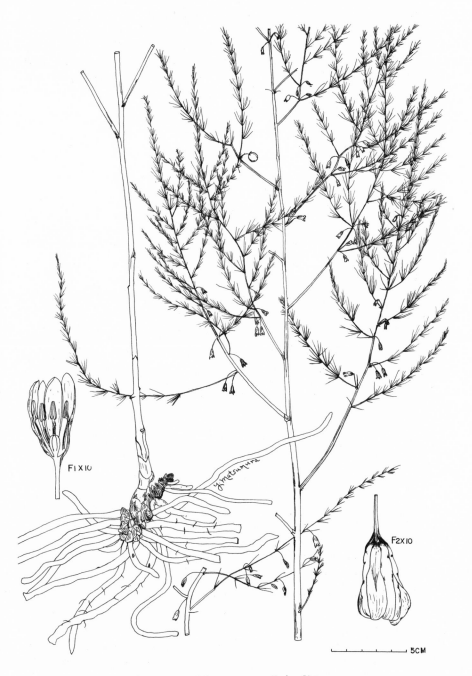

F1 X 10

F2X 10

5CM

ASPARAGUS *(Asparagus officinalis)*

cultivated in this country. It has a way of escaping to roadsides, thickets and wasteground, often well away from dwellings and settlements. Many people have a hobby of collecting this wild asparagus for cooking, canning and freezing.

Use:

The young shoots have provided favorite food since the beginning of history and undoubtedly were used long before that. They are boiled or pressure cooked and eaten in a variety of ways, often with butter or creamed, but are sometimes pickled (Coon, 58). Many people consider asparagus to be the queen of cultivated vegetables. The Europeans seem to like their asparagus blanched; this is done by covering the shoots and preventing the green color from developing. This procedure seems to keep them tender longer but it may affect the taste to some degree.

The seeds of the plant have been roasted and ground and have often been used as a substitute for coffee, although Fernald & Kinsey (84) stated they are said to be poisonous at times. It might be better to leave the seeds alone or at least try them carefully!

References (to numbers in the bibliography):
58, 68A, 84, 93, 134, 158.

Equisetum arvense
HORSETAIL, SCOURING RUSH

Description:

This plant has no true flowers, but reproduces by spores or spreads by underground rootstocks that often bear tuber-like swellings; the spore-bearing shoot lacks green color, is unbranched, has circles of toothlike leaves at intervals and is terminated by a cone which bears the reproductive spores; the sterile shoots come along later, they are branched, with whorls of smaller toothlike leaves, the whole unit resembling a green-colored horsetail.

Horsetail grows on plains, thickets and banks, often in sandy places where the ground is moist. It is widely distributed throughout the Western hemisphere, and is fairly abundant in our area.

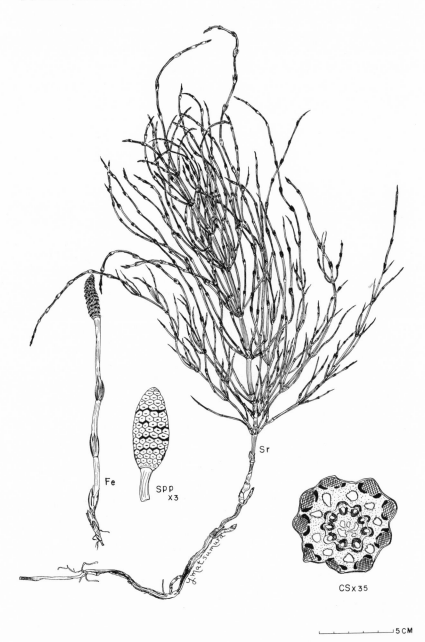

Fe Spp Sr CSx35 5CM
×3

HORSETAIL *(Equisetum arvense)*

Use:

This plant is listed in most books on poisonous plants as causing trouble to livestock when eaten. However, Dr. N. Oshima, a colleague of ours, stated that he has often eaten the cone-bearing shoots in Japan. Since he was still very much alive at the time we talked with him, we decided to try them ourselves.

We gathered the reproductive shoots just before the cone scales loosened, and removed the teethlike leaves from the stems. These stems were boiled in water which soon became very yellow in color, so we thought it wise to change it several times. A good initial experiment would be to boil them 25 minutes (at 5000 ft.) with 3 or 4 changes of water. We ate them with salt, pepper and butter. The taste was fairly pleasing but not very distinctive. The Indians were reported to have eaten the peeled stems, the base of the plant, the roots and the tubers, either raw or cooked. We have not done this and hesitate to advise it in view of the unfavorable reputation of the plant. The plant might be worth trying with reasonable care in cases of emergency.

Some of the horsetails were utilized by drying the green stems, grinding them to a powder and using the product as mush or thickening. This powder has also been used to make a tea, and we have seen it for sale in local grocery stores.

Related Species:

Several species have been used as food. Most of them soon develop a scratchy, tough stem-covering and this would limit their usefulness. *Equisetum laevigatum, E. hyemale* and *E. fluviatile* have been reported to have been so utilized. (Morton, 166; Fewkes, 85; Uphof, 240; Castetter, 43; Hedrick, 117; Johnson, 134; Coon, 58).

References (to numbers in the bibliography):
  A. As a poisonous plant—5, 59, 79, 98, 141, 167.
  B. As a food plant—5, 8, 57, 107, 193, 227, 240, 242.

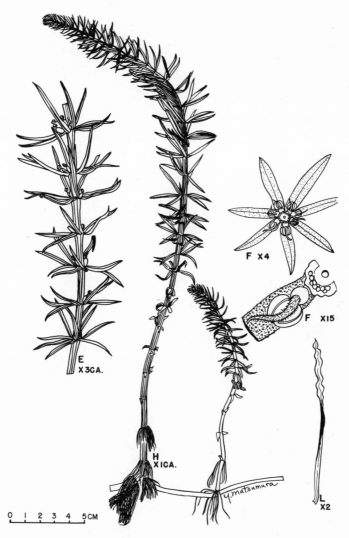

E
X3CA.

H
X1CA.

F X4

F X15

L
X2

0 1 2 3 4 5CM

y.matsumura

MARESTAIL *(Hippuris vulgaris)*

Hippuris vulgaris
MARESTAIL

Description:

Stems weak and limber, 8 inches to 2 feet long; leaves about
⅜ to 1¼ inch long; flowers small and inconspicuous; fruits about
⅛ inch long.

Growing in water of swamps and ponds, usually at least partly submerged. Scattered in the northern part of North America, south in the Rocky Mountains to New Mexico.

Use:

This is a water plant (aquatic) that has been often used by the Indians, particularly in Alaska. They gathered the shoots and used them as a potherb or to make soup. Since the parts are tender, they can be gathered in any stage. Even when the ponds and lakes are frozen over, the upper part of the plant may protrude and can be gathered for food (Heller, 119). Because it is one of the few food-producing water plants and because it might provide sustenance in winter, we have included it here.

Related Species:

Hippuris tetraphylla has been used in similar fashion in the Northwest.

References (to numbers in the bibliography):
4, 119.

Pteridium aquilinum (Pteris aquilina)
BRACKEN FERN, BRAKE

Description:

Plants with creeping, rather thick blackish rootstocks, hence growing in patches; fronds (leaves) 1 to 6 feet tall; frond blades 1 to 3 feet long, the stalk usually shorter.

Pastures, open woods, burned-over areas, on open slopes and in woods. This is a cosmopolitan species, our varieties usually found in shaded, rather moist slopes in the mountains.

Use:

This is a fern that is widely used as food in many countries of the world. According to Professor Oshima, one of our colleagues, it is commonly eaten in Japan. The young fronds in "fiddlehead" condition are collected, boiled and then often dried in the sun.

So

Rh

5CM

BRACKEN FERN *(Pteridium aquilinum)*

The dried product is stored for use during the winter. The underground rootstocks are sometimes broken up and the starch extracted; this is known by the name of "warabi" starch. It is often used to make confections, and the ancient city of Nara (once the capital of Japan) is famous in this respect. In Siberia and Norway, the uncoiled fronds have been employed in brewing a kind of beer. The young fronds and the rootstocks have often been used in many countries, especially in times of food shortage. It was a favorite edible plant with our North American Indians and, at least at one time, appeared in the markets of cities in the eastern part of the United States.

It should be mentioned, before proceeding, that the bracken fern is listed as being poisonous to livestock, at least to some degree (Durrell, Jensen & Klinger, 79; Anderson, 5; Core, Reitz & Gillespie, 59; Muenscher, 167; Fernald & Kinsey, 84; Dayton et al., 74; Wherry, 247; Oswald, 179; Kearney & Peebles, 138; Kingsbury, 141). The mature leaves, especially in hay, seem to be the offenders. It might be well to go slow on eating bracken in any stage, until you are sure you are not sensitive to it.

We have certainly had no bad effects from eating the young leaves or rootstocks. We took the uncoiling fronds when they were about 4 to 7 inches tall, cutting off the very base if it seemed tough, and also the curled up tops. We then removed the woolly hairs by drawing them through our fingers, this often done under water. We boiled these stalks about 30 minutes, changing the water twice and served them in any of the various ways that asparagus is prepared. We found them somewhat mucilaginous and more or less bitter tasting, not pleasant, but at least edible. They appeared best when creamed or fried in bread crumbs.

The rootstocks have been cooked and found, by us, to be tough and unpalatable. The Indians dried them, then ground them to a meal (or ground them and then dried the meal) and used this meal in various ways. They are also said to have eaten the young fronds raw.

This is a fairly good emergency food plant, but not flavorful enough to warrant our recommending it for general use. Bracken may be fairly abundant locally, but ferns in general are rather rare in this climate, and it seems a shame to root them up under ordinary conditions.

Related Species:

We have only one species of *Pteridium* in the area, but at least two varieties are present. Some forms are reputed to contain more starch in the rootstocks than others.

References (to numbers in the bibliography):

5, 8, 13, 26, 29, 32, 38, 52, 57, 58, 74, 79, 84, 90, 91, 93, 99, 102, 107, 112, 115, 117, 119, 129, 134, 138, 158, 164, 167, 179, 181, 182, 191, 198, 204, 211, 212, 225, 227, 228, 230, 240, 243, 253, 256.

Smilacina spp. (*Vagnera* spp.)
FALSE SOLOMON'S SEAL, SOLOMON'S PLUME

Description:

Plants from thick, spreading rootstocks; stems unbranched; leaves without teeth or lobes, several-nerved; flowers in rather simple to compound clusters, the 6 segments rather small, white in color; berry roundish, 1- to 2-seeded, red to purplish-black in color, often with dark dots or stripes, to $1/4$ inch in diameter.

Woods, thickets or open meadows. Throughout most of temperate North America and two species widespread in the entire Rocky Mountain area.

Use:

The berries of the False Solomon's Seal are edible either raw or cooked. They are rather bittersweet and the flavor may be somewhat disagreeable to some tastes. The Indians are said to have used them a great deal, and they should provide good emergency food for anyone. However, they should be utilized cautiously at first, because some writers report them to be laxative when taken in quantities.

The young tender shoots are used as a potherb or as a substitute for asparagus. The Indians ate the rootstocks, first soaking them in lye to free them from their disagreeable taste, then parboiling them to get rid of the lye. These starchy rootstocks are sometimes used to make a pleasant pickle according to Fernald & Kinsey (84).

The species of False Solomon's Seal are all reasonably edible, but we do not rate them high on our desirable, edible plant list.

E.S

Rs

y. Matsumura

⊢——⊣——⊣——⊣ 5 CM

FALSE SOLOMON'S SEAL *(Smilacina stellata)*

Related Species:

The Rocky Mountain area has 2 species rather widespread, *Smilacina racemosa* with a compound flower cluster and *S. stellata* with a more simple flower cluster. They are used in similar fashion.

References (to numbers in the bibliography):
5, 43, 84, 93, 117, 158, 166, 181, 217, 221.

Smilax herbacea (Nemexia herbacea, N. lasioneuron) Greenbrier, Carrion Flower

Description:

Stems not woody, up to about 6 feet tall, climbing by several to many pairs of tendrils which are located at the base of the leaf stalks; leaves 1½ to 4 inches long, broad and veiny; flowers in round clusters, individual flowers many in the cluster, rather small, greenish in color; berries ¼ to ⅜ inch in diameter, blue-black in color.

Meadows, woods, thickets and edges of clearings. Widespread in the eastern part of the United States with the western variety extending from Montana to Colorado.

Use:

The berries of this plant were eaten by the Indians and are said to have a pleasant taste according to Gilmore (95) and Medsger (158). Certainly, they would be worth trying, especially in an emergency. The young shoots look somewhat like asparagus, and are used in similar fashion. They grow rapidly and, like asparagus shoots, soon pass out of the tender stage. They can be boiled and eaten with butter or served with a cream sauce. These shoots are reported to be very palatable with a delicate pleasant flavor. The flowers have a fetid odor when fresh, hence the name carrion flower.

Related Species:

The variety that is in the Rocky Mountain area is *Smilax herbacea* var. *lasioneuron*. It has longer leaf stalks, a short-hairy lower leaf surface (instead of hairless) and black-colored berries

GREENBRIAR *(Smilax herbacea)*

(instead of blue), all of which distinguish it from the species itself, which grows in the eastern part of the United States.

References (to numbers in the bibliography):

84, 93, 95, 158, 240.

CHAPTER V: SALADS (like Lettuce)

THE USE of wild plants for making salads is closely related to their value as potherbs or as young shoots except, of course, the salads are used in the uncooked condition. The problem is the same in regard to the correct identification of very young plants, but here it is even more acute since cooking will sometimes render harmful plants edible. The same advice that was given in Chapters III and IV is repeated here:

1. Collect and dry (by pressing) some of the young plants in "salad" condition.
2. Allow other plants to mature to form flowers or fruit.
3. Identify (or have identified) these pressed mature plants.
4. Mount the juvenile and mature pressed plants together on a cardboard. You are now ready for next season.
5. Next year compare the young plants with this pressed material.

The problem of contamination from sprays, bacteria, organic material, various insect stages, animal parasites, etc., is very serious since the product is eaten raw. The leaves or shoots can be washed, and allowed to stand in water to give them crispness. It is possible to dissolve a halazone tablet in some water and soak the plant parts in this. Some people dry this wet material by swinging it vigorously in a mesh bag or basket before it is used. The leaves or shoots can be torn into pieces of the desired size; it is best not to cut them with a knife or scissors, unless this is necessary.

The material should be dry, crisp, and cold when used. Most people recommend a highly seasoned dressing on these salads since many of our native plants have a somewhat "wild" taste. The dressing should be added just before the salad is served. If the plants are blanched for at least several days by excluding the light from them in various ways, the parts become more tender and lose much of any bitterness that might otherwise be present. Pieces of the root parts can be brought into the cellar or basement in the fall and planted in earth-filled tubs or boxes. The young shoots and leaves growing from the roots may produce salad material at intervals throughout the winter.

Many of us like to use a mixture of native salad plants, some with a bland taste, others with a sharp flavor. Under survival conditions, the duckweeds (*Lemna* spp., *Spirodela* spp.) that often float on the surface of the still water of ponds, lakes and rivers can provide copious and palatable material for salads (Ney, 175; Klein, 142), although lack of space precluded formally including them here. The raw leaves of native plants, when used in salads, probably will be low in actual numbers of calories, but their value in providing vitamins is well known. Such food is rather seasonable but is often present in great abundance at least for a short period. Native salads can certainly give you some new and interesting taste sensations. Some you may like, others you may not like, but you can select what you will from nature's great market.

Plants sometimes used as salads but illustrated or described under another chapter.

Calochortus spp. VI.   *Oenothera strigosa* III.
Caltha leptosepala III.   *Plantago major* III.
Campanula rapunculoides VI.   *Portulaca oleracea* III.
Capsella bursa-pastoris III.   *Rhus glabra* IX.
Cichorium intybus IX.   *Sisymbrium* spp. III.
Cirsium spp. VI.   *Stellaria media* III.
Cymopterus spp. VI.   *Taraxacum officinale* III.
Epilobium angustifolium III.   *Thlaspi arvense* III.
Erythronium grandiflorum VI.   *Tragapogon porrifolius* VI.
Hemerocallis fulva III.   *Typha latifolia* VI.
Malva neglecta VIII.

Erodium cicutarium
ALFILERIA, HERONBILL, STORK'S BILL, FILAREE

Description:
    Annual or sometimes perennial acting plants, since during very early spring the leaf rosettes may already be established, ready to

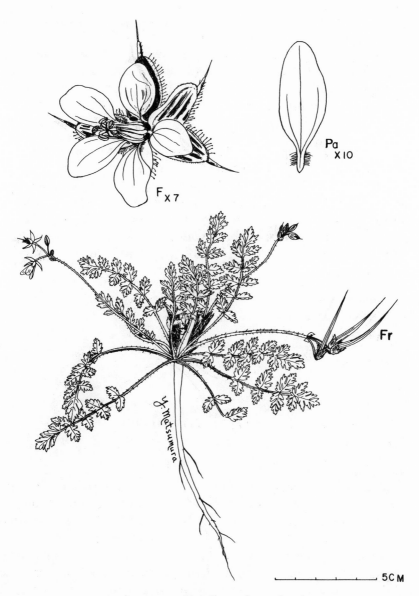

ALFILERIA *(Erodium cicutarium)*

elongate into flowering at the first hint of warm weather; leaves
filmy and fernlike; petals pink or rose-colored, each about ⅛ to ⅜
inch long; fruit becoming 1 to 2½ inches long, (shaped somewhat
like a heron's bill).

Widespread in North America. Grows on plains, mesas and slopes often in lawns, gardens, fields and waste places as a weed. The plant may flower well through the growing season, but is most noticeable in this area in the spring.

Use:

This species has been used when young, either raw or cooked. It can be used as a salad, worked in to good advantage with other plants like lettuce. If you boil it for greens, we suggest that you select young tender parts and try boiling them for about 25 minutes (at 5000 ft.). This plant was much used by certain Indian tribes. It is abundant in some seasons in some localities, often present in large quantity early in the season, just when other foods may be scarce.

Related Species:
We know of none.

References (to numbers in the bibliography):
57, 84, 93, 117, 140, 182, 243.

Heracleum lanatum (H. maximum)
Cow Parsnip

Description:

Stems 2½ to 7 feet tall (our drawing giving a rather inadequate idea of the complete plant); leaves with large segments (leaflets), these sometimes over a foot long; flowers white, borne in double clusters (umbels); fruits about ⅜ to ½ inch long.

Plants growing in moist ground, often in ditches and partial shade. Widespread in the United States and also through the Rocky Mountain area from the plains almost to timberline in the mountains.

Use:

This husky, rank-smelling plant is often found in abundance. It was much used by the Indians as food. They ate the cooked roots, which are said to taste like rutabaga, but at least one writer,

YL

FI x5CA

In

F2 x6

x 1/2

M. Matsumura

R

BL

FC

Fr x3

CFr x6

x3

UL

x 1/2

5CM

COW PARSNIP (*Heracleum lanatum*)

(Standley, 214), suggested they may be poisonous. The base of the plant is said to have been used as a substitute for salt. The young tender shoots were used as a salad or as a potherb. We tried the shoots boiled for 30 minutes (open kettle at 5000 ft.), changing the water once. The taste was fair but a suggestion of the rank and unpleasant (to us) odor still lingered. If the shoots are too mature the fibrous outer coat should be peeled off before cooking.

The older stems, say just before the flower clusters unfold, can be peeled and the tender inner tissue eaten raw or cooked. We found them edible but still with a lingering, rank, unpleasant taste. We suggest changing the water once or twice when cooking these parts.

This would be an excellent survival plant, particularly in the mountains. Some of our collaborators couldn't relish it in any condition, but others did not mind it at all. It is not on record how hungry they actually were when the plant was tried.

Related Species:
None in our area.

References (to numbers in the bibliography):
5, 26, 32, 52, 56, 57, 58, 65, 74, 77A, 84, 100, 107, 117, 119, 138, 167, 190, 191 209, 212, 214, 217, 221, 227, 228, 240, 243, 256.

Lactuca scariola (L. serriola, L. integrata)
PRICKLY LETTUCE, WILD LETTUCE

Description:
Annual or possibly biennial plants; stems upright, 1 to 3½ feet tall; leaves usually bearing weak spines on the main rib below, as shown; flowers yellow when fresh, often fading to blue-purple in age, crowded 6 to 8 together in a headlike structure that is about ¾ inch long; seeds (achenes) with a hairy parachute like a dandelion.

Fields and waste places, growing as a common weed over most of the United States and southern Canada.

Use:
When the seedlings are young and tender this lettuce, and related species of wild lettuce, are used in salads. The young leaves can

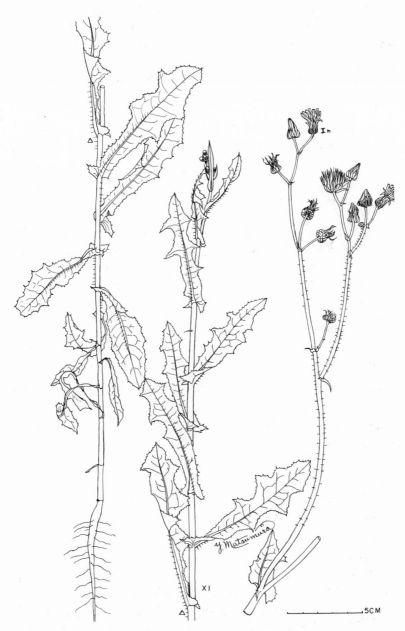

PRICKLY LETTUCE *(Lactuca scariola)*

be cut into strips with scissors or a sharp knife and may be mixed with other plants. Several people we know relish the plant this way, but we could not get used to the bitter taste, this reminding us of dandelion leaves. Perhaps a report by Kingsbury (141), that cattle in Wyoming were poisoned by eating large quantities of the young plant prejudiced us against it.

The young plants can be used as potherbs. They take little cooking; we boiled them 10 minutes (at 5000 ft.) with one change of water. The result was voted edible, but somewhat unpalatable due to a bitter aftertaste. We advise mixing the wild lettuce with other blander tasting species until you are certain you will enjoy this background of bitterness.

As with many other species, the plants can be blanched by excluding the light for a time. This can be done with straw, canvas or by inverting a tub over them. Plants treated in this way will be more tender and will lose at least some of their bitterness. The species of wild lettuce are often very abundant locally and at times can provide plenty of food material.

Related Species:
Lactuca canadensis, L. pulchella and *L. ludoviciana* are reported to be used in similar fashion.

References (to numbers in the bibliography for all species of *Lactuca*):
11A, 31, 42, 49, 56, 68A, 79, 84, 93, 112, 134, 138, 141, 158, 181, 220, 225, 240.

Montia perfoliata (Claytonia perfoliata, Limnia perfoliata)
MINER'S LETTUCE, INDIAN LETTUCE

Description:
Annual plants with sprawling stems about 2 to 6 inches long or in favorable spots even longer; basal leaves long-stalked, only 2 stem leaves present, these opposite and their bases partly or completely joined to each other; petals $\frac{1}{8}$ to $\frac{1}{4}$ inch long, white to pink.

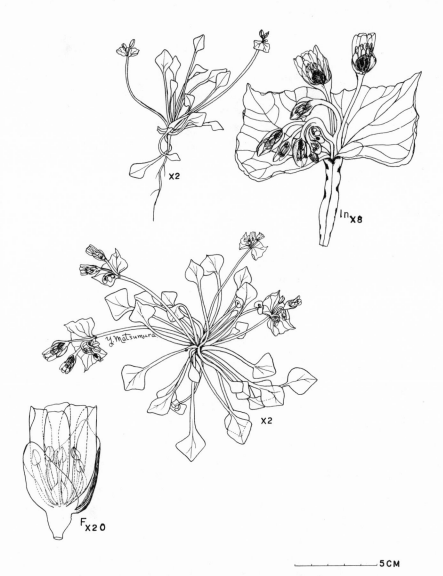

|——————|————|————|5CM

MINER'S LETTUCE *(Montia perfoliata)*

Moist banks and slopes, often in partial shade. This is a western plant that comes into the Rocky Mountains east to northeastern Arizona, eastern Utah and the Black Hills of South Dakota.

Use:

This was a well-known food plant to the Indians and to the early white settlers. According to Hedrick (117), it has been cultivated in France; also our Indians may have cultured or at least encouraged its growth in their immediate area (Osborne, 178).

In the spring the young plants may be used raw as a kind of salad. The shoots and leaves can also be cooked as "greens" and are reported to be excellent. The two contrasting kinds of leaves makes it a plant easy to recognize and it was very popular during the gold rush to California, hence the name "miner's lettuce". It was one of the fresh native plants that could be used to cure and avert scurvy.

Related Species:
A rather succulent relative, *Montia chamissoi,* is present in the Rocky Mountain area and deserves a trial.

References (to numbers in the bibliography):
8, 18, 26, 52, 57, 107, 117, 119, 138, 178, 189, 204, 227, 228, 240.

Oxyria digyna
MOUNTAIN SORREL, ALPINE SORREL, ROUND-LEAVED SORREL

Description:
Low perennial plants with thick fleshy taproots; stems 2 to 12 inches tall; leaves about ⅜ to 1⅜ inches across; flowers small, inconspicuous, reddish to greenish in color; fruit ⅛ to ¼ inch long, broadly winged.

Found among rocks, often in wet places, usually above timberline in our mountains. Canada south to New Hampshire, New Mexico and California. In the Rocky Mountains the plant reaches to northern New Mexico and northern Arizona.

Use:
The rather fleshy leaves can be eaten raw and have the characteristic, pleasantly sour taste of sorrel. Some recommend using them only when young, but we have found them good tasting even when the plants were in fruit. The raw leaves when nibbled on help to quench thirst, and we found them tender and crisp. They are

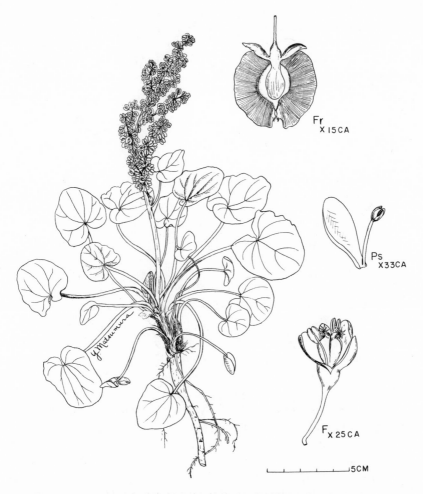

Fr
X 15 CA

Ps
X 33 CA

F
X 25 CA

5 CM

MOUNTAIN SORREL *(Oxyria digyna)*

favorites in salads, especially when mixed with other plants. The Indians used to chop them up with other leaves like those of water cress, *(Rorippa nasturtium-aquaticum)* and allowed the mixture to ferment like sauerkraut. They were said to be very fond of it.

Mountain sorrel can be used as a potherb. Again, some recommend taking the younger plants, but we used them in all stages. We boiled the young plants and leaves for 10 minutes (at 5000 ft.). The odor reminded us of cooking rhubarb. We ate the "greens" with butter, salt and pepper and found the taste very good indeed. As one of us remarked, "It tastes like spinach with vinegar." The sour taste probably is an oxalate; certain plants high in such substances will sometimes cause poisoning to livestock when eaten to excess. We know of no incident where this plant poisoned human beings. In any case, when eaten in reasonable amount we consider this one our very best edible species, especially since it grows in the high mountains where few other edible species are found.

Related Species:

None. The other sour-tasting sorrels belong to plants often not even related to mountain sorrel.

References (to numbers in the bibliography):

4, 5, 8, 26, 84, 107, 117, 119, 140, 158, 182, 187, 214, 228, 240.

Rorippa nasturtium-aquaticum (R. nasturtium, Nasturtium officinale, Sisymbrium nasturtium-aquaticum)
WATERCRESS

Description:

Growing submerged or at least partly submerged in water; petals white, each 1/8 inch long or slightly longer; pods about 3/8 to 1 1/4 inches long.

In water or mud, often in springs or in gently flowing streams. Apparently coming to this country from Europe and now spread over all North America. In the Rocky Mountain area seldom found above 8000 feet elevation.

Uses:

Watercress is a famous edible plant and sometimes appears for sale on the markets. Many people, especially those of foreign extraction, try to secure this plant for flavoring all their soups or meat dishes. Its use in salads is well known and it is often mixed with other plants such as brooklime (See *Veronica americana*). Diced apples and olives have also been used with it. The taste is

WATERCRESS *(Rorippa nasturtium-aquaticum)*

rather peppery or "bitey," but nonetheless pleasing to most people.

Watercress also makes a good potherb, alone or when mixed with other plants that may be more bland in taste. It can be cooked and used almost exactly as you would spinach. Try using it with rice or in a white sauce. An interesting herb butter can be made by mixing cress, parsley and chives with your butter or margarine. A tomato aspic salad is worth trying. Use 1 package of lemon jello (gelatine), 1 package lime jello, tomato juice for liquid and chopped watercress and walnuts. Sopher (212A) gave an interesting recipe for soup.

POTATO AND WATERCRESS SOUP

1 lb. potatoes	½ cup milk
1 bunch watercress	4 cups water
1 tablespoon butter	Salt and pepper to taste

Peel potatoes and boil until done. Strain off water and rub the potatoes through a sieve, then put back in the water again. Add finely chopped cress and cook for 5 minutes. Put in milk and butter, seasoning to taste, and heat for a few minutes.

The soup can be served with a sprinkling of chopped fresh watercress on top.

The leaves of the watercress can be dried, ground and used on the top of other foods as a mild seasoning like pepper. Watercress-leaf tea has been for sale in one of the area's grocery stores. This plant is rather abundant and should be used more widely. It is considered to be a good source of vitamins and is listed as an efficient antiscorbutic. It is available for long seasonal periods, sometimes even during the winter, since often the cress will be green and healthy under the ice. One reason it is not more popular is that many people are afraid that the fresh plants were contaminated, say, by nearby cattle or pigs. Some recommend that it be taken from near the mouth of a fenced in spring or from a stream with a sandy bottom. The fresh young shoots can also be soaked for a time in some water-purification substance such as halazone tablets. Another difficulty is that the shoots have a very superficial similarity to the water hemlock (See *Cicuta douglasii*), which is deadly poisonous.

Watercress is a justly famous edible plant. Hedrick (117) mentioned that in ancient times Xenophon strongly recommended its use to the Persians, and the Romans used it with vinegar as a remedy for those whose minds were deranged; hence the Greek proverb, "Eat cress and learn more wit." We have never noticed any such effect on ourselves; perhaps we have never eaten enough of it.

Related Species:

Several related species have been used in the same ways as watercress. They include *Rorippa palustris* (Hedrick, 117; Medsger, 158) and *R. islandica* (Kearney & Peebles, 138) as well as the famous horseradish (*R. armoracia*), the grated root when mixed with vinegar and certain seasonings is commonly found on grocery shelves. (Muenscher & Rice, 168; Gillespie, 93; Medsger, 158; Fernald & Kinsey, 84).

References (to numbers in the bibliography):

11A, 18, 42, 52, 56, 57, 58, 82, 84, 92, 99, 112, 117, 122, 134, 138, 140, 146, 158, 168, 181, 194, 205, 212A, 219, 225, 227, 228, 240, 244.

Rumex acetosella
SHEEPSORREL, RED SORREL

Description:

Perennial plants from creeping rootstalks; stems 4 to 24 inches tall; leaves 1 to 6 inches long; flower clusters turning reddish in age, but individual flowers small and not at all conspicuous; fruit 3-winged, small, not much over 1/24 inch long.

Plants of old fields, roadsides and waste places, often acting as a weed. Now widespread throughout the most of North America. In our area from low elevations up to timberline in the mountains.

Use:

All the species of this group (genus *Rumex*) may contain varying amounts of oxalates which have sometimes caused poisoning to livestock when eaten to excess. There is probably no danger to human beings when taken in ordinary amounts, in fact the sour

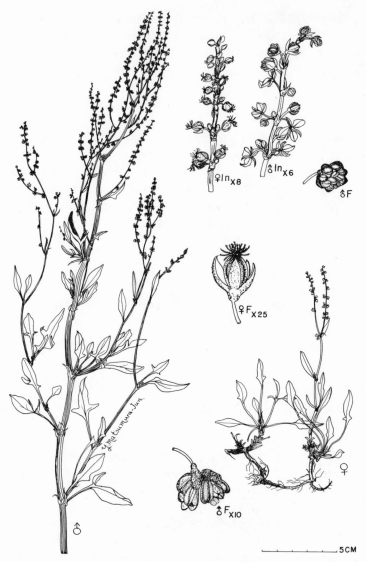

Sheepsorrel *(Rumex acetosella)*

taste provides one of the main desirable features of the plants. Because of it, sheepsorrel has always been a favorite in seasoning almost any other food. It has long been used for that purpose in France, a country justly famous for its flavorful food. Egg omelets can be almost completely cooked, then chopped sorrel leaves can be sprinkled on the top. Soup can be flavored by the addition of the diced leaves. A well-known sorrel soup recipe is given by several authors. We give it as recorded by Fernald & Kinsey (84):

Sorrel Soup

Wash about a handful of sorrel and put in a pan with a little water (not covered). Cook slowly for 30 minutes. Put 4 cups of milk with a small whole white onion in a double broiler. Add 2 teaspoons of butter and 2 tablespoons of flour (blended to avoid lumps) to the hot milk. Let stand, add sorrel and strain. Season to taste. This serves about 6 people.

The young fresh leaves are much used in this area as an ingredient in salads, often with lettuce or sometimes chopped and added to cottage cheese. We have found that they make a good garnish for a sandwich. A puree may be easily made by using this plant. Jam and jelly can even be obtained from it (Rexford, 194) as well as pies (Stratton, 225). A beverage can be made from sorrel, steeping the leaves in water and cooling the liquid. This is said to be a refreshing drink but does not keep for very long periods. The young leaves can be chewed in moderation by the hungry traveler, so it certainly makes a fairly good emergency food. We have found that the leaves and shoots are best before flowering has proceeded very far. Fortunately, in our area certain plants fail to flower readily so that desirable leaves may be available throughout the whole growing season.

Related Plants:

A similar plant *(Rumex acetosa)* is grown in various parts of the world, particularly in Europe and Asia under the name of garden sorrel.

References (to numbers in the bibliography):

8, 13, 38, 42, 58, 77A, 79, 84, 93, 99, 112, 121, 132, 140, 141, 151, 167, 168, 181, 194, 219, 225, 228, 243.

Sedum spp.
STONECROP, ORPINE, QUEEN'S CROWN, KING'S CROWN

Description:

Perennial plants with fleshy succulent stems; leaves thick and fleshy, margins smooth or toothed; flowers in terminal dense or loose clusters, rose, rose-purple, white or yellow in color; fruit becoming dry, of 4 to 5 clustered podlike structures.

These plants often along rocky cliffs, streams and meadows. The various species are widespread in North America and in the Rocky Mountain area at almost all elevations.

Use:

The young leaves and shoots of several stonecrops are eaten as a salad or boiled as a potherb, especially in the North. *Sedum rosea* (not present in our area), commonly called "roseroot" has been used in the Arctic. Our related species, *S. rhodanthum,* commonly called "queen's crown" (see figure) has rose-colored flowers clustered in a terminal head. We have eaten the leaves both raw and boiled for 15 minutes, finding them very acceptable when taken young. *S. integrifolium,* commonly called "king's crown" has a terminal cluster of dark rose-purple flowers. We have eaten the young shoots often, sometimes cutting them into small pieces and mixing them with lettuce for a salad. It also makes a good potherb, but like queen's crown the older leaves take on a rather bitter taste and become fibrous. The common yellow-flowered stonecrop *(S. stenopetalum)* has no record of edibility, but we tested it out raw and cooked, finding it as good or even a little better than the others.

The stonecrops can be listed as providing acceptable food when the parts are young. They should be valuable in an emergency since they can be eaten raw to allay hunger and thirst. We advise they be taken in moderate amounts, especially if the leaves are mature, as one of us reported a slight nausea upon consuming a rather large quantity of the yellow stonecrop.

Related Species:

Any species of stonecrop should be tried carefully if the parts are young and tender.

STONECROP *(Sedum rhodanthum)*

References (to numbers in the bibliography):
56, 187, 228, 240.

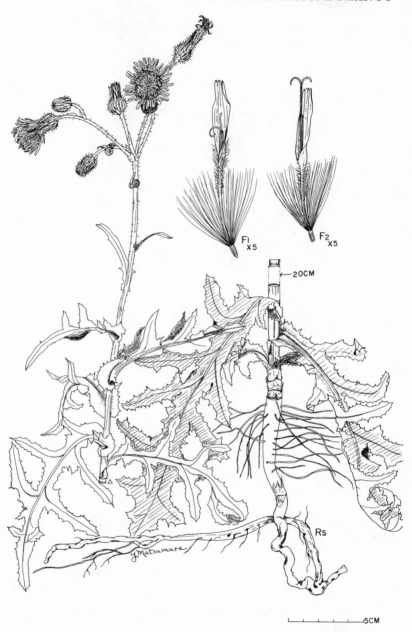

SOWTHISTLE *(Sonchus arvensis)*

Sonchus spp.
SOWTHISTLE

Description:

Plants annual or perennial from creeping rootstalks; some or all of the leaves lobed from the sides, the bases partly clasping the stems; flowers clustered in heads like a dandelion, but with several to many heads to one stem (instead of just one), yellow in color; fruits seedlike, with long hairs at the top.

Fields, gardens, roadsides and waste places, usually acting as weeds. The various species are now widespread over the United States and the Rocky Mountain area, mostly at lower elevations.

Use:

The sowthistles have milky juice and a rather bitter taste, this latter intensifying as the parts mature. They have been eaten since Greek and Roman times and were mentioned as esculents by Dioscorides and Pliny. Sowthistles seem to be more popular as food plants in other parts of the world than in this country. The raw young leaves have been used as a salad, especially when worked in with those from milder tasting plants. Try blanching the young growth by inverting a basket over several plants or covering them with straw or canvas. The blanched yellow or whitish shoots will be more tender and less bitter. Of course, many people learn to relish this bitter taste.

The young shoots can be cooked like spinach. We prefer to change the water at least once and mix the greens with blander tasting ones. Some writers have said that the peeled young stems and roots are edible. If you like dandelion greens then you will probably enjoy eating sowthistles.

References (to numbers in the bibliography):

31, 33, 38, 66, 84, 93, 99, 112, 117, 122, 134, 149, 158, 165, 181, 219.

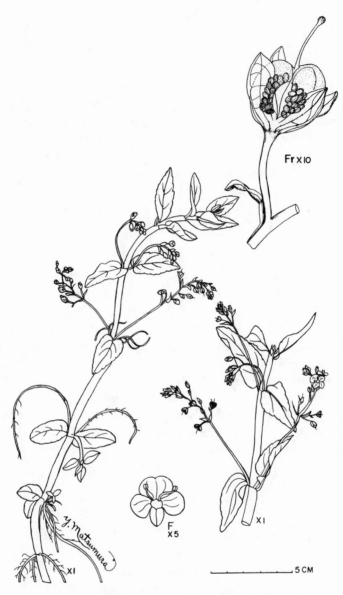

AMERICAN SPEEDWELL *(Veronica americana)*

Veronica americana
AMERICAN SPEEDWELL, AMERICAN BROOKLIME

Description:

Perennial plants; stems erect to prostrate, about 4 to 24 inches long; leaves about ¾ to 3 inches long; flowers rather small, ⅛ to ¼ inch across, blue to nearly white; fruit a small, podlike, flattened capsule with 2 compartments, 2-notched at the apex.

In shallow water or very wet ground. Widely distributed in North America and the Rocky Mountain area.

Use:

This speedwell is used like watercress (See *Rorippa nasturtium-aquaticum*) in many parts of the world, especially Europe and Japan, many thinking it equal to that species as a salad plant. We have used it many times and find it always has a distinctly bitter taste; this is so pronounced that we try to mix it with other plants. You may enjoy this suggestion of bitterness when you use it alone, especially with the addition of some robust dressing. Like any fresh, green-salad plant it is antiscorbutic and healthful (Medsger, 158). We used the young, rapidly growing shoots.

We have tried the plants as potherbs, boiling them for about 15-20 minutes (5000 ft.). They were tender but still had the after-taste of bitterness noticed in the raw shoots. We suggest a couple of water changes during the boiling process to help tame them down, in any event, we like to use them diluted with other greens.

Related Species:

There are several related species that should be tried. These are perennial plants that grow in water or wet soil and have the flower clusters axillary to the ordinary leaves (not terminal on the main stems). The species in our area include *Veronica scutellata, V. anagallis-aquatica* and *V. salina.*

References (to numbers in the bibliography):
84, 93, 140, 158, 240.

Viola spp.
VIOLET

Description:

Perennial plants; stems varying from rather long to very short; leaves from narrow to broadly heart-shaped, the latter shape very common; flowers solitary on the stalks, varying from yellow, white, rose to purple in color, showy, with a short spur or sac at the base (but inconspicuous nonshowy flowers often borne later on, at, or below the surface of the ground); fruit a podlike dry capsule opening along 3 lines.

Use:

Apparently all species of violets are edible, even the garden varieties. We have tried about ten native species and found them all good, with no objectionable flavor or harsh bitterness in any of them. Jaeger (132) mentioned that violets are cultivated for food in the gardens in Europe and we know of a few people in this area who raise them for salads. The young leaves and flower buds are used raw. A favorite mixture of ours consists of head lettuce, halved cherry tomatoes, peeled fresh carrots, shredded violet leaves and other native salad plants as available. A few drops of vinegar can be used as a dressing. The leaves and buds are best in the spring, but even in late summer young leaves can be selected that will make an acceptable salad. We have found raw violet leaves tender and good but perhaps just a bit flat tasting when eaten alone.

The leaves and flowers can be boiled to make an acceptable potherb. Again we like to use them mixed with other plants of more pronounced taste. Violets are often used to thicken soup, especially in the southern part of the United States where they may be called "wild okra."

The flowers can be candied like rose petals and have been used to give a flavor to vinegar. As outlined by Sopher (212A), the latter procedure is very simple. The flowers are crammed into a bottle, as many as can be conveniently forced in, then white wine vinegar is

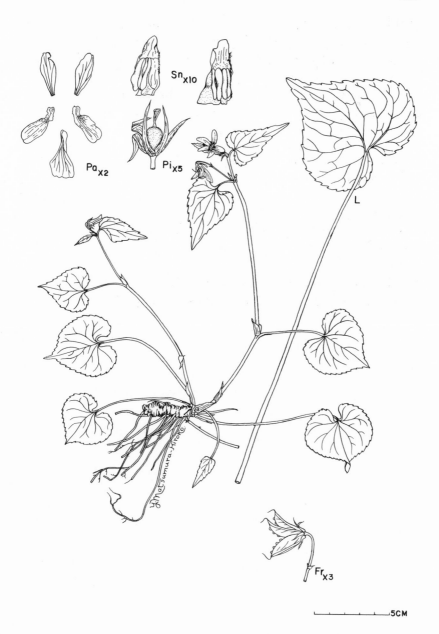

Sn ×10

Pa ×2

Pi ×5

L

Fr ×3

5CM

VIOLET *(Viola canadensis)*

added. This is corked and allowed to stand for about 4 weeks. Then the vinegar is strained and used as "violet vinegar."

The violet leaves make a good substitute for tea. In fact, many of the old timers in this area fondly recall that they drank delicious violet-leaf tea when they were children (Bagdonas, 11A). We have tried tea made from several species including *Viola canadensis, V. rugulosa, V. nuttallii, V. nephrophylla* and *V. papilionacea.* Long boiling does not make the tea bitter, and a little added sugar improves the taste to us. Violet-leaf tea is for sale in a few food stores of this area.

Related Species:

Any species of *Viola* would be worth trying; some will be better than others.

References (to numbers in the bibliography):

11A, 57, 77A, 84, 93, 112, 132, 206, 212A, 243.

Chapter VI: ROOTS AND UNDERGROUND PARTS (like Radish)

These below-ground structures are very useful as sources of food in many native plants. For one thing, they are available the year round if one knows where and how to locate them. In fact, many such roots and underground parts are at their very best in the fall or winter. However, using them poses a problem as to the correct identification of the plant, since the plant stems at that season may have withered, the flowers will have disappeared, and only the old parts of the plants remain above ground. The root parts often look much alike on different species, and the possibility always exists that material from harmful plants may have been gathered by mistake. Even the Indians seemed to have been sometimes guilty of this error. This becomes of particular importance when one notes that poisonous substances, when present, are often concentrated in the underground parts of the plant. Of course, if they are gathered in the spring or summer when flowers are present (to aid in recognition), this special problem is not so acute. *Do not use the underground parts of any plant unless you are sure of the species involved.*

Another advantage is that root parts often provide comparatively large amounts of reasonably nutritious food. Also, they can be stored for a reasonable length of time, and can be carried from areas where they are readily available to other parts of the country. This may be of special value in food-emergency situations. Of course, they are rather heavy but they can be easily sliced, dried in the sun, then be readily transported. Such dehydrated root parts keep for months or even years according to our experiences; when soaked again in water, they cook into a palatable food.

The term "root or underground parts" is used here to include any thickened structure borne by the plant below the ground level. Such structures as rhizomes (cattail), tubers (potatoes), corms (crocus) and bulbs (onions) are included in this general concept. By utilizing these edible underground parts, the Indians and the early pioneers were able to survive during many periods of serious food shortage, especially when these occurred in the winter time.

Plants where the underground parts are used, but illustrated or described under another chapter.

Agropyron repens VIII.
Allium cernuum IX.
Capsella bursa-pastoris III.
Helianthus annuus VIII.
Hemerocallis fulva III.
Monolepis nuttalliana III.

Oenothera strigosa III.
Osmorhiza spp. IX.
Pteridium aquilinum IV.
Smilacina spp. IV.
Taraxacum officinale III.

Arctium minus
BURDOCK, SMALLER BURDOCK, COMMON BURDOCK

Description:
Plants from thick, fleshy taproots; stems stout, branched, 1¾ to 7 feet tall; leaves egg-shaped but variable from top to bottom of the stem, margins rather wavy but not toothed or lobed, often very large, gray-hairy beneath; flowers enclosed in a burrlike head about ⅝ to ¾ inch wide, the individual flowers pink to rose in color.

This plant is a weed of fields and waste places, often found around barns and dwellings, probably because the burrs catch in the hair of animals or the clothing of people and may be carried in from outlying areas. It is widespread in the United States and the Rocky Mountain area, mostly near cultivated places or around ranch buildings, usually not growing above 8000 ft. elevation.

Use:
The burdock is widely used as a food throughout the world and has been actually cultivated for that purpose in Europe and Japan. In the latter country it is much used in preparing sukiyaki. It does have a strong, rank taste and an odor objectionable to some people, especially if it is not properly prepared. The young leaves and

BURDOCK *(Arctium minus)*

shoots can be gathered to use as a potherb like spinach, or they can even be eaten raw as a salad. We have never tried them and would suspect the taste might be rather strong. The young stems and leaf stalks are said to be good if peeled of every shred of the rind which would probably be bitter tasting. The inner pithlike material may be eaten raw or it may be better if boiled with one or two changes of water.

The roots of this plant have long been used, especially those on the young plants; these may bear only the leaf rosette but no flowering stalk. We have prepared them by peeling off the outer layer or rind. The young roots seemed tender inside but seemed to take quite a bit of boiling since cooking for 30 minutes in an open kettle (at 5000 feet elevation) did not do the job. It is wise to slice the roots crosswise into segments for quicker cooking. We found these young roots tender and they were agreeable tasting, with the addition of butter, salt and pepper. We also followed (our illustrator) Matsumura's recommendation and tried some with sesame seed and soy sauce; these were very flavorful. The older roots had developed fibers and were not so good. Roasted and ground burdock roots are for sale in a grocery store of this area, for use as a tea or coffee substitute.

The burdock may not be as abundant in the Rocky Mountains as it is farther east, but it certainly makes a good food plant if gathered at the right time and prepared properly. It would be of value as an emergency food, but unfortunately it may not be abundant in wilderness areas where it might be needed. The roots can be dug and stored for future use should this be necessary.

Related Species:

Arctium lappa is similar to our burdock, but its vegetative parts are larger. It is used in the same way.

References (to numbers in the bibliography):

13, 56, 57, 58, 84, 90, 92, 93, 99, 112, 117, 134, 146, 158, 164, 181, 219, 221, 225, 244.

Calochortus gunnisonii and *C. nuttallii*
Mariposa Lily, Sego Lily, Segolily Mariposa

(These 2 plants are similar in appearance and use; they are figured on the same plate and described together.)

Description:

Plants growing from deep-set, thick-scaled bulbs, often with an additional swelling on the stem about at ground level; stems erect, unbranched except at the top, varying from 4 inches to over a foot tall; leaves narrow and grasslike; flowers large, often up to 3 inches wide, whitish, cream colored to purplish tinged or even varying to a light yellow, the petals about as broad as long; fruit a narrow, dry pod (capsule) with 3 inner compartments bearing seeds.

These plants are in the western part of the United States from the Black Hills of South Dakota to New Mexico and west; some of the species in Arizona and California having orange- or red-colored flowers. They grow on open slopes, plains and meadows or in partial shade, from low elevations in the Rocky Mountains nearly up to timberline.

Use:

This was an important food plant to the Indians and the early pioneers. In fact, it is credited with saving the lives of many Mormon settlers, especially during the fall of 1848 when the crops were damaged by a horde of crickets (Bennion, 24). In gratitude, one of the species *(C. nuttallii),* was made the state flower of Utah under the name sego lily. Incidently, a statue in honor of the sea gulls that helped destroy the crickets, stands on the temple grounds in Salt Lake City.

The whole plant is edible and has been used as a potherb, but is hardly bulky enough to provide much material. The seeds have been ground as food and the flower buds have been eaten raw as a kind of salad. However, it is the thick-scaled bulbs that are the real delicacy and the source of a good food supply. These bulbs are rather small (rarely over 1 inch in diameter), and are borne about 5 or 6 inches underground. They break off readily from the

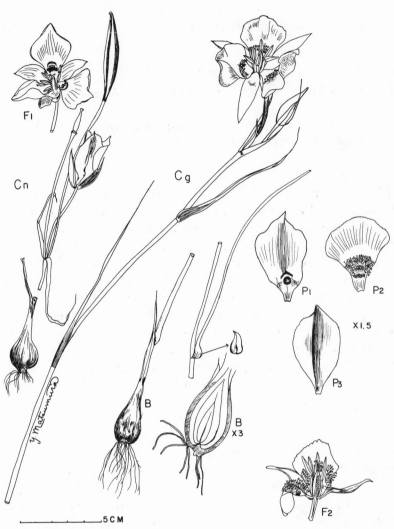

MARIPOSA LILY (*Calochortus gunnisonii & C. nuttallii*)

stem and may be easily overlooked in the ground. It is not an
easy matter to secure an adequate amount but it is certainly worth
the effort. To prepare: the bulbs are washed and the outer husk or
coat removed. They can be eaten raw, with salt to flavor, and have
a pleasant starchy taste somewhat like a raw potato. The bulbs can
be boiled for 15-30 minutes, or they can be fried or baked as one
would potato tubers. They have a crisp nutlike texture, a pleasing
flavor, and are one of our favorite native foods. Colyer (56), once

placed 8-10 raw bulbs on a 12-inch pizza pie and cooked the mixture about 20 minutes, reportedly with good success. Other special uses of the bulbs will occur to the experimental cook. The only drawback to the use of these plants, other than the difficulty of finding enough bulbs, is the fact that they are beautiful plants and using the underground parts would tend to eradicate them. For this reason we think that they should be used sparingly if at all, except in times of emergencies. The bulbs can be stored for future use should this be necessary.

Other Species:

As far as we know, all the species of *Calochortus* are edible. *C. macrocarpus* (Steedman, 217; Coville, 65; Anderson, 5) and *C. flexuosus* (Jaeger, 132; Dodge, 77), are listed in the literature.

References (to numbers in the bibliography):

12, 14, 18, 26, 43, 49, 50, 56, 74, 83, 85, 97, 103, 117, 138, 157, 158, 181, 182, 204, 227, 228, 239, 240, 249, 256, 259.

Camassia quamash (C. esculenta, Quamasia quamash) COMMON CAMASS, BLUE CAMASS, WILD HYACINTH

Description:

Plants from onion-like bulbs, these $\frac{1}{5}$ to $1\frac{1}{4}$ inches broad, usually with blackish coats but white inside; stems about 1 to 2 feet tall; leaves grasslike; flowers in narrow clusters; flowers 6-parted, blue-purple in color, each segment about $\frac{3}{8}$ to 1 inch long; fruit a short dry pod (capsule).

This is a plant of the western United States from Montana to British Columbia and California. It is found only in the western part of the Rocky Mountain area. It grows on moist open meadows.

Use:

This plant was an important food source of the Indians. It has been reported that many local Indian wars were fought over the collecting rights to certain meadows where camass happened to be abundant. The only drawback was that bulbs of the death camas

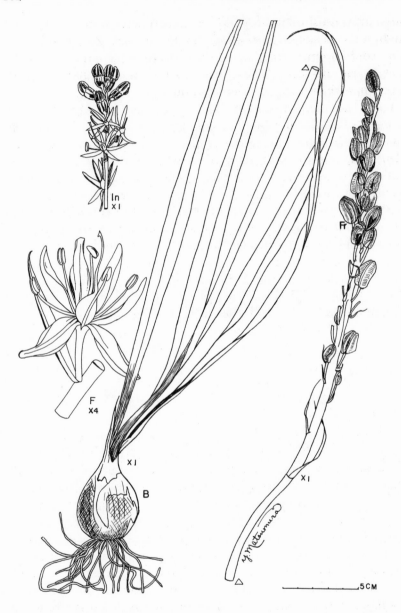

COMMON CAMASS (*Camassia quamash*)

often grew on similar sites and apparently were sometimes mixed in by mistake, often with fatal results. (Check *Zygadenus* spp.) This could occur particularly if the collections were made after the flowers had dropped. (The camass has blue flowers, but the death camas has whitish to cream colored ones).

One reads conflicting accounts of just when the bulbs were collected, but apparently they are edible at any season. It is better to take them in flower when the plants are conspicuous and readily identified, but we have used them when the pods were almost full sized. The Indians sometimes boiled the bulbs down to form a syrup, but usually baked them in pits with the "fireless cooker" method they so often used. The pit was dug according to the amount of material (perhaps 6-10 feet wide and 2-3 feet deep) and lined with stones. Then a fire was built inside and stones allowed to get very hot. The stones were then covered with a layer of grass or other vegetation, the bulbs placed in the pit, covered with another layer of grass and finally with dirt. Sometimes water was poured on the mass, with a hole left for the steam to escape. A fire was sometimes built on the top to keep things good and hot. After from 12 hours to 3 days the pit was opened. The bulbs came out brown or blackish in color, and apparently were rich in sugar content. They were eaten at once or allowed to dry for storage. The bulbs could also be pounded into cakes which could be sun-dried for future use.

We found the raw bulbs were crisp and quite palatable although we must admit not exceptionally so. We boiled them for 25 minutes and found them pleasant tasting, but they were somewhat gummy and mucilaginous, annoying us somewhat by sticking to the teeth after chewing. We roasted the bulbs in aluminum foil at 350°F. for 45 minutes and thought that they were about the same as boiled. The Indian method of steaming and roasting sounds the best to us. Camass bulbs seem to be lacking in starch but they are high in sugar content (Yanovsky & Kingsbury, 256), and although their actual nutritive value may not be exceptionally high, they certainly remain an important potential source of food available over a period of several months of the year. But best beware of the death camas bulbs!

Related Species:

Several related species occur in the western United States and some like *C. leichtlinii* (usually with white flowers), have been used as food.

References (to numbers in the bibliography):

5, 14, 26, 32, 49, 74, 97, 115, 121, 132, 143, 158, 174, 181, 182, 183, 191, 193, 204, 213, 217, 219, 224, 227, 228, 236, 252.

Campanula rapunculoides
CREEPING BELLFLOWER, HAREBELL

Description:

Plants with slender, creeping rootstocks, these in turn from central thickened roots; stems erect, $1\frac{1}{3}$ to $3\frac{1}{3}$ feet tall; leaves 2 to 6 inches long; flowers nodding, $\frac{3}{4}$ to $1\frac{1}{4}$ inches long, blue or purple-blue in color, each more or less bell-shaped.

Fields, roadsides, waste ground and ditches, usually acting as a weed. In this area often cultivated as an ornamental plant, often in borders and along fence rows from where it spreads out into the lawn and becomes a serious pest. The plant is more common in the eastern half of the United States, but now is spreading into the Rocky Mountain area.

Use:

Our plant is a relative of *Campanula rapunculus*, which has for years been cultivated in gardens in this country and Europe under the name of "rampion." The young leaves and shoots of rampion are used as a salad, a potherb, or the roots can be boiled, roasted or fried. Our plant can be utilized in the same ways and makes a very acceptable substitute. We used the enlarged taproots and scraped off the thin rind. The roots were only up to $\frac{1}{2}$ inch in diameter, so they did not provide much bulk. In addition, some of the larger ones were rather stringy and fibrous even after cooking. However, it was not at all difficult to secure a mess of good ones since the plants grew abundantly in large patches. We boiled the roots for 20 minutes and found them very palatable with a "nutlike" taste. Some of these boiled roots were fried in butter and

CREEPING BELLFLOWER *(Campanula rapunculoides)*

these were very good indeed. Since this is a vigorous weed there seems little danger of eradicating it from an area by utilizing it as food.

Related Species:

We have several species of *Campanula* in our area, but none of them have enlarged root parts and we have no record as to their use as food.

References (to numbers in the bibliography):

84, 93, 102, 117, 124.

Cirsium spp. (*Carduus* spp.)
THISTLE

(Note: The species figured is the "common thistle or bull thistle" but the other kinds look, and feel, about the same.)

Description:

Stems variable, from very short to over 6 feet tall in the various species; leaves usually lobed, with the teeth and lobes ending in spines or at least the tip ending in a spine; flowers clustered in spiny, burrlike heads, usually white, pink or reddish in color; fruits (seedlike) with a parachute of hairs.

Thistles are widespread throughout the United States. In the Rocky Mountain area we have about 20 to 25 species, ranging from lower elevations to above timberline. Thistles are poorly understood botanically and good specimens in the collections are rather rare. Anyone who has handled one will understand why!

Use:

Thistles were often used as food by the Indians and have been credited with saving several early explorers from starvation (Havard, 115). We have used the very young leaves raw as a kind of salad and they were just fair. Thistle-leaf tea is for sale by some companies. The young tender roots of several species have been used by us. The young stems were peeled and the pithlike inner

THISTLE *(Cirsium lanceolatum)*

part eaten raw or cooked. We have eaten the roots and crown of *Cirsium drummondii;* we boiled them for 15 minutes, and used salt and butter or salt and vinegar as a seasoning. The older roots were a bit fibrous, but the crown of the plant was mild and pleasant tasting, providing some enjoyable meals. Horses nip off the flowers of some species and it has been reported that these may also be edible for human beings. We thought they were rather fuzzy or cottony tasting when eaten raw. The seedlike fruits can also be eaten raw, but we found them rather bitter. This bitter taste is reduced by roasting them. Thistles in spite of their forbidding exterior can provide food, especially in times of emergency. Avoid patches treated with weed killers.

Related Species:

As far as we know any species of thistle can be used as food if taken in the right stage and suitably prepared.

References (to numbers in the bibliography):

11A, 56, 57, 84, 88, 93, 103, 115, 146, 158, 206, 228, 240, 243, 256.

Claytonia lanceolata (C. multicaulis, C. multiscapa, C. rosea)
WESTERN SPRING BEAUTY, LANCELEAF SPRING BEAUTY

Description:

Plants from underground, tuber-like structures (corms), these from rather small to at least 1½ inches in diameter on older plants; stems to 8 inches tall; leaves to 4 inches long the basal ones, when present, longer than the two on the stem; petals white or pink in color, each ¼ to ½ inch long.

This plant grows on rich soil, often along valleys and sometimes in partial shade. It is found throughout the Rocky Mountain area and west to the Pacific, from low elevations to almost timberline in the mountains.

Use:

The tuberous corms were much used by the Indians and seem to us to be rather high in starch. When eaten raw they were crisp

F
X5CA

F₁
X4CA

Cl

B

R

Cm

F2
X3.5

⊢————————⊣5CM

WESTERN SPRING BEAUTY *(Claytonia lanceolata)*
AND ALPINE SPRING BEAUTY *(Claytonia megarrhiza)*

like potatoes, not at all displeasing but not very flavorful to our
taste. We boiled them for 25 minutes (at 5100 feet), some peeled
and some with the jackets left on. The peeled ones were somewhat

like potatoes, perhaps even better tasting. The peel came off readily on the whole ones after cooking, but we thought it imparted a slightly "earthy" taste to the contents. The spring beauty is an attractive spring flower, seldom growing abundantly and it does seem a shame to use the corms extensively except in real emergencies.

Related Species:

C. *virginica* and C. *caroliniana* are similar plants of the eastern United States and also produce edible corms which can be used. A far northern species, C. *tuberosa,* is used by the Eskimos according to Heller, (119).

References (to numbers in the bibliography):

5, 26, 49, 50, 92, 99, 115, 158, 183, 217, 219, 240, 252, 256.

Claytonia megarrhiza
ALPINE SPRING BEAUTY

Description:

Plants from long thick, fleshy, purple-red taproots; stems not much over 4 inches tall; leaves numerous, varying from nearly round to narrower in some forms, up to 2 inches long; petals white to pink in color, each ¼ to ⅜ inch long.

Slopes and rockslides of the higher mountains of Colorado to Montana and west to Washington. Usually found above 10,000 feet in the Rocky Mountains.

Use:

We have eaten both the roots and the rosettes of leaves of this plant. The leaves, when eaten raw, are not displeasing but we must admit they are not particularly flavorful. However, we felt that they could be used to good advantage as a mixture in a salad.

The cooked young leaves, to our notion, made an acceptable potherb. We suggest boiling them for 10-15 minutes (at 5000 feet elevation); the water does not need changing. We boiled the roots for 30 minutes. They tasted very nice except for a fairly strong "earthy" taste. We advise peeling the roots before cooking and suggest trying them baked. This plant should be an excellent survival plant if one were needed at higher elevations in the mountains.

References (to numbers in the bibliography):
115, 117.

Cymopterus spp. (*Phellopterus* spp.)
Biscuit Root, Corkwing, Wafer Parsnip, Wild Celery

This group, consisting of about a dozen species, are all very similar and therefore it is hard to distinguish any particular one. They are limited to the western part of the United States and are widespread over the Rocky Mountain area. The following description applies to all of them.

Description:
Plants from elongated but thickened taproots; stems short, with the leaves from near the base; leaves variable but always more or less filmy and fernlike; flowers in characteristic clusters (umbels), these always double as shown; individual flowers small, petals white, yellow or reddish-purple; fruit of 2 halves, each half with 2 or more longitudinally running wings.

These plants grow on open plains and hills, often on dry soil and appear fairly early in the season. Some of them grow only on the eastern slopes, others only on the western side of the Continental Divide.

Use:
Note: These plants belong to the Carrot or Umbel Family (*Umbelliferae* or *Ammiaceae*) which also contains several poisonous members. They all may have a superficial resemblance, but fortunately the resemblance is not very close. (See *Conium maculatum* and *Cicuta douglasii*.) These poisonous ones are taller plants with some of the leaves inserted on the upper part of the stem.

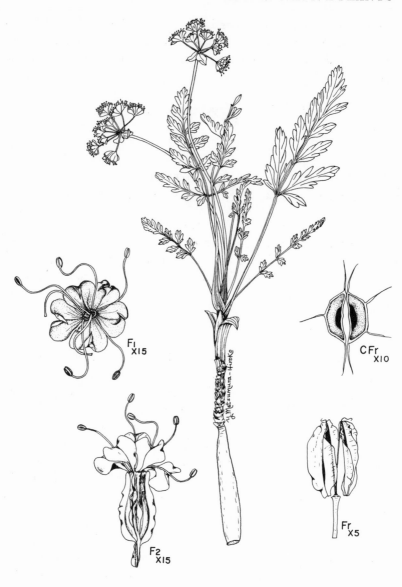

BISCUIT ROOT *(Cymopterus bulbosus)*

As far as we know all the various species of biscuit root produce edible roots, although the Indians claimed some had bitter leaves that they used in flavoring. Certainly, it would be worthwhile to try all the species.

The upper part of the plant in the early stages has been used raw as a salad, like celery, or it has been cooked as a potherb. All kinds of *Cymopterus* would be worth trying, although the water might have to be changed several times when cooking the reputed bitter-tasting varieties. The roots of *Cymopterus purpurascens* are still used by the Ute Indians and we have tried them several times. The Indians, particularly the children, ate the young roots raw in the spring when they are said to be more tender and sweet. We gathered the roots later in the season, peeled them and tried them raw. They were slightly sweet, but on the whole starchy like potatoes, not very pleasant tasting but quite acceptable. We baked the roots for about 40 minutes in a moderate oven and ate them with butter and salt. Some of the older roots were a bit fibrous, but the younger ones were good. We also boiled them for about 30 minutes (open kettle at 5000 feet elevation). The taste was pleasant and some of us liked them best cooked this way. This plant probably is at flavor peak in the spring and from our experience we would advise using the younger plants only. In any event, this looks like an excellent survival plant. It is acceptable raw, may be found in dry areas where other edible plants may be scarce, and is available at all seasons of the year. The Indians ground the roasted roots of biscuit root to make a meal that they used like cornmeal.

Related Species:

Probably all species of *Cymopterus* could be used but *C. bulbosus, C. purpurascens, C. montanus, C. fendleri, C. purpureus, C. newberryi* and *C. longipes* are mentioned particularly in the literature as having edible qualities.

References (to numbers in the bibliography):

13, 43, 49, 50, 56, 83, 115, 117, 138, 158, 164, 218, 227, 239, 240, 249, 259.

Cyperus esculentus
FLATSEDGE, CHUFA, NUTGRASS

Description:

Plants grasslike perennials with rootstocks bearing tubers; stems 10 inches to 2½ feet tall; leaves narrow, not over ⅜ inch wide; flowers in compound clusters but the smallest unit (spike) with many scales in 2 opposite rows, each scale bearing an inconspicuous flower.

This plant is found in moist ground and appears often in fields as a weed. It is now widespread in the United States and is found here and there in the Rocky Mountain area, but only locally abundant.

Use:

This has been a famous food plant since ancient Egyptian times, and the tubers still appear on the markets in many parts of Europe. These tubers are somewhat sweetish and nutty tasting, but they do have a rather tough, dry rind that should be removed before eating. They are commonly boiled, peeled, then eaten with butter and seasoning, but are sometimes candied or ground into a palatable and wholesome flour. To make a drink, the tubers are mashed, sugar and water added, and the material is strained and chilled. This would be an excellent survival plant since the inner base of the stems can be eaten raw and the tubers can either be used raw or they may be baked in the fire. Even though flatsedge can become a noxious weed in places, it may also have its beneficial side.

Related Species:

The inner base of the young stems could be utilized for any species of *Cyperus*. In addition, there are several others with tuber-like thickening at the base of the plant or else bearing tubers at the end of slender rootstocks. These include *Cyperus fendlerianus, C. schweinitzii, C. rotundus* and *C. setigerus*. A variety of our plant, *C. esculentus* var. *sativus* is cultivated in the southern part of the United States for its edible tubers under the name of "chufa."

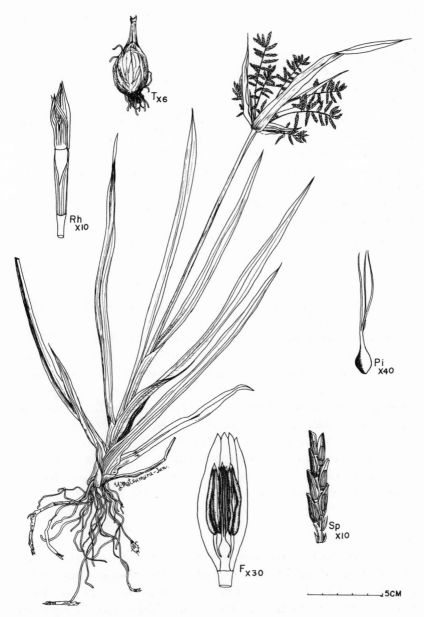

FLATSEDGE *(Cyperus esculentus)*

References (to numbers in the bibliography):
2, 13, 18, 84, 93, 99, 115, 117, 138, 158, 240, 243.

Daucus carota
WILD CARROT, QUEEN ANNE'S LACE

Description:

This plant appears to be a biennial and has a fairly thick tap-root; stems solitary (one to a root), 6 inches to 3 feet tall; flowers in characteristic clusters (compound umbels); petals small, white to pink or rose-purple, the latter especially on the flower in the center of each small cluster; fruit of 2 halves, about ⅛ inch long, becoming burrlike.

Valleys and fields, particularly in waste places. Introduced as a weed in all parts of North America. It does not seem to be very common and widespread throughout the Rocky Mountain area, except locally as in the Black Hills of South Dakota.

Use:

This is the plant that by breeding and selection produced the well-known garden carrot. The wild forms have rather bitter tops that have caused cows consuming them to produce similar tasting milk. Wild carrots cause dermatitis on contact with some people, especially when the plants are wet, but cultivated carrots will sometimes have the same effect. We once knew a student who had trouble convincing her doctor that she had this allergy to carrots. She clinched the matter by using a cut carrot root to draw a picture on her arm of a round face with its tongue sticking out in a most impolite fashion. The next day at the resulting doctor's examination there were at least two red faces present in the room.

It has been reported that the roots of wild carrots are sweeter than their cultivated counterpart (Morrell, 163). We collected wild carrot roots in the latter part of July and found them tough and stringy, certainly not edible in the raw state. Perhaps if used in the spring, or if only the first-year plants were selected, this would be a good root food. The dried and roasted roots have been ground or diced in small pieces, and have been brewed into a substitute for coffee. This plant was extensively used by the Indians and should be kept in mind as an emergency food. It belongs to the same family as some very poisonous species (See *Cicuta douglasii*

In.1
X1

X1

In.2
X2

Fr
X15

F
X10

5 CM

WILD CARROT *(Daucus carota)*

and Conium maculatum) and looks like them in many ways, so it should be used with caution.

Related Species:

A related plant may be in our area, especially in the southern part. It is *Daucus pusillus,* and was used in similar fashion by the Indians (Castetter, 43; Uphof, 240; Elmore, 83; Underhill, 239; Kearney & Peebles, 138).

References (to numbers in the bibliography):
18, 38, 59, 84, 93, 117, 134, 163, 167, 240.

Erythronium grandiflorum (E. parviflorum)
DOGTOOTH VIOLET, FAWNLILY, TROUTLILY, ADDER'S TONGUE

Description:

Plants with deep-seated, tuber-like swellings (corms); stems about 6 to 13 inches tall; leaves only 2 to a stem, about 4 to 8 inches long; flowers one to several to a stem, each ¾ to 1⅝ inches long, golden yellow in color.

This species ranges westward from Wyoming and Colorado. In the Rocky Mountain area it is found up to timberline.

Use:

This characteristic and lovely plant is certainly too beautiful to gather indiscriminately as food. The leaves and corms can be used raw as a kind of salad, but they should be tried carefully as some writers say they have an emetic effect. The limited amounts we have tried had no such action. The young plants have been boiled as a potherb and are said to be good.

The corms are deep seated and it is hard to dig out a reasonably sized mess. To make it worse they tend to snap off easily and may often be lost in the soil. They have a nice, crisp, chewy taste when eaten raw. We boiled them for varying times, but found 25 minutes (at 5000 ft.) to be about right. They had a very pleasant crisp taste and we liked them very much. This plant is locally abundant

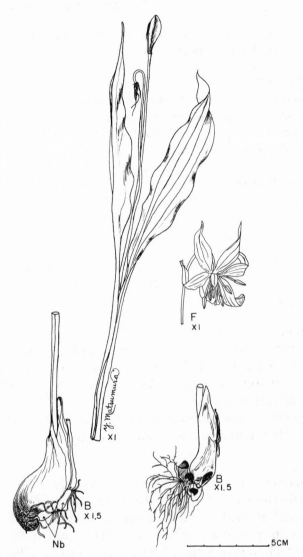

DOGTOOTH VIOLET *(Erythronium grandiflorum)*

but the corms are hard to dig, and the plant is really too lovely to destroy. Consequently we must agree with practically everyone else on the subject who always advise that dogtooth violet should be used only in times of emergency. Remember, if you eat it raw, take it easy at first!

Related Species:

A yellow-flowered dogtooth violet of the eastern United States
(E. americanum) has been used in the same fashion as our plant
(Morton, 164; Bale, 13; Gillespie, 93; Medsger, 158; Gordon, 99;
Grieve, 102; Fernald & Kinsey, 84; Oswald, 179; Palmer, 181). A
western species *(E. oregonum)* was reported by Kingsbury (141) to
have apparently caused poisoning to poultry.

References (to numbers in the bibliography):
    26, 117, 132, 217, 256.

Ipomoea leptophylla
Bush Morning Glory

Description:

Perennial from a deep-seated, enormous root, this sometimes
up to 1 foot thick and 4 feet long; stems erect or rather sprawling,
1 to 4 feet long; leaves 1 to 6 inches long; flowers 1½ to 3 inches
long, pink-purple to rose-colored.

Plains and dry banks, especially on sandy ground. South Dakota
and Montana to Texas and New Mexico. This plant is found in
the eastern edge of the Rocky Mountain area, seldom above 6000
feet.

Use:

The Indians apparently used the roots as food, but the various
writers on the matter uniformly called it a "starvation food by no
means palatable or nutritious." Maybe the Indians were deliberately keeping something from them, for we found it to be one of
the very best plants we have ever tried. Perhaps these reporters
used too old a root, for they do become woody in age. We selected
one about 3 inches in diameter and sliced it into pieces about ½
inch thick. These slices had a tougher outer rind which we removed, leaving a bright white core about 1½ to 2 inches across.
We ate this raw and found it to be crisp, tender and sweet, making
an excellent salad.

Then we boiled the slices for over an hour in an open kettle

BUSH MORNING GLORY *(Ipomoea leptophylla)*

(at 5000 ft. elevation). The taste was good but apparently they lost some of their sweetness in the boiling process. The slices were still rather crisp and not at all mushy, like over-boiled potatoes sometimes become. We also roasted some for about 1 hour and 20 minutes in a moderately hot oven. The taste was excellent, rather crisp and sweet, making this one of the most palatable of all the wild foods we have ever tried.

As an experiment, we cut the root core into thin slices and dried them in the sun. After a couple of years these dried slices appeared to be about in their original condition. About a month after drying we soaked some of these slices in water for 30 minutes, then fried them slowly in butter. The taste was quite palatable.

This plant appears to be a highly desirable food plant, both for general use and in an emergency. It is locally abundant on sandy soils, such as sand dunes, and even a small root yields an amazing amount of food product. The roots we tried had two annual rings, which may mean they were in their third years growth. Younger plants may be even better, but we would suspect older, larger roots would be tough and woody.

Related Species:

Ipomoea pandurata has a similar habit of growth and produces similarly enlarged roots. It grows in the eastern part of the United States, where it is known as wild potato vine. The Indians used the root as food. (Ginter, 97; Medsger, 158).

References (to numbers in the bibliography):
    26, 97, 117, 158, 162, 182, 240, 242.

Lewisia rediviva
BITTERROOT, BITTERROOT LEWISIA

Description:

Plants from thick, fleshy roots; leaves thick and fleshy, becoming ¾ to 1¼ inches long; petals 12 to 18 in number, each ¾ to 1 inch long, rose to white in color, the flowers rather large and showy.

Stony hills, ridges and slopes. Montana to British Columbia, south to Colorado and northern California. Found in the Rocky Mountains south to northern Colorado and Utah.

FX1 CA

X1

Y.Matsumura

0 _____ 5 CM

BITTERROOT *(Lewisia rediviva)*

Use:

This is a lovely plant, chosen to be the state flower of Montana. The roots were highly prized by the Indians and some rather exaggerated statements concerning them appear in print. For example, Palmer (182), said that they abounded in concentrated nutriment, a single ounce of the dried article being sufficient for a meal. One also finds the statement in print, that a bag of the roots was worth as much to the Indians as a horse. Of course they do not state how big the bag was or how good the horse was! The roots were dug in the spring when the plants were in flower. Perhaps the plants were easier to find at that season, but another advantage was that the rind, or outer layer of the roots, slipped off easily then. This covering apparently contains most of the bitter tasting substance, and probably was discarded before cooking. The core was usually cooked in water and became swollen, exuding a mucilaginous substance. We collected the plants in flower in early June and found the covering of the root separated fairly easily then, by using our fingernails or a knife blade. The inner core was bright white and rather brittle. For the benefit of the botanist let us state that it appeared that this bark was made up of phloem and cork, and the core was composed of xylem tissue. We boiled the cores for 20 minutes, changing the water once. The roots became soft and swollen. We ate them with butter, salt and pepper. The taste was good, but a bitter background tardily appeared. This is always disappointing—like thinking you have won a prize only to find out later you haven't!

It seems a shame to dig up such a lovely plant and since the roots aren't too palatable anyway (to us) we suggest that bitterroot be used only in time of emergency.

Related Species:
   None.

References (to numbers in the bibliography):
   5, 26, 32, 74, 107, 115, 117, 132, 138, 158, 181, 182, 198, 204, 213, 217, 227, 228, 234, 236, 240, 252, 256.

Lilium umbellatum (L. montanum)
Lily, Western Orange Cup Lily

Description:
   Plants from flattened, globe-shaped bulbs, these with thick, fleshy scales; stems 1 to 2 feet tall; flowers 1 to 3 to a stem, each about 2 to 3 inches long, brownish to orange red in color, with dark spots near the base.

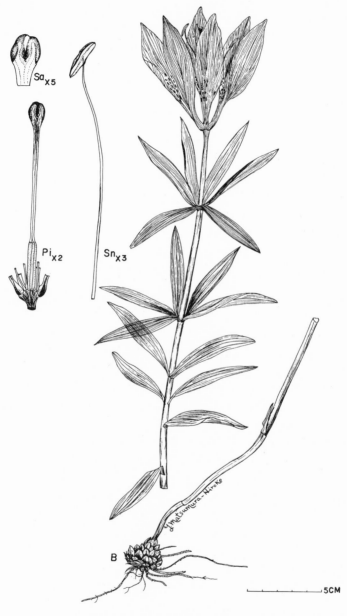

LILY (*Lilium umbellatum*)

In dry open woods or moist thickets. Ohio to Alberta, south to New Mexico and Arizona. Scattered in the mountains of the Rocky Mountain area.

Use:

Many of the species of *Lilium* produce bulbs that are edible and are often used both in this and in other countries. They seem to be extensively used in Japan. Makino, in his flora of Japan, listed *L. maximowiezii,* with the comment that the underground parts are edible and lacked the bitter principle found in the others.

Our American Indians ate the bulbs of several species of lily. According to report they were utilized as we would cook potatoes, for example; they were often used to thicken soup. Fernald & Kinsey (84), suggested that all our native species are edible, having a starchy and slightly sweetish taste. Practically everyone who ever wrote on the matter called attention to the fact that lilies are so beautiful and usually so scarce, that it would be folly to gather them in large quantities for food. For that reason we have never even tried our plant, but we would have no hesitancy in eating it in a food emergency. We bought a jar of lily bulbs put up in syrup for sale at a neighborhood grocery store. They were imported from Japan and our colleague, Dr. N. Oshima, guessed they were from a native species now in cultivation. They had no pronounced taste but were crisp and slightly spicy. We did not particularly care for them. The flavor of the cooked bulbs is said to resemble roasted chestnuts with a slight bitterness which renders them agreeable (Anderson, 5).

Related Species:

Lilium columbianum, L. philadelphicum and *L. superbum* are mentioned particularly in the literature as providing a source of food.

References (to numbers in the bibliography):

5, 84, 93, 184, 194, 240.

Nuphar polysepalum (Nuphar luteum ssp. *polysepalum, Nymphaea polysepala)*
COWLILY, POND LILY, SPATTERDOCK, YELLOW WATERLILY

Description:

Plants from thick rootstocks which are anchored in the soil at the bottom of a lake or pond; leaf blades 8 to 16 inches long, usually on long stalks which let them float on the surface, but sometimes actually raise them in the air; flowers large, the individual segments ¾ to 1¼ inches long, yellow in color but often tinged with red; fruit large, often hen's-egg size, becoming leathery and podlike, containing many large seeds.

Growing in lakes, ponds or slow streams. Black Hills of South Dakota to Alaska, and south to southern Colorado and Utah. In the Rocky Mountain area it is commonest in high mountain lakes, often to about timberline.

Use:

Cowlily rootstocks are buried in the mud, often in water 4 to 5 feet deep. The Indians would dive for them and would bring up chunks as much as 2 feet long. These were usually boiled or baked. The rind was then removed and the spongy, glutinous, slightly sweet contents were used in various ways, often with meat. The AF Manual (2), suggested peeling the fresh rootstocks, cutting the centers into thin slices and allowing them to dry. These slices can then be ground or pulverized. Then the meal can be soaked in water, the water poured off carefully, and this repeated several times; this is said to remove the strong taste. The meal or flour can then be dried and used in various ways, such as making gruel or in thickening soup. These rootstocks are said to be stored in muskrat houses, which cache the Indians often raided. In time of emergency this could be done by anyone. They are usually collected in the fall, but would be available at any season when the water was not frozen solid.

The fruit pods contain numerous seeds which have been used in various ways. For example, try drying the large pods and pound-

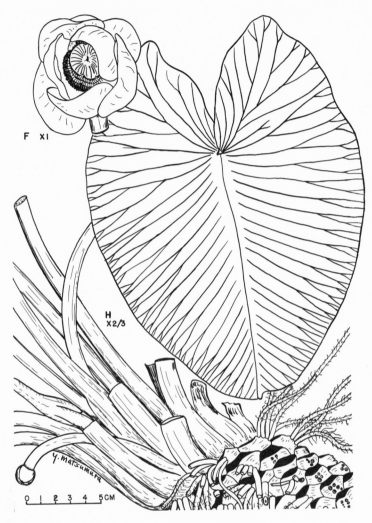

COWLILY *(Nuphar polysepalum)*

ing out the hard seeds which can then be further dried in the sun. The pods can also be broken open in a pan of water and the seeds separated from the sticky pulp by washing, then dried in the sun. These seeds can be stored for winter use to be processed when needed. In any case, when you need them you can parch the seeds in a frying pan over a slow fire, stirring the seeds as you would do in popping corn. They may pop open slightly, somewhat like unenthusiastic popcorn. These parched seeds are pounded or lightly ground and the hard shells removed by winnowing, shaking or by picking them out with the fingers. The kernels can be ground up to make a meal, or after additional parching can be eaten like peanuts. The meal can be used in various ways. Norton (176) suggested using 2 cups of boiling water, stirring in 1 cup of the meal. Boil for 15 minutes stirring constantly and then simmering it with very low heat for an hour. This can be eaten hot like mush or cooled, sliced and fried in butter.

The various species of cowlily formed one of the important foods to the early Indians, especially in the Northwest. It can be an emergency food of no small importance, and the rhizomes or seeds may be available in just the places where food may be desperately needed.

Related Species:
Nuphar advena of the eastern United States is used in similar fashion.

References (to numbers in the bibliography):
2, 26, 57, 84, 93, 99, 117, 132, 140, 174, 176, 181, 182, 204, 219, 224, 227, 228, 240.

Orogenia linearifolia
INDIAN POTATO, GREAT BASIN OROGENIA

Description:
Plants from tuber-like roots resembling those of radishes; leaves and flower stalks small, only about 2 to 6 inches tall; leaflets about 5/8 to 2¾ inches long; flowers in characteristic round or flat-topped clusters (umbels), white in color; fruits about ⅛ inch long.

Open mountain sides and ridges, often in sandy or gravelly soil. Montana to western Colorado, then west to Utah and Washington.

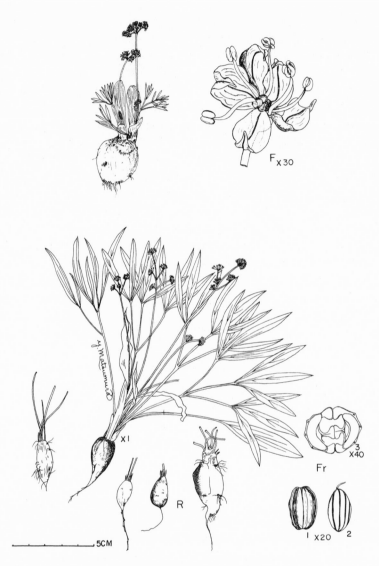

INDIAN POTATO *(Orogenia linearifolia)*

Use:

The tuber-like roots vary in shape from being almost globular to about the shape of icicle radishes. They vary in size from ¼ to about 1½ inches in diameter. The thin outer coat can be removed; since it has a slight bitter taste you may wish to do so. We found this was unnecessary for our taste. If you like baked potato jackets, you probably will prefer to have the coat of this root left on. The raw roots had a pleasant crisp taste, with the general flavor of the parsley family. We then sliced and fried these raw roots in butter. We all pronounced them very good, somewhat nutty tasting, not really like fried potatoes, but possibly even better.

We boiled the unpeeled roots for 20 minutes and found them good, as we expected. We also baked them about 20-30 minutes at 350 degrees F. and again thought them excellent. They can undoubtedly be served in any of the ways potatoes have been used. One of our students who lived on a ranch in western Colorado told us that this plant is known as a harbinger of spring and is called "pepper plant" in the area. It certainly produces palatable food, but has one drawback, at least in the area in which we have collected it. The roots are rather small, the plants scattered, and it took a real effort to secure a large sized mess. However, this plant is reported to be much more abundant in some localities than it was in the patches we located. Like most plants bearing their food underground, it is available for most of the year. One certainly should not go hungry in places where it grows.

Related Species:
    None.

References:
    Strangely enough this plant is not recorded as a food source in any of the books and magazines that we examined. It seems to be well known to many people in the area where it grows, as being very good to eat. For example, May (157A), said that his brother's children near Steamboat Springs in northwestern Colorado are fond of eating the raw roots and call the plant "pepper and salt." Professors Cottam and Flowers of the University of Utah told us that the roots are favorite "nibbles" for their students on field trips near Salt Lake City. The Indians surely didn't overlook such a flavorful source of food but apparently they didn't care to talk about it to the ethnobotanists.

Perideridia gairdneri (Carum gairdneri, Atenia gairdneri)
YAMPA, WILD CARAWAY

Description:

Plants from a solitary root or from clusters of tuber-like roots; stems 1 to 3½ feet tall; smallest leaf divisions about ¾ to 6 inches long; flowers small, white in color; fruit about ⅛ inch long.

Meadows, valleys and slopes. Canada, south to New Mexico, Arizona and California. In open meadows or in partial shade, often very abundant locally in the Rocky Mountain area.

Use:

This was a favorite root food among the Indians, often mentioned as the one they liked the best. This is not surprising to us, as it is also one of our favorite edible native plants. The roots tend to taper both ways, are rather small in size (⅝ of an inch in diameter being a good-sized one) and are covered with a thin brown skin. The plant is abundant only in local areas, as for example in the drainage valley of the Yampa River in northwestern Colorado. The Indians were said to have swarmed into that area each fall to gather the roots of what they called "Yampa." The plant gave its name to the whole valley, the river that flows through it, and the town of Yampa. In fact, Dawson (72) pointed out that when several names were considered for the proposed new state, the name "Yampa" ran close competition with the finally selected "Colorado".

The Indians were said to have gathered the roots and placed them in baskets in running water. Then the squaws would tread them with bare feet to remove the outer skin. This sounds like one of the well-known wine-making stories. The early pioneers, notably Lewis and Clark and John Fremont, learned the value of this plant from the Indians. Even today many people in the Yampa Valley make at least limited use of the plant that gave the name to the area. We have tried these roots in many ways and they seem to get better every time we eat them. They have a sweet, nutty, parsnip-like flavor when eaten raw, with a percentage of sugars

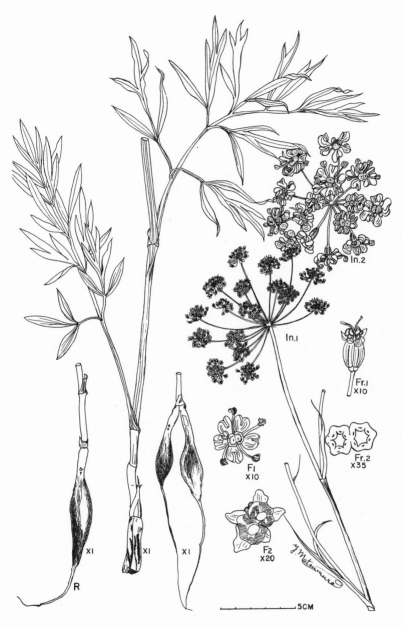

YAMPA *(Perideridia gairdneri)*

that equals or surpasses the starch content (Trimble, 234; Yanovsky & Kingsbury, 256). As one of us remarked, "They taste like parsnips—if parsnips only tasted good."

The outer peel is thin and we have found it unnecessary to remove it. We have cooked the roots by several methods. They were boiled for 25 to 35 minutes (at 5000 ft.), depending on their size, and it was found that the peeling separated readily if this is desired. We usually ate them with butter, pepper, and just a little salt. They were very good, but it is our feeling that some of the sweet taste is removed in the boiling process. The leftover boiled roots can also be fried. We liked the roots when baked in a 350 degree F. oven for 40 minutes. They were crisp, sweet and tender with a delicious taste. In fact, any of the many recipes for cooking ordinary potatoes would certainly work for Yampa roots. Here is one we liked.

CREAMED YAMPA ROOTS

Make about 1 cupful of sauce using:
1 tablespoon butter or other shortening
2 tablespoons flour   1/16 teaspoon pepper
3/4 teaspoon salt   1 cup milk

Melt butter, add flour, salt and pepper and mix well. Add milk slowly and bring to the boiling point, stirring constantly to avoid lumps. Stir in about 1 cup of cut up, boiled and peeled Yampa roots.

CANDIED YAMPA ROOT

Heat some butter with brown sugar and drop in whole, boiled, peeled roots. Then stir over fire until they are coated or candied. The taste may be almost too sweet for some palates.

We found the roots dried readily in the sun, either whole or when split longitudinally. The dried product seems to keep indefinitely, but we have found this difficult to do because several of us around the laboratory have formed the habit of nibbling on them. We let the pieces soak up in the mouth a bit before chewing; the flavor is aromatic and sweet. The sliced roots, when soaked in water for half an hour and when fried in butter, have a taste we would describe as "sweet, tender and good." The Indians were said to grind up the roots to form a sort of meal which could be used in various ways. Yampa is a close relative of caraway and the seeds (fruits) have also been used as seasoning.

This plant is locally abundant, the roots are easy to dig, they do not need peeling, they are delightful tasting raw or cooked, and they dry readily for storage. On the other hand they are rather small, do not store well in fresh condition like potatoes, our experience makes us suspect they are not so palatable during their active growing season, and lastly, they belong to the same family as some deadly poisonous plants (like *Conium maculatum* and *Cicuta douglasii*). Of course they do have some superficial resemblance to them. However, the resemblance is not very close and this is surely one of our best edible plants. If the roots could be enlarged by selection or breeding surely Yampa roots could be cultivated and marketed. What a shame that this delicious taste sensation has been almost lost to mankind!

Related Species:
Wild caraway *(Carum carvi)* resembles Yampa very closely. Its use in seasoning is well known.

References (to numbers in the bibliography):
5, 18, 26, 49, 65, 72, 74, 88, 89, 97, 107, 113, 115, 117, 138, 158, 182, 183, 204, 213, 227, 234, 240, 256.

Polygonum bistortoides (Bistorta bistortoides, B. linearifolia)
AMERICAN BISTORT, WESTERN BISTORT

Description:
Perennial from fleshy, horizontal rootstocks; stems 8 to 28 inches tall, erect, unbranched; basal leaves 4 to 8 inches long, stem leaves shorter, each sheathing the stem at the base; flowers in a cluster, only one to a stem, this cluster about 1/2 to 1 3/8 inches long and around 1/2 inch thick; individual flowers white to light rose in color, about 1/8 inch long.

Moist or wet meadows and swamps at high elevations in the mountains, seldom below 8000 feet, often above timberline. Canada, south to New Mexico, Arizona and California.

Polygonum viviparum (Bistorta vivipara) VIVIPAROUS BISTORT:

This is a smaller species with shorter and of course smaller but still fleshy rootstocks; stems 4 to 12 inches long; basal leaves ¾ to 4 inches long; flower cluster about ¾ to 3 inches long and about ⅜ inch thick; flowers pale rose to white in color, at least the lower ones replaced by small bulblets.

This species is found with the other one in our area.

Use:

For the two species: The two kinds have similar uses but the American Bistort has the advantage of producing larger rootstocks. The young leaves can be used as a potherb and are said to have a pleasingly tart taste. The rootstocks have often been used by the Indians, some tribes esteeming them highly. We ate some of the rootstocks raw and thought them starchy and rather pleasant, with no bitter taste to the rind or contents. Some of the older ones were slightly fibrous and we would recommend cooking them. It does not seem necessary to peel them, which would be difficult to do in any case, since the surface is so rough and irregular. However, we must admit this peel does not improve the appearance of the cooked product.

We boiled them for 40 minutes and ate them with salt, pepper and butter, peel and all. The taste was rather starchy, but very pleasant. One of us compared the flavor to that of the water chestnut of Japan. We also wrapped the rootstocks in aluminum foil and baked them for 40 minutes in an oven at 300 to 325 degrees F. When eaten with butter, salt and pepper they were judged to be an excellent food, with a sweet, pleasant, nutty taste.

Our two species are often abundant, the rootstocks are borne shallowly in the soil (although rather hard to dig), so they are fairly easy to secure in quantities; they are edible raw and are very palatable cooked. These plants would be excellent to try on a camping or fishing trip, and make a good emergency food in the higher elevations in the mountains.

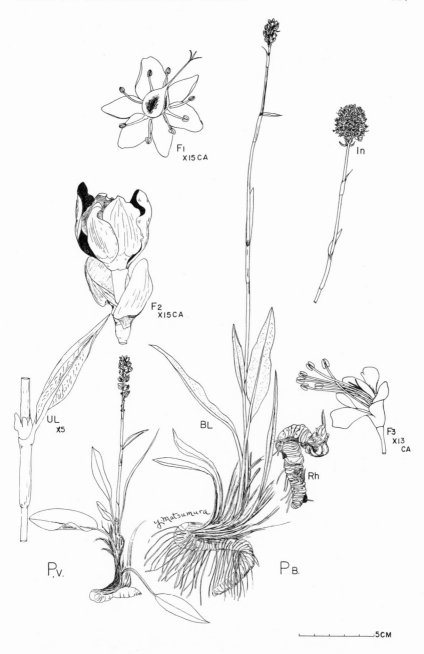

F1
X15 CA

F2
X15 CA

In

UL
X5

BL

F3
X13
CA

Rh

y.matsumura

P.v.

P.B.

5CM

BISTORT *(Polygonum viviparum & bistortoides)*

Related Species:

Some species of *Polygonum,* called "Smartweeds," have an acrid juice in the stems and leaves (Campbell et al., 40; Muenscher, 167; Kearney & Peebles, 138), but these species all have two or more flower clusters to a stem and have only a distant resemblance to our two plants. Even some of these, such as *Polygonum persicaria,* have been used as a salad or as a seasoning. (Fernald & Kinsey, 84; Kephart, 140; Stratton, 225; Medsger, 158.) The Japanese Knotweed *(P. cuspidatum),* with broad leaves cut off square at the base, is often planted as an ornamental and sometimes runs wild, even becoming weedlike. The young shoots have been cooked like asparagus and the rootstocks boiled or baked (Gillespie, 93; Gibbons, 92; Harris, 112; Fernald & Kinsey, 84).

The seeds of several kinds of *Polygonum* have been used as food after being parched and ground into meal but they would surely be tedious to gather in quantity. (Blankinship, 26; Uphof, 240; Coville, 65; Harris, 112; Mal'tsew, 151; Fernald & Kinsey, 84; Gillespie, 93; Chestnut, 52; Colyer, 56.)

References (to numbers in the bibliography):
    84, 102, 103, 117, 119, 187, 198, 228, 240.

Potamogeton spp.
PONDWEED, FISHWEED

Description:

Plants growing in water, in some species at least the stems arising from buried rootstocks or tubers; leaves varying from narrow and grasslike to broad, often both kinds on the same stem, leaves submerged or floating; flowers inconspicuous, in elongated narrow clusters (spikes) which are sometimes lifted in the air above the water.

In water, the various species widely distributed in the Northern Hemisphere.

Use:

The thickened rootstocks and tubers of certain species of pondweed have sometimes been used as food. Situated as they are at the

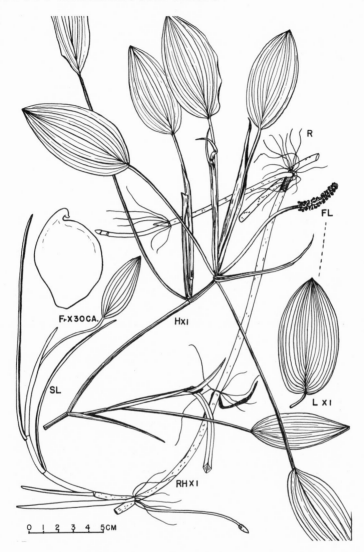

PONDWEED *(Potamogeton natans)*

bottom of ponds and streams, they are somewhat inaccessible. However, on the favorable side, the plants are rather easy to recognize and could hardly be mistaken for anything of a poisonous nature. Sometimes ponds, streams or irrigation ditches, which during the early part of the season support a growth of pondweeds, will dry

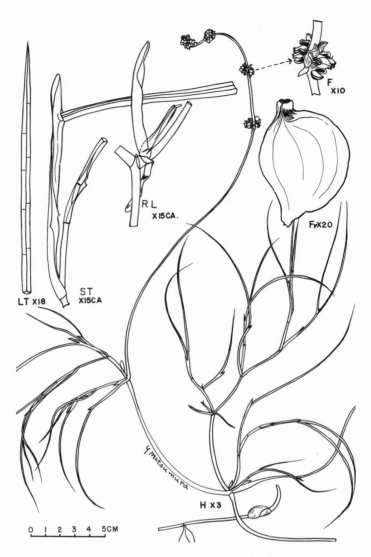

LT X18 ST X15CA R L X15CA. F X10 Fr X20 H X3

0 1 2 3 4 5CM

PONDWEED (*Potamogeton pectinatus*)

up in late summer and autumn. The underground parts then
become relatively accessible. For example, Mr. Comes, who does
research on aquatic weeds for the federal government, told us that
he and his crew often ate the tubers of *Potamogeton pectinatus*,
commonly called Sago pondweed or fennel-leaf pondweed. They
seem to have hard hulls or rinds which were readily cracked off.
The contents were eaten raw and were said to taste somewhat like

nuts. Hussey (129) & Fernald & Kinsey (84) stated that the thickened underground parts of *P. natans,* commonly called floating-leaf pondweed, are edible both to human beings and to animals. In any event, the pondweeds might well furnish emergency food in quantities. We have several different kinds in the Rocky Mountain area including the two illustrated, *P. natans* and *P. pectinatus.*

Related Species:
Probably all pondweeds could be utilized, particularly if they produce thickened underground structures.

References (to numbers in the bibliography):
Already given.

Potentilla anserina (Argentina anserina, A. argentea) SILVERWEED, SILVERWEED CINQUIFOIL

Description:
Plants perennial with thickened roots; main stems very short but producing long runners like a strawberry, these up to 2 feet long; divisions of the leaves (leaflets) ⅜ to 1¾ inches long; leaves silvery-hairy below or on both sides; flowers borne singly; petals yellow, ¼ to ⅜ inch long; fruits of many seedlike structures (achenes) borne in a cluster.

Moist or wet, usually open ground. Widely distributed in the cooler portions of the Northern Hemisphere.

Use:
The roots of this plant have often been utilized for food in various parts of its range, particularly by the North American Indians. In western Scotland they are said to have supported the entire population of certain areas for several months, in times of acute emergency. We had heard the roots described as having a taste of chestnuts and by others with possessing a parsnip flavor. We washed the roots and ate them skin and all, although this outer covering could be easily rubbed off if desired. We tried them raw, finding the taste good, with a nutty, somewhat starchy flavor. The

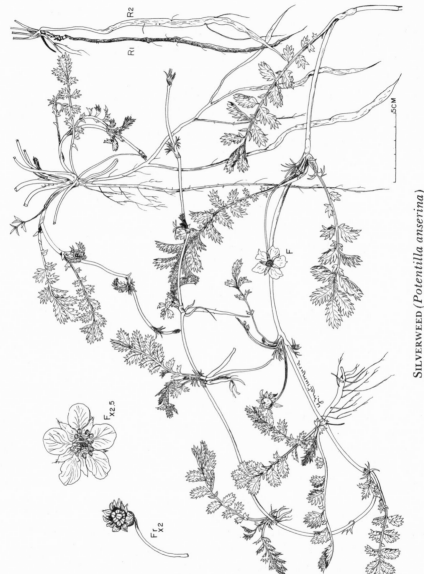

SILVERWEED (*Potentilla anserina*)

"sweetish" taste often described for the roots was not particularly noticeable to us. They would certainly make an excellent salad or relish ingredient. We then boiled them for 15 minutes and used them with salt, pepper and butter. They retained their crispness and flavor; we voted that they were excellent food. We did not detect any special hint of "parsnip" flavor about them.

This is an excellent survival plant for several reasons. It is widespread in the mountains, often present in abundance in parks, along streams and in clearings—just the places where food might be desperately needed. It can be eaten raw or cooked, and the roots will keep for at least a reasonable time. On the other side of the ledger, the roots are rather small, those $\frac{1}{2}$ inch thick would be rather large ones in our experience, and are reasonably hard to dig since they are often found over 6 inches deep in the soil. One thing about it, the plant has striking characteristics, making it easy to identify. We refer specifically to the solitary, yellow flower, the runners and the unusual leaves.

Related Species:
A shrubby relative *(Potentilla fruticosa)* is common in the Rocky Mountains, even appearing occasionally in cultivation under the name of "shrubby cinquifoil." The leaves have been used as a substitute for tea (Porsild, 187; Fernald & Kinsey, 84; Uphof, 240; Anderson, 4).

References (to numbers in the bibliography):
26, 84, 107, 117, 138, 140, 158, 217. 228, 229, 240.

Psoralea esculenta (Pediomelum esculentum)
COMMON BREADROOT, INDIAN BREADROOT, PRAIRIE TURNIP, PRAIRIE POTATO, SCURFPEA

Description:
Plants perennial from swollen, deep-seated roots; stems stout, 4 to 12 inches long; leaf divisions (leaflets) $\frac{3}{4}$ to $2\frac{1}{2}$ inches long; flowers about $\frac{1}{2}$ to $\frac{5}{8}$ inch long, blue-tinged; pod short, only about $\frac{1}{4}$ inch long.

Prairies and plains on open, often rocky ground. Canada south to Missouri, Texas and eastern Colorado. Comes into the eastern part of the Rocky Mountain area.

Use:

The starchy, tuber-like roots furnished a well-known food to the Indians, and the early white settlers soon discovered their value. In fact, the roots were sent back to France in about the year 1800 by Lamare-Picquot, an early explorer, with the expectation that the plant would become a valuable cultivated crop (Dayton et al., 74). Although this fond hope did not materialize, the breadroot has always been famous as a food producer in this country and has sustained many a starving person for a time. For example, Ginter (97), said that John Colter, one of Lewis and Clark's men, while escaping from the Blackfeet Indians, lived for a whole week entirely on the roots of breadroot. The Indians dug the roots in July or August when the tops were browning, peeled them, and cooked them in various ways. Sometimes they were boiled, often they were baked, occasionally they were dried in the sun and stored. They could later be ground into a meal for seasoning other food, thickening soup, making gruel or they were formed into cakes for making bread. In 1895, Havard (115), had some of these roots analyzed by C. Richardson who listed them as containing 70% starch, 5% of sugar and 9% of nitrogenous matter. Subsequent analysis, (Yanovsky & Kingsbury, 256), had a higher percentage of sugar and a lower one of starch, perhaps because of differences in the time of gathering.

We have found that the roots peeled easily, had a bright white inner core and a fairly thin outer covering. We consider that they are reasonably edible raw, rather tough to chew perhaps, but with no pronounced taste of any kind, certainly not a bad one. We boiled the roots in a pressure cooker to save time and gave them 30-40 minutes at 15-lbs. pressure. The taste was pleasant, being a mixture of nutlike and potato-like, but not at all strong flavored. We also roasted the root cores. These were wrapped in aluminum foil and placed for about 2 hours in an oven set at 375 degrees F. The taste was good but we thought they were somewhat better boiled.

COMMON BREADROOT *(Psoralea esculenta)*

We also cut some of the cores into thin slices, using a pocket knife, and let them dry on the window ledge. They certainly keep for any reasonable length of time, perhaps indefinitely, for 3 years later we soaked them in water for an hour and fried them in butter. They were slightly tough to chew as compared with fried potatoes, but had a pleasant, though not a pronounced taste.

This plant appears to us to be an excellent edible species, particularly in times of emergency. The tuberous root is fairly large, often being larger than a hen's egg. On the other hand, the plant does not seem to be very abundant, at least in our area, and it seems to us that it often grows in soil that is so hard that it is difficult to dig out the roots.

Related Species:

At least three other tuberous-rooted scurfpeas are in the area and have been reported to be edible. *P. hypogaea* is in eastern Colorado and New Mexico (Hedrick, 117; Grinnell, 103; Medsger, 158), and the rather small root is reputed to be as good or better than the common breadroot. The two others, *P. mephitica* and *P. castoria,* may be found in the southwestern portion of the Rocky Mountain area and were well known to the Indians (Palmer, 183; Uphof, 240; Maisch, 150). Another eastern species, *P. cuspidata,* was probably eaten (Dayton et al, 74) but the times we have tried it, the roots were too bitter to be pleasant eating. *P. tenuiflora* has running rootstocks instead of tuberous roots and has been used as food by the Kiowa Indians, although the herbage has caused poisoning to livestock (Vestal & Schultes, 242; Muenscher, 167; Kearney & Peebles, 138; Stevens, 219).

References (to numbers in the bibliography):
   26, 57, 74, 84, 88, 89, 94, 95, 96, 97, 102, 115, 117, 125, 127, 132, 138, 140, 150, 158, 174, 181, 182, 204, 219, 240, 253, 256.

Sagittaria latifolia
COMMON ARROWHEAD, SWAMP POTATO, TULE
   POTATO, WAPATOO

Description:

This is a variable plant in general habit, but it is always perennial with long rootstocks that bear tuber-like structures; the leaves are always arrow-shaped, the thin expanded parts (blades) 4 to 16 inches long; flowers medium large, up to 1 inch wide, white in color; fruit a cluster of small seedlike structures.

Shallow water of streams and margins of lakes. Widespread in the most of the United States. Mostly at lower elevations in the Rocky Mountain area.

Use:

The tubers are borne at the end of the slender rootstocks and may actually be located some distance from the main cluster of the stems of the parent plant. These tubers become much larger in the fall than is indicated in our drawing, and are said to reach the size of a man's fist. In our area we seldom get them larger than a hen's egg and they are often much smaller. They are solid and white-colored inside, covered with overlapping scales and are borne well below the soil surface, sometimes as much as a foot deep. This creates a problem when you attempt to collect an adequate supply. Arrowhead tubers were widely used by the North American Indians and the early explorers soon learned to eat them. For example, Lewis and Clark described how the Indian squaws waded into the water, sometimes up to breast-deep, dragging a canoe. The women would dig out the tubers with their toes, and the tubers, being light, would rise to the surface of the water to be collected later and thrown into the boat. The Indians would also raid muskrat caches in order to obtain a supply. Anyone in a bathing suit or hip boots, wielding a strong rake or potato fork, can obtain a good supply without too much labor.

Some people claim that these tubers can be eaten raw, but we have never cared for them that way. First, they have a distinctly bitter taste that may be unpalatable, although this seems to be more concentrated in the peeling. Even individual tubers seem to vary in the relative amount of this bitterness. Secondly, one may run a certain danger of contamination by eating them raw. We boiled them for about 15-30 minutes, removed the outer scales and ate them with salt, pepper and butter. We considered them excellent food, something on the order of potatoes, with little, if any, of the bitter taste remaining after cooking. We also roasted them for about 30-40 minutes at 375°F., wrapped in aluminum foil, and liked them even better. The Indians used to use their favorite

COMMON ARROWHEAD (*Sagittaria latifolia*)

pit method for cooking them. This is described by Norton (176) as follows:

Duck or Chicken and Wapatoo Imu

Wrap the duck or chicken (a leg of lamb will do) in some large leaves such as rhubarb or arrowhead. Wash the tubers. Dig a pit larger than the meat. Line this with stones about fist size and build a hot fire on them. When the stones are white hot, scrape out the embers, line the pit with a thick layer of grass or leaves, set the wrapped meat in place and surround with the arrowhead tubers. Cover with more leaves and grass, then a wet burlap sack and finally with warm earth from about the pit. After about one to two hours the pit may be opened and the meal served.

As Hopkins (127) suggested, arrowhead tubers would make a "superb" dish for a picnic supper. The guests can dig their own supply of tubers, wrap them in aluminum foil and roast them in a bed of hot coals if they don't care to use the "imu" method.

The name "Wapatoo" apparently comes from the name of an island in or near the Columbia River where arrowheads grew in abundance, and were an important source of food to the Indians. This plant is much used in the Orient and certain species are said to be cultivated in China and Japan. Matsumura told us of its use in certain Japanese ceremonies:

1. New Year Ceremony
Boil the tubers for 10 minutes with a little salt. Discard the water and boil with soy sauce for 5-10 minutes.

2. Special Ceremony
Boil tubers as above, mix with 2 or 3 pieces of chicken, soy bean sauce or paste, mushrooms, carrots and burdock roots, stirred egg, soy sauce and sugar. Place in a bowl, cover it and put it in a steaming pan for 5 minutes. One would assume that the chicken, carrots and burdock roots were cooked first and some water or chicken stock was added as he stated that this produces a kind of soup called "Chawanmushi." This is apparently a semiliquid product according to a statement by Oshima.

We followed Matsumura's suggestion of boiling the partly cooked tubers with a mixture of soy sauce and water; it did seem to improve the flavor somewhat. The Indians used to boil them, then string them up to dry for later use. We cut some of the raw tubers in slices and allowed them to dry in the sun. Some three years later we found them quite palatable when allowed to soak in the mouth, or when they were soaked in water for about an hour, then fried in butter. The bitter taste did persist to some degree and we concluded that the Indian method of drying the boiled tubers was superior. It has been reported that a flour can be obtained by grinding up these tubers.

The arrowhead plant is available for food throughout the whole year, even in winter if one is hardy enough or hungry enough to dig for it. The tubers are good boiled, fried or roasted; in fact, in any way that potatoes are prepared; they work in well with almost any other food. Certainly the arrowhead is well worth remembering in case of emergency, particularly since it is easy to recognize, and could hardly be mistaken for any harmful plant.

Related Species:

Any of the species of *Sagittaria,* especially the ones with arrow-shaped leaves, are worth testing out as food, providing, of course, they produce tubers of reasonable size.

References (to numbers in the bibliography):

5, 13, 14, 18, 26, 29, 32, 57, 60, 65, 75, 84, 91, 92, 93, 94, 95, 96, 97, 99, 103, 112, 115, 127, 132, 134, 138, 140, 143, 158, 162, 176, 182, 194, 204, 208, 209, 210, 211, 219, 224, 227, 228, 240, 253.

Scirpus acutus (S. occidentalis, S. lacustris in part)
TULE BULRUSH, COMMON TULE, GREAT BULRUSH

Description:

Plants perennial, spreading by thick, scaly rootstocks, these bearing relatively thick roots; stems thick, 5 to 12 feet tall; spikes ¼ to ¾ inch long; seedlike fruits somewhere between ⅛ and ¼ inch long.

This plant found in wet ground or shallow water. It is widespread in Canada and the United States and scattered over the Rocky Mountain area, usually at lower elevations.

SP

Nb

Rh

Nb

F
x20

5CM

Tᴜʟᴇ Bᴜʟʀᴜsʜ *(Scirpus acutus)*

Use:

The Indians used this plant very extensively. In the spring they gathered the young shoots which were just coming up, and ate them raw or cooked. They are described as being white, crispy, juicy and nourishing. Even later in the season the base of the stems provided palatable, if somewhat tougher, chewing. When the bulrush was in flower the pollen was collected and often mixed with meal to make bread, mush or pancakes. Later on the seeds could be beaten off into baskets or pails, ground into a similar meal and used in the same fashion as the pollen. In the fall there might even be a new growth of young shoots ready for the taking. The old stems were used to weave into mats or baskets. The scaly rootstocks were available in all seasons of the year. They were eaten either raw or cooked; sometimes they were dried thoroughly in the sun, then pounded into a kind of flour. The Indians made a sweet syrup by bruising the rootstocks, boiling them for several hours (some writers say up to 15), then pouring off the sweet liquid. Certainly this was an important food plant to many Indian tribes.

We liked the younger rootstocks best, the ones ending in a new bud. These were peeled and eaten raw; they had no pronounced taste which was good or bad, but appeared to us to be nourishing. Yanovsky & Kingsbury (256) found that a closely related species *(Scirpus validus)* had as much as 8% sugar and 5.5% starch in its rootstocks, but less than 1% protein. We found that even the older rootstocks could be eaten raw although they were a bit fibrous.

We also peeled the rootstocks and boiled them for 30 minutes (5000 feet), eating them with salt, pepper and butter. We concluded they made a very satisfactory dish. Tule bulrush seems to us to be one of the very best survival plants we have in our area. It is often locally very abundant and the parts are relatively bulky. For example, the rootstocks can be almost 1 inch in diameter; the only disadvantage is that they do require some arduous digging. Various edible portions of the plant are available throughout every season of the year. There is no need to go hungry in any season, even in winter, if a swamp is nearby where bulrushes grow.

Related Species:
Scirpus validus is a closely related, but less bulky species, that

is found throughout our area and has similar uses. *S. paludosus* is a bulrush with triangular stems and rootstocks, these often forming tuberous enlargements which have been used as food.

References (to numbers in the bibliography):

13, 18, 32, 49, 50, 57, 65, 75, 84, 93, 95, 96, 99, 103, 115, 117, 138, 158, 166, 181, 182, 183, 198, 240, 243.

Solanum jamesii
WILD POTATO

Description:

Perennial plants with slender rootstocks, these bearing globe-shaped to flattened globe-shaped tubers somewhat like the garden potato; stems 4 to 12 inches tall; leaves with 5 to 9 divisions (leaflets); flowers 1/2 to 3/4 inch across, normally white in color; fruit a berry.

Mountains and valleys. Texas to Arizona and north to southern Colorado and Utah.

Use:

The tubers are borne at the ends of the rootstocks, and vary from about the size of an average grape to over one inch wide. They have breathing pores scattered on their surfaces (lenticels) and a few "eyes," these mostly clustered at the end opposite the attachment. They have a corky, thin peel like a small, ordinary potato. The Indians ate them raw, boiled or baked. The rather bitter astringent taste was counteracted by eating them along with a kind of special clay, which may also have prevented stomach disturbance. A typical Navajo recipe was given in Young (259).

MASHED WILD POTATOES WITH FOOD CLAY

1 quart wild potatoes
2 heaping tablespoons of food clay
salt to taste
Boil potatoes until tender. Drain and mash between grinding stones. Dissolve the food clay in a little water and add to the

WILD POTATO *(Solanum jamesii)*

potatoes as they are being mashed. Mix well. Mold into small loaves and serve hot or cold with goat's milk or mutton broth.

We agree with the astringent taste reported, at least for the ones we have tried. The tubers have a crisp potato taste and odor when raw, with the bitterness concentrated mostly but not completely near the peel. We have tried boiling them 20-35 minutes, both with the peels left on and removed. They were quite edible either way, but some of the bitterness remained, this somewhat less in the peeled ones. We would suspect that they would be best roasted, but have never tried them that way nor have we eaten them with clay. In any case, wild potatoes raw or cooked would be a reasonably good emergency food if eaten in moderate amounts. Like cultivated potatoes, the tubers keep whole for several months, or they can be sliced, dried, and ground into a flour.

Related Species:

Another tuber-bearing, wild potato *(Solanum fendleri)* is found in southern Arizona and New Mexico, possibly farther north into Colorado. It has been used in the same fashion as the one described above.

References (to numbers in the bibliography):

12, 43, 45, 67, 83, 85, 97, 115, 138, 158, 173, 182, 218, 220, 239, 240, 248, 249, 259.

Stellaria jamesiana (Alsine jamesiana, A. curtisii)
CHICKWEED, STARWORT

Description:
Perennial plants with creeping rootstocks, these with small to fairly large tubers or swellings at intervals along them; stems 8 to 20 inches tall; leaves 2 to 4 inches long; flowers white in color, the petals about ⅛ to ¼ inch long, each deeply lobed at the apex; fruit a dry capsule.

Moist woodlands and among shrubs. Wyoming to Texas and westward. In our area often found among sagebrush or under oak brush, inclined to grow in somewhat moist loamy sites.

Use:

The size of the tuber-like swellings vary from plant to plant, from one habitat to another, perhaps from spring to fall. They seem to be larger when the plant is growing in rich loamy soil. We have found them up to ⅞ inch wide and 1½ inches long in the summer, but perhaps they may be even larger in the late fall. The "tubers" are usually borne from 1 inch to 4 inches below the soil surface, have a thin, light-brown rind, and a tender rather mealy texture inside, much like that of a potato.

We do not remove the rind from these thickened structures and enjoy eating them raw. They are tender and crisp, slightly sweet, but with a pleasant spicy taste. We have been told that they are favorites with many children of the areas where this chickweed is abundant. We have boiled them for varying times depending on the texture, sometimes as little as 10 minutes, and found them very good indeed with the sweet taste still remaining.

We have also fried the "tubers" in butter, either whole or split longitudinally. They seemed to have the taste of fried food in general, fairly sweet, rather tender, and very satisfactory indeed. We have baked them for 40-60 minutes at about 300° F. and decided they were sweet and pleasant tasting. Apparently they make an excellent substitute for potatoes, cooked in any of the ways we utilize that vegetable.

We cut some of these thickened roots in cross-sections, and longitudinally, then dried them in the sun. About two years later we soaked them in water for an hour and fried them in butter. The taste was sweet and pleasant, not as tender as potatoes, but nice and chewy.

This is a very good survival plant. The "tubers" are available for most of the year, even in winter. We must admit that they are usually rather tedious to dig, but once secured they are good raw or cooked. As near as we can figure it out the Ute Indians used this plant a good deal, but they may possibly have been referring to a related species in their conversations with us.

Related Species:
See *Stellaria media*

CHICKWEED *(Stellaria jamesiana)*

References (to numbers in the bibliography):
56, 157A.

Tragopogon porrifolius
SALSIFY, VEGETABLE OYSTER, OYSTER PLANT

Description:

Biennial or perennial plants from fleshy taproots; milky juice present in the fresh parts; stems hollow in the center, about 1 to 3 feet tall; flowers purple or rose in color, crowded into a dandelion-like head which is about 1¼ to 2 inches long; fruits seedlike, with a slender projection at the top, this bearing a parachute of fuzzy hairs.

Fields, gardens and waste places. This is a widely, if not commonly, cultivated plant in the United States. In the Rocky Mountain area it commonly escapes from cultivation, often along ditches and roads.

Use:

This plant is often cultivated for its unusual flavor, which is thought by some people to resemble that of an oyster. In cultivation the roots become quite large, resembling those of parsnips. These roots can be dug in the fall and preserved in sand in the cellar for later use, and will keep for at least a limited time. Some prefer to leave them in the ground and dig them up as needed during the winter.

The roots are prepared in many ways: boiled, fried, baked, stewed or made into a soup. Start by washing and scraping the roots. If they are to be kept awhile it may be wise to place them in cold water to which a little vinegar or lemon juice has been added, this prevents discoloration. Slice or dice them, and boil until tender; then you can use them in any way you wish. We enjoy them made into a cream soup like potato soup. In general, utilize them in any of the countless ways that you would potatoes. The young shoots are sometimes eaten raw in salads, but you may like them better prepared like spinach or asparagus. The water can be changed one to several times if the taste is too bitter for you.

Related Species:

Several yellow-flowered species of *Tragopogon* are weedy and often become abundant in certain localities. The ones in our area,

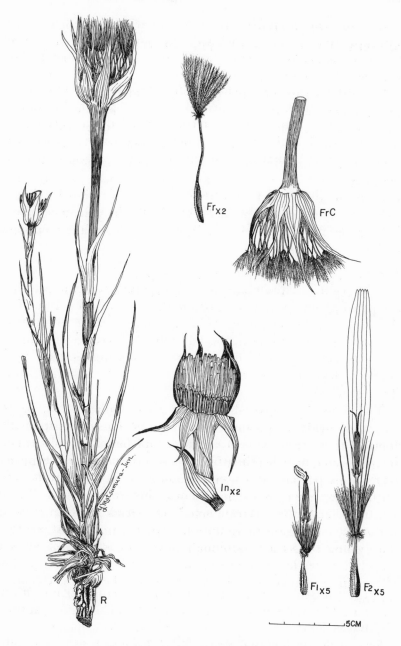

Fr x2

FrC

In x2

Fl x5

F2 x5

5CM

SALSIFY *(Tragopogon porrifolius)*

T. pratensis and *T. dubius*, are very similar to each other in general appearance and are discussed together here. We have read that these plants, often called "wild salsify" or "goatsbeard," are preferred by some to the purple-flowered one and have been actually cultivated in other parts of the world. We have tried our species several times, prepared as one would handle the purple one, hoping these more plentiful plants would provide an acceptable substitute. The results were seldom very favorable. We tried them from spring to late fall and usually found the roots relatively small, fibrous, woody and tough. Perhaps in cultivation they may be different, but on the basis of those we have experimented with we can recommend them only as emergency food. Try the small roots in the spring and you may have a higher opinion of the yellow salsify.

References (to numbers in the bibliography):

13, 38, 56, 57, 77A, 84, 99, 102, 117, 121, 134, 138, 158, 181, 219, 240, 243, 244.

Typha latifolia
COMMON CATTAIL

Perennial plants with thick underground rootstocks; stems 3½ to 8 feet tall; leaves ¼ to 1 inch wide; spikes variable in length, but the lower, seed-bearing, hairy portion about 4 to 12 inches long, the pollen-bearing upper portion about as long; fruits seed-like, bearing hairs, very many crowded together.

In marshes, shallow lakes, ditches and stream borders in moist or wet places. Widely distributed in Eurasia and North America. Scattered over the Rocky Mountain area, usually below 8000 feet.

Use:

This is probably the most famous of all the edible plants of the Northern Hemisphere. It has been called "an outdoor pantry." The Boy Scouts of this area have a saying, "You name it, we'll make it with cattails" (Bagdonas, 11A). Certainly no one should starve or even go hungry in an area where cattails are abundant. They were favorite plants with the Indians, who used them as food throughout most of the year. The young shoots were pulled or cut from the rootstocks in the spring when they were about 4 to 16 inches long. The outer leaves were peeled away, leaving the tender golden-yellow inner portion; these were eaten raw or in salads. We found them delicious when chopped with lettuce, tomatoes and cucumbers. These young shoots can be used as a potherb, as they are in Russia, where they are called "Cossack asparagus," or they can be cooked in other various ways, even made into a kind of soup. Even when the shoots are 1 to 2 feet long they can still be utilized. These young shoots are more prevalent in the springtime, but do appear throughout the summer and fall. Try boiling them for 25-35 minutes, serving them with butter and seasoning. We consider them excellent in flavor.

As the season progresses the young flower stalks begin to appear. These spikes can be taken out of their sheaths and cooked in various ways. When boiled for 20 minutes you can eat them like roasting ears, nibbling the flowers off the tough inner stalk. The flowers, especially the pollen-producing ones on the upper part, can be scraped off and used alone, or as flavoring or thickening for other foods.

When the plants have further ripened, but the pollen has not been shed, we have sometimes stripped off these pollen-producing flowers by hand, often gathering several pounds in an hour or two. These young flowers can be used to make muffins, cookies, biscuits or pancakes, when mixed with wheat flour in equal proportions. They can be preserved for future use by spreading them out on a flat pan. Put this in a preheated oven set at about 350 degrees F. and roast the flowers until they are perfectly dry, stirring them frequently to avoid burning. They can then be stored for long periods in a dry, closed container, and can eventually be used in the same way as the fresh ones. After the pollen starts to be shed it can be collected by shaking the flowers in a container. A surprising amount of this yellow dust can often be collected in a reasonable length of time. If this pollen is shaken in the can, the chaff and insects will rise to the top and can be removed. This pollen, when mixed with flour, can be used like the flowers for making muffins, cookies, biscuits, cakes or pancakes. Pancakes made with cattail pollen are famous. Try the following recipe as given by Norton (176).

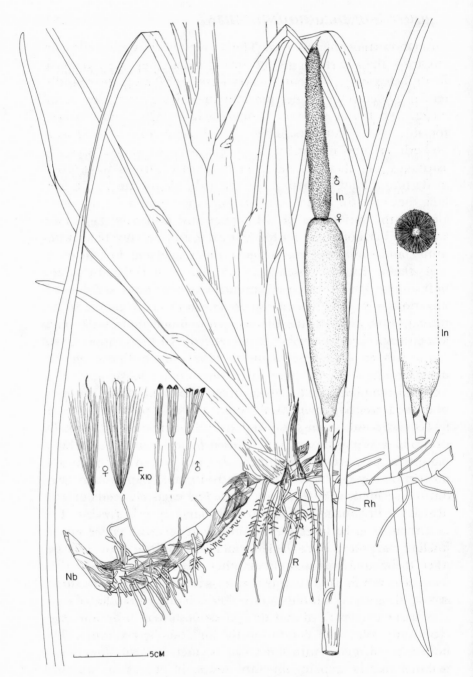

$\mathring{\circ}$ In
$\female$

In

$\female$ F$_{X10}$ $\mathring{\circ}$

Rh

Nb R

5CM

COMMON CATTAIL *(Typha latifolia)*

CATTAIL FLAPJACKS

2 cups cattail pollen (or flowers)	½ cup evaporated milk
2 cups wheat flour	1½ cups water
4 teaspoons baking powder	1 tablespoon syrup
1 teaspoon salt	bacon drippings
2 eggs	

Beat eggs, add milk, water and syrup. Mix and add dry ingredients, beating until mixture is creamy. Add bacon drippings. Fry in a hot greased pan over the camp fire. Makes about 20 cakes.

After the tops of the cattails have turned brown in the fall the rootstocks are available for food. In fact, they are available at any time, but seem to us to be richer in starch at the end of the growing season. They are usually found about 3-4 inches below the soil surface. We like the young rootstocks best; these are the ones that have a bud at the end ready to form the new growth in the spring. The outer peel should be removed and the central white core, often ⅜ to ½ inch in diameter, will be found to make up about 50% to 60% of the rootstock. These cores can be eaten raw; they have a pleasant starchy taste, but contain harsh fibers that interfere somewhat with the enjoyment of eating them; we think they are better boiled or baked.

Cattail rootstocks are fairly high in starch content; this is usually listed at about 30% to 46%. This can be extracted to form a flour which compares favorably with that from wheat, corn and rice in percentages of fats, proteins and carbohydrates. The flour can be secured in at least two ways. The rootstock cores can be dried, then pounded in a metate or ground up in a grinder. The fibers can then be sifted out and the flour secured. Water can be used in the process since the flour will readily settle to the bottom; then the liquid is poured off. Another method suggested by Gibbons (92) was to fill a large container with cold water then shred, manipulate and crush the cores with the hands in the water until the fibers are separated and washed clean. Then strain out these fibers and allow the flour to settle for about 30 minutes. The water can then be poured off and fresh water added again. After another half hour pour off the water again. The flour will still have enough moisture so that it can be worked like dough.

The buds at the end of the young rootstocks have a lump of starchy material in their centers where they join the main rootstock; this starchy mass is also present after the buds develop into young shoots; it is greatly fancied by many people. Cattail flour is a potential source of food for the population since this plant covers many thousand acres in the United States. Classen (54) figured that one acre of cattails would yield about 6,475 pounds of flour. This flour would probably contain about 80% carbohydrates and around 6% to 8% protein. It does appear that this is a potential source of food, produced by land not suitable for growing most other crop plants. Harvesting the rootstock cores would be a problem and we do not expect the production of cattail flour to become a major industry. As a source of emergency food these rootstocks are ideal.

The Indians would sometimes eat the tiny seedlike fruits, by burning off the bristles. This process would roast or parch the "seeds," which could then be rubbed off the spike. Sometimes the down was pulled off the spikes and spread on a flat rock. This was burned and the minute "seeds" swept up to be used as food. Finally, the cattail down was sometimes stripped off the spikes and used to provide padding in pillows, blankets and for the Indian cradle board. Certainly, there is no more useful edible native plant than the cattail.

Related Species:

The narrow-leaf cattail *(Typha angustifolia)* is also widely distributed and can be used like the common species. It is not so abundant in our area and the edible parts are smaller.

References (to numbers in the bibliography):

2, 11A, 13, 14, 16, 26, 38, 43, 49, 52, 54, 56, 57, 58, 65, 66, 77A, 82, 84, 90, 92, 93, 97, 98, 99, 107, 112, 117, 119, 127, 129, 130, 132, 135, 138, 140, 141, 146, 149, 158, 162, 165, 166, 176, 179, 181, 183, 194, 204, 206, 219, 227, 228, 239, 240, 243, 249, 253.

Valeriana edulis
EDIBLE VALERIAN, TOBACCO-ROOT

Description:

Plants perennial with large thickened taproots, something like those of a carrot, these often branching below; stems erect, 4 to 24 inches tall; flowers small, yellowish to whitish, about 1/24 to ⅛ inch long; fruit small and seedlike.

Moist open places or in dry meadows and slopes. Canada, south to South Dakota, New Mexico and Arizona. Widely scattered in the Rocky Mountain area, where it may sometimes grow in partial shade.

Use:

The roots of this plant are fairly large, often over a foot long and over 2 inches thick; they are reasonably easy to dig out with a shovel or spade. Sometimes they are quite abundant, such as in the partial shade of aspens, and it is seldom difficult to secure a reasonable amount. Many people feel that a large enough supply (for them) can be secured without digging at all. Perhaps they have never been hungry enough to appreciate the peculiar taste and odor of this plant. The roots are rather inelegantly described by some observers to taste a good deal like chewing tobacco and to have the odor of unwashed feet!

The Indians used this valerian a great deal and seemed to like it very much. They considered the raw roots to be poisonous, which may well be the case. They often baked them in their "fireless cookers." These were pits dug in the ground and lined with stones. A fire was made in the pit, then raked out and the pit lined with fresh grass on all 4 sides with the roots in the center. The roots were also dried and ground into a kind of flour for making bread or for thickening soup. Fremont (88) found the plant extensively used and has this to say about the matter: "I ate here, for the first time, the kooyah, or tobacco-root, the principal edible root among the Indians who inhabit the upper waters of the streams on western side of the mountains. It has a very strong and remarkably peculiar taste and odor, which I can compare to no other vegetable that I am acquainted with, and which to some persons is extremely offensive. It was characterized by Mr. Preuss as the most horrid food he had ever put in his mouth; and when, in the evening, one of the chiefs sent his wife to me with a portion which she had prepared as a delicacy to regale us, the odor immediately drove him out of the lodge; and frequently afterward he used to beg that when those who like it had taken what they desired, it might be sent away. To others, however, the taste is rather an agreeable one, and I was afterward always glad when it formed an addition to our scanty meals. It is full of nutriment; and in its unprepared state is said by the Indians to have very strong poisonous qualities, of which it is deprived by a peculiar process, being baked in the ground for about two days."

We have tried the roots in the late spring, middle summer and fall and have tentatively concluded that fall is probably the poorest season in which to gather them for food, since the roots were more fibrous then, and apt to be worm eaten. We have boiled them for varying times with changes of water, soaked them in sodium bicarbonate solution, baked them in aluminum foil for up to two hours—in fact, tried them in every way we could imagine. In general, all we can conclude is that we agree with Fremont's cartographer, Mr. Preuss, as quoted above. It should be added that "Valerian Root Tea" is sometimes prepared for sale from this or a related plant.

We are including the plant in spite of its objectionable taste and odor because it is available in fairly large quantities in case of dire emergency. Possibly all of us could learn to like it after prolonged use. After all, there are people who are just crazy about Limburger cheese!

Related Species:

Other species of *Valeriana* were probably used by the Indians and should be tried in an emergency. These do not have the large vertical taproots of the one described above.

References (to numbers in the bibliography):

18, 26, 56, 65, 74, 77A, 88, 115, 117, 138, 140, 158, 164, 182, 183, 240.

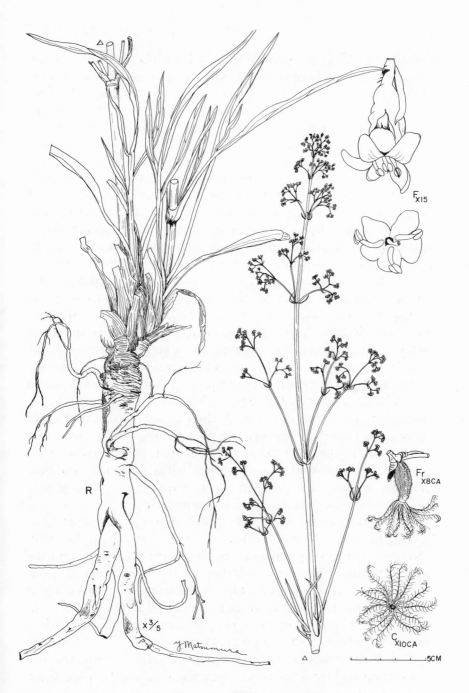

R

x³/₅

J. Matsumura

F
X15

Fr
X8CA

C
X10CA

5CM

EDIBLE VALERIAN *(Valeriana edulis)*

Chapter VII: FLESHY FRUITS (like Apples)

FLESHY FRUITS are rather conspicuous and are often brightly colored; this makes them rather easy to locate in the fields and forests. They seem to be the commonest food that is avidly seized upon by people lost in the wilderness, at least to judge by occasional newspaper accounts. Eating such fruits does create a certain problem in identification, for when they are ripe the characteristic flowers that preceded them have usually faded away. Of course, most fruits are definitely characteristic in themselves, and easy to recognize once you become familiar with them. Many of them are closely related to commonly cultivated ones like raspberry and strawberry. Fortunately, only a very few berries in our area are seriously poisonous. One of them is the baneberry *(Actea)*, which has attractive shining red or white fruits, the other is poison ivy *(Rhus)* with waxy white berries. The best way to proceed is to learn these poisonous plants in all their growth phases, and avoid their fruits entirely. Then you can eat, with reasonable safety, any other palatable berry in the Rocky Mountain area. A safe general rule would be to avoid all red or white fruits, sticking to the blue or black colored ones, but then you would miss out on some very delicious ones like those of the wild strawberry.

Fleshy fruits are often very seasonable, lasting but a short time. Trying to gather them often turns out to be a race with the birds. However, some fleshy fruits do remain on the twigs even into the winter and may be handy to gather, especially in times of emergency. Such a fruit would be that of the wild rose *(Rosa)*. These become dry and withered, but can be softened in the mouth or in water, and they seem to us to provide some taste and nutrition, even when a layer of snow is on the ground.

Such fleshy fruits are relatively high in water content, and under certain arid conditions this characteristic could be a life saver. They may be relatively low in actual number of calories, but do have the reputation of being high in essential vitamins. Usually, one of your recipes for cultivated fruits will do equally well for the most of the wild ones, especially if the two plants are somewhat related. If you wish to make jam or jelly from wild berries, it is wise to try a small amount first to see if the addition of pectin is necessary.

Fleshy fruits are sometimes locally abundant, but are hard to store, at least under primitive conditions. Under survival conditions it would be wise to avoid gorging too heavily on them; consider drying a portion of them in the sun for future use. The Indians manufactured their famous pemmican using various native berries. This was made in several ways, but the fleshy fruits were commonly mixed with dried lean meat which had been pounded to a powder-like consistency. Then melted fat was poured over the mixture and allowed to solidify. The product may not sound very appetizing to many of us, but this concentrated food played an important part in the exploration and settlement of the wilderness, especially in the North.

One thing can be said for eating wild, fleshy fruits. Most of them have a tangy and delicious taste; this is usually much more pronounced than that of their cultivated counterparts. If you do try them extensively you are in for some new and different taste sensations.

Plants with fleshy fruits but illustrated or described in another chapter.

Arctostaphylos uva-ursi IX.   *Smilax herbacea* IV.
Smilacina spp. IV.

Amelanchier alnifolia
Serviceberry, Juneberry, Shadblow, Sarviceberry

Description:
Shrubs or small trees to 14 feet tall; leaves oval to nearly round with toothed margins; flowers in clusters longer than broad; petals white, rather narrow about ¼ to ⅜ inch long; fruit apple-like, but

SERVICEBERRY *(Amelanchier alnifolia)*

only ⅜ to ⅝ inch in diameter, purple-red to black when ripe.
  Stream banks, moist hillsides, in woods or on open slopes, from
Nebraska west to Oregon and western Canada. Locally abundant
in the Rocky Mountains.

Use:

The different kinds of serviceberries all have edible fruit, but they vary in size of the product and the relative amount of pulp present. Even in the same species one can notice differences among races or even between individual trees. The amount of rainfall for the season or the moisture in the site where the plant grows affects this fruit size. The Indians used these fruits in large amounts. They can be eaten fresh, the only objectionable feature being the large seeds which may be bad tasting to some, but are said by some people to add to the flavor. The fruit can be dried and used as one would use raisins. They tend to dry on the plant and late in the season can be picked, eaten raw, or cooked into a puree or jam. Cooking makes the skins and seeds more palatable after this drying.

The Indians pounded the fruit, spread out the mass and let it dry in large cakes for future use. These cakes were used particularly to flavor stews and puddings, but they can be cooked by themselves. The serviceberry fruits were often used in making "pemmican," a discussion of which appears at the beginning of this chapter.

The fresh fruit can be used in any of the various ways that any fleshy fruit can be utilized. It makes good pies and may be canned for this purpose. Mrs. John May made an excellent jelly using the recipe on the package of Certo or Sure-Jell, substituting the word "serviceberry" for "sour cherry," and she has sold it commercially in this area. The color is a rich dark purple and has the consistency of any other jelly. The taste to us was like apple jelly, but milder and blander. For this reason some recipes for serviceberry jellies and jams suggest adding the juice of something more tart, like chokecherries, apples, plums, or lemons.

Douglass (77A) gave a recipe for steamed pudding. For each individual serving use ¼ cup fresh serviceberries, ¼ cup sliced peaches and 2 teaspoons sugar. Mix and place in the bottom of a large custard cup. Then make a dough, using 1 tablespoon biscuit mix (Bisquick), 1 tablespoon sugar and 1 tablespoon milk. Mix this together and drop on top of fruit mixture. Cover and put in steamer for 50 to 60 minutes.

Many similar recipes are in print using various fruits for which this fruit can be substituted. It seems a shame that this plant isn't used more, in view of its historical importance to the Indians and to early white settlers. Colyer (56), stated that the Ute Indians preferred to use the fruit of some serviceberries before it turned red or purple. In any event, this fruit would be an excellent emergency food either raw or cooked, and would be available over a period of several months.

Related Species:

A. utahensis, A. florida, A. prunifolia, A. canadensis have all been listed by various authors as having desirable fruit (Palmer, 182; Newberry, 174; Holmes, 125; Whiting, 249; Elmore, 83; Castetter, 43; Hardy, 107; Heller, 119; Colyer, 56).

References (to numbers in the bibliography):

A. For *A. alnifolia*—5, 26, 49, 50, 52, 65, 73, 83, 100, 103, 117, 145, 158, 183, 214, 240, 256, 258.

B. For *A.* spp.—6, 8, 18, 43, 56, 58, 74, 77A, 84, 92, 93, 98, 99, 132, 138, 157A, 182, 204, 219, 227, 228, 239, 244, 254.

Berberis repens (B. aquifolium, Odostemon aquifolium)
CREEPING BARBERRY, OREGON GRAPE, CREEPING MAHONIA, HOLLY GRAPE

Description:

Stems less than a foot long, creeping and rooting along their length; leaves compound (pinnately), the leaflets about 1 to 4 inches long, thick, evergreen, with spiny marginal teeth; flowers small, yellow in color, borne in clusters; berries about ⅓ inch long, nearly round, black or blue-black in color.

This plant grows on hills and slopes, often in partial shade, from Montana to New Mexico and west to the Pacific Ocean. It is found scattered in the Rocky Mountain area, usually in rough or mountainous country.

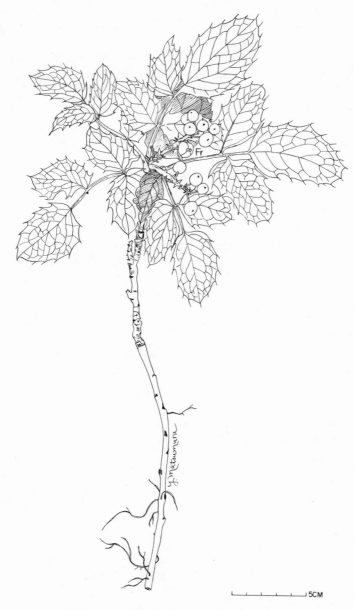

⌞___⌞___⌞___⌞___⌞ 5CM

CREEPING BARBERRY *(Berberis repens)*

Use:

The fruits of this plant have been used for a long time by the Indians and the early white settlers. Some people do claim they have a bitter taste, and Durrell, Jensen & Klinger (79) have this species listed in their poison plant bulletin. However, those we have tried have all been free from any objectionable flavor or taste. Perhaps local races vary in this respect, or possibly certain unfavorable seasons may cause this reportedly bitter taste. Certainly the berries are favorites with many people. They can be eaten raw or made into jelly, jam or wine. Some people use them fresh to make a kind of "lemonade-like" drink. Littlebee (146) described soaking the fruits in salt water, then pickling them in scalding vingar.

We have eaten several batches of jelly made from this fruit by ourselves or by several interested collaborators, and found the taste rather tart, but very good. Some of the jelly was made by using half apple juice to half barberry juice. Colyer (56) used this mixture and followed the Sure-Jell recipe for concord grape jelly. The flavor was distinctive, but certainly would be pleasing to most people.

Related Species:

The barberries form 2 groups, one with thick, evergreen, spiny edged leaves, the other with thinner leaves that drop in the autumn, the spines being on the twigs instead of the leaf edges. Many of them in both groups are favorites for jelly and jam making. For example, *B. fremontii, B. nervosa, B. trifoliata, B. vulgaris* and *B. haematocarpa* have been used by Indian and white people for years.

References (to numbers in the bibliography):

14, 26, 36, 56, 57, 58, 65, 74, 77A, 138, 146, 157A, 162, 227, 240, 243.

Chenopodium capitatum (Blitum capitatum)
STRAWBERRY BLITE, BLITE GOOSEFOOT

Description:

Annual plants; stems simple or branched from the base, up to 2½ feet all; leaves about 1 to 3 inches long; flowers rather inconspicuous in dense clusters, the flower parts in age becoming conspicuously red and fleshy so that the cluster resembles a berry.

Fr
×10

Fr
×3.5

×1.

y. Matsumura

5CM

STRAWBERRY BLITE *(Chenopodium capitatum)*

Rocky soil, moist valleys, often in partial shade, throughout most of the United States.

Use:

This plant is a sister species to *Chenopodium berlandieri* (see Ch. III), and the young leaves and tender shoots have long been used in similar fashion as a potherb. However, at least the older parts are rather bitter in some plants and would require several changes of water (Douglass, 77A). Kephart (140) stated that it is sometimes cultivated for greens, indicating how widely the plant has been used.

The fleshy fruit clusters are used raw or cooked. We found them sweet, but rather insipid and seedy. They should constitute a fairly good emergency food. Sometimes children have been attracted to the bright red clusters, and in one case the anxious parents called a doctor, a county agricultural agent and a plant taxonomist in quick succession to check on the possible poisonous character of the plant!

Related Species:

Another related plant, *C. overi (Blitum hastatum)* produces similar fleshy clusters that should be edible.

References (to numbers in the bibliography):
    11A, 49, 84, 117, 119, 140, 228, 243.

Fragaria spp.
WILD STRAWBERRY

Description:

The wild strawberries can be easily recognized because of their resemblance to the garden varieties in type of fruit and in general appearance. The plants are always low, with hardly any true stems showing above ground except as they may put out characteristic runners that take root and spread the plants over, instead of under, the ground; leaves always of 3 leaflets; flowers with white petals; fruits like those of the garden strawberry, but typically much smaller.

Wild strawberries are found in most parts of Canada and the United States. They may grow in the open or in the shade.

Use:

Surely almost everyone knows and loves the wild strawberry. The cultivated varieties were bred from the wild ones and when

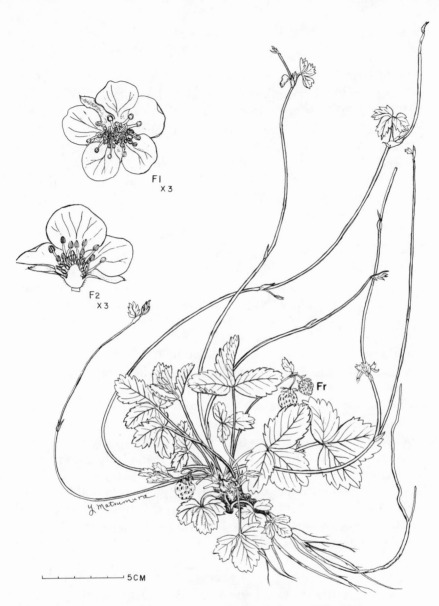

F1
×3

F2
×3

Fr

5CM

WILD STRAWBERRY *(Fragaria ovalis)*

the horticulturists increased the size of the fruit many of us felt
they left behind some of the fragrance and flavor of the wild ones.
Someone has said (the remark attributed to Dr. Butler by Izaak
Walton), "Doubtlessly God could have made a better fruit than
the strawberry but doubtlessly God never did!"

In this area the fruits of the wild strawberries are hard to find in abundance. For example, one may find a tangled mat of numerous plants growing in open spots, but apparently not producing berries. Sometimes one finds scattered plants in shade or in partial shade with a comparative abundance of fruits. These patches are well to mark for future years. If you strike a favorable spot it isn't too hard to secure as much as a pint or more, that is, if you have will power enough to keep from eating them as you pick them.

Another possible disadvantage is that wild strawberries do not keep well fresh. Colyer (56) noted that the Navajo Indians have mastered the trick of drying the fruit without changing the color or even greatly reducing the size. These have been displayed at the Northern Navajo Fair at Shiprock, New Mexico. As you probably know there are now on the market ready-to-eat cereals with dried strawberries included in the package.

Wild strawberries can be eaten fresh, with shortcakes, made into preserves and jams or used to flavor other preparations, in general, in the same ways as you would use the garden type. Your various recipes for cultivated strawberries will work well here and we will not take space to give our many special ones. Boorman (29), gave a couple of recipes for what is called "strawberry soup," but they turned out to be a kind of drink made from the crushed berries, sugar, cream and various other things like grated cucumbers and peanuts. If you wish special recipes for the wild variety check in Angier (6), Gibbons (92) and Littlebee (146). Mrs. Douglass (77A) contributed the following directions for a special use of wild strawberries.

MOLDED RICE WITH STRAWBERRY HARD SAUCE

Molded Rice	1 cup milk
½ cup rice	½ teaspoon salt
1 cup boiling water	1 tablespoon sugar

Put water, milk and salt in a double boiler. Add rice and cook until tender, usually about 40 minutes. Add sugar and mold.

Strawberry Hard Sauce
½ cube (⅛ lb.) of butter or margarine
Powdered sugar   ¾ cup wild strawberries
Cream butter with fork and add as much powdered sugar as
possible. Add strawberries and mix gently. Serve the hardsauce
over the molded rice.

All the recipes we have ever seen sounded good to us; it is hard
to see how anyone could spoil a food preparation including wild
strawberries.

The leaves of the wild plant are said to brew an excellent tea
and we have seen this for sale in at least one local grocery store.
The leaves should be picked, dried, and tea made in conventional
fashion. Cheney (51) suggested using 1 heaping teaspoon of dried
leaves to a cup (and one for the pot) and pouring on boiling water
to steep for 3 to 6 minutes. Szczawinski and Hardy (228) advised
2 handfuls of leaves to 1 quart boiling water. A little experimenting will surely give the right combination to suit your taste.

Related Species:
All the species produce edible berries. *Fragaria ovalis, F.
americana (F. bracteata), F. virginiana, F. vesca, F. cuneifolia*
have been mentioned in the literature.

References (to numbers in the bibliography):
  6, 18, 26, 29, 38, 51, 56, 57, 58, 65, 77A, 83, 84, 92, 93, 99, 107,
132, 134, 138, 146, 151, 158, 182, 212A, 219, 228, 239, 240, 243,
254, 258.

Gaultheria humifusa
WESTERN WINTERGREEN, CREEPING WINTERGREEN, CHECKERBERRY, TEABERRY

Description:
Evergreen shrub with depressed prostrate branches; stems only
about 8 to 10 inches long; leaves thick, about ⅜ to ¾ inch long;

corolla short, vase-shaped, about ⅛ to ¼ inch long, white (not shown on drawing); fruit a rather dry berry about ¼ inch wide, becoming red in color when mature, especially when exposed to light.

Mountain slopes and valleys, often in moist soil near bogs and lakes. Alberta, Canada, to Colorado, west to the Pacific.

Use:

The related species of *Gaultheria* in the eastern United States and Canada are much better known as food plants than is our representative of the group. However, many people will swear by the western wintergreen as an all around useful plant. Consider. First, the young leaves are pleasant to chew when hiking in the mountains, since they leave a cooling sensation of mint or menthol. They can also be gathered, cleaned and used fresh or dry as a tea. This has a mild flavor with a sensation somewhat like menthol again. One of us found it a pleasant pallative for a raw sore throat or a head cold. Secondly, the fruit can be used to make a jam. Try the following recipe of Mrs. Douglass (77A).

GAULTHERIA JAM

3¾ cups crushed fruit pulp
7½ tablespoons lemon juice
1 package powdered pectin (like Sure-Jell)
5 cups suger
Crush about 6½ cups of fresh berries or grind them in a food chopper to eventually yield the 3¾ cups pulp. Add lemon juice and mix pectin with pulp. Place over high heat and stir until it boils hard. Stir in sugar and bring to a full rolling boil and boil 1 minute. Remove from heat and alternately skim and stir for 15 minutes to prevent fruit from floating. Pour into scalded glasses and seal at once with hot paraffin. Makes about 8 medium glasses.

Such a jam is red in color with a spicy odor which was not really pleasing to most of us. The taste itself was not objectionable, but the spicy odor and taste may take a bit of getting used to for many people. By substituting fresh peaches for half the wintergreen berries, a better tasting jam may be secured. In any

Fr
x5

|_____|_____|_____|_____|_____| 5 CM

WESTERN WINTERGREEN *(Gaultheria humifusa)*

case, try the berries as jam or cooked in pies, maybe the rather pungent, spicy flavor will make a devotee of you.

Related Species:

The eastern wintergreen *(Gaultheria procumbens)* is much used where it grows and at one time was sold in some of the eastern markets. The northern plant, Sallal *(G. shallon),* is eaten regularly by the Indians.

References (to numbers in the bibliography):

13, 51, 58, 75, 77A, 92, 93, 99, 100, 117, 158, 164, 174, 181, 182, 240.

Juniperus scopulorum (Sabina scopulorum)
ROCKY MOUNTAIN JUNIPER, RED CEDAR

Description:

This is a bushy shrub or a medium-sized tree, often with several trunks; leaves scale-like, 1/24 to 1/8 inch long; some plants producing only pollen, others only fruit; fruit blue with a whitish coating, about 1/8 to 1/4 inch wide.

Dry rocky ridges, foothills and bluffs. Grows from Alberta to British Columbia in Canada and south to New Mexico and Arizona.

Use:

The junipers have a characteristic, rather displeasing, resinous odor and taste, but fortunately the fruit has less of this than do other parts of the plant. These berry-like fruits vary among the different kinds in size and thickness of pulp. The Indians used these fruits in the late summer or fall, and ate them raw or cooked. They have a high percentage of sugar and are sweet to the taste. The cooking process can be either boiling or roasting. We have tried them raw and found they were strong flavored, but not actually inedible. Since we did not care for the taste we did not try to cook them. However, a few were used to flavor meat and imparted a taste somewhat like sage. As is well known, the berries of some junipers are used to flavor gin. The fruit and the young shoots have been used to make a kind of tea. It may be healthful, but we found it rather potent for our taste, although it is for sale in one grocery store in this area.

The Indians used to dry the fruits, and stored them for the winter. These berries could then be ground into a meal and used to make mush or cakes. They could also be roasted and ground to make a substitute for coffee. Another use they found for the plant was to burn the green leaves, put boiling water on the ashes and use the strained liquid as a flavor for various other foods. In times of acute food shortage the Indians would sometimes peel off the inner bark of the trunk, and chew it to avoid actual starvation. Juniper berries have a thin layer of wax that can be removed by

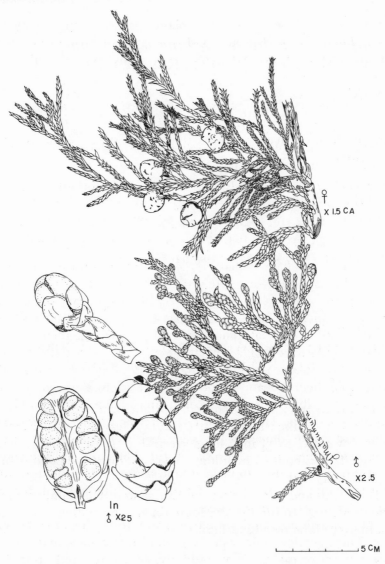

X 1.5 CA

X2.5

In
♂ X25

⊢――――――――――⊣ 5 CM

ROCKY MOUNTAIN JUNIPER *(Juniperus scopulorum)*

boiling and skimming them or by allowing the water to evaporate. With patience a usable amount of fragrant wax can be secured.

The junipers are often very abundant; the berries are available through at least part of the winter, and the bark more or less at all times. For these reasons, this plant is an excellent emergency food. The fact that the odor and taste are not pleasing to many people is not a serious argument against its use as a survival plant.

Related Species:

All the species of *Juniperus* can be tried. *J. communis, J. monosperma, J. osteosperma (J. utahensis), J. deppeana (J. pachyphloea)* have been listed in this respect, the last two being recommended particularly.

References (to numbers in the bibliography for all species of *Juniperus*):

2, 11A, 12, 14, 18, 37, 43, 45, 49, 57, 58, 67, 79, 83, 84, 98, 107, 117, 122, 130, 132, 138, 164, 172, 173, 182, 183, 195, 204, 206, 217, 228, 239, 240, 242, 243, 248, 249, 254, 256, 259.

Lycium pallidum
WOLFBERRY, PALE WOLFBERRY, DESERT THÓRN, BOX THORN, RABBIT THORN, TOMATILLA

Description:

This is an intricately branched, upright shrub with spreading, spiny branches, the whole 3 to 6½ feet tall; leaves ⅜ to 1⅝ inches long; flowers ⅝ to ¾ inch long, greenish in color or tinged with purple; berry about ⅜ inch long, red or reddish-blue because of a whitish waxy coat.

Dry plains and hills. Texas and Colorado to Utah and Arizona, also in Mexico. In the Rocky Mountain area extending north into southern Colorado and southern Utah.

Use:

The fruits of this plant were much used by the Indians of the Southwest. The berries were eaten fresh or were dried for winter use. They were also cooked into a syrup or sauce; sometimes this thick sauce was spread out on rocks where it was allowed to harden. This material was then stored for future use, later to be recooked into a sauce or soup. These berries are said to have a bitter as-

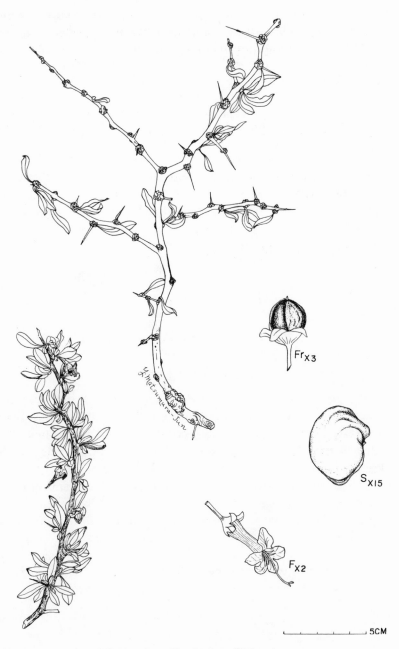

Fr x3

S x15

F x2

5CM

WOLFBERRY *(Lycium pallidum)*

tringent quality; the ones we have tried certainly lived up to their reputation. The Indians often mixed the raw or cooked fruit with clay (often equal amounts of each). This was said to get rid of the bitter taste. Apparently this plant helped the Indians over many a critical period and might well do the same for anyone.

Related Species:

Lycium halimifolium, commonly called Matrimony Vine, is variously listed as poisonous to animals or used as a potherb by human beings (Gillespie, 93; Fernald & Kinsey, 84; Durrell, Jensen & Klinger, 79; Muenscher, 167). The berries of the southwestern *L. torreyi* (Bailey, 12) and *L. fremontii* (Curtin, 66; Kearney & Peebles, 138) were used in the same manner as the plant illustrated.

References (to numbers in the bibliography):

18, 43, 83, 85, 128, 138, 173, 195, 204, 218, 220, 239, 249, 259.

Opuntia spp.
PRICKLYPEAR, TUNA, INDIAN FIG

Description:

Stems in joints or segments, these commonly flattened as in the illustration, but round in cross-section in some kinds, (these often called "candelabra cacti"), these stem segments bearing patches of spines, the spines of two general kinds, borne together: large ones that are stiff and sharp like a needle, and many minute ones (glochids) hardly big enough to see without a lens; leaves very small but fleshy, borne with the spine clusters and soon falling away leaving only a scar behind; flowers relatively large and showy, usually pink, purple, rose, reddish or yellow in color, petals and stamens many (11 or more) to a flower; fruit dry or fleshy, borne below the flower (inferior) instead of within or above it.

Use:

The cacti are plants of many uses, especially the ones with pulpy fruits which are very important in Mexico. There they are

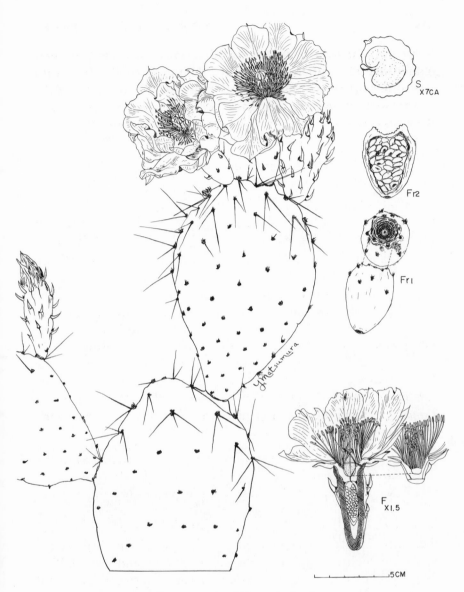

PRICKLYPEAR *(Opuntia* spp.)

sold in the markets as "tuna," secured from plants that may have
been cultivated. Some of our wild species have fruits that have
a much thinner layer of pulp between the rind and the seeds, but
they are still edible, although they do vary considerably in palatability. As far as we know no cactus is poisonous. In fact, many

kinds have been used as emergency cattle feed, after the spines are burned off with a blow torch. Spineless varieties of prickly pear have been developed for possible cultivation.

The large spines are a nuisance of course, but, except in rare instances, are not dangerous. The minute, barbed, bristle-like spines (glochids) are the ones to be feared. They may penetrate and work into the flesh, causing trouble for days afterwards. We once saw a public speaker holding a prickly pear in his bare hands in order to demonstrate his message more effectively. Out of curiosity we made a point of observing him the next day and found, as we expected, that both of his hands were red and swollen. Colyer (56), found these bristles in ninety per cent of the feces examined in studying the ancient Indian Ruins at Mesa Verde National Park. She then courageously tried eating some of the fresh fruits with bristles intact and strangely enough, beyond a pricking of the tongue, the bristles produced no special ill effect. The Indians are said to have rubbed off the spines but we were never able to get rid of the bristles either in that fashion or by burning them off. Anyone who has viewed these sharp-pointed little needles under a strong lens, with their lateral rows of barbs standing out like the ones on a fishhook, will surely use extreme caution in handling any part of the plant afterwards. Try burning them off if you wish, rubbing them off with leather gloves or scraping them off with a knife. In any case be respectful of them, even though you may not be able to see them.

The fruit can be split down one side, opened up, and the central seeds removed. The pulp layer can then be scraped away and eaten raw if you wish. You should find it sweet and gelatinous; at least the native kinds we have tried were very pleasant. The pulp is used in various ways as would any fleshy fruit. Here is a recipe for cactus jelly (Douglass, 77A).

PRICKLY PEAR JELLY

Wash and scald fruits. Remove spots but not prickles. Cut in halves and cook 15 minutes barely covered with water. Pour in bag and squeeze out the juice.

3 cups cactus juice   ½ cup lemon juice
1 package powdered pectin (such as Sure-Jell)

4½ cups sugar

Mix juices and pectin. Place over high heat and stir until the mixture comes to a full rolling boil. Add sugar. Boil hard 1½ minutes stirring constantly. Remove from heat, skim, pour into scalded glasses and seal immediately with paraffin.

The Indians often dried the pulp in the sun. We tried this and after an interval of years we found it still in good condition. It can be used in any of the ways that dried fruit of any kind can be prepared for the table.

The seeds can be dried and stored for future use. The Indians parched them, ground them to a meal and used this in gruel or cakes. The young stem segments can be peeled and the contents eaten raw. We found them watery and mucilaginous, so much so that it was actually difficult to chew the pieces. This combined with a rather sour taste made us conclude that it would be much better to eat them only in cases of extreme need. The segments can be roasted or boiled, and the peel separated. Then the contents can be further prepared in various ways. One of us ate them sliced and mixed with scrambled eggs, pronouncing them "pleasant tasting."

The cacti can be life savers in the desert, providing both liquid and food in extreme emergencies. The use of the barrel cacti in providing water is well known and has undoubtedly saved many lives.

Related Species:

All the species of this genus *(Opuntia)* and in fact any cactus should be edible at least in the young stages of the vegetative phase. Any fleshy-fruited *Opuntia* would be worth a trial. The ones that have been of special value in our area are *Opuntia humifusa, O. phaeacantha, O. engelmannii* and *O. whipplei.*

References (to numbers in the bibliography for all species of *Opuntia*):

2, 5, 11A, 12, 14, 18, 26, 43, 56, 57, 66, 68A, 73, 74, 77A, 83, 84, 85, 93, 95, 96, 103, 107, 108, 115, 117, 125, 138, 140, 158, 162, 164, 173, 174, 181, 182, 192, 195, 197, 199, 206, 216, 217, 218, 219, 220, 228, 239, 240, 241, 242, 243, 244, 249, 259.

Squaw Apple *(Peraphyllum ramosissimum)*

Peraphyllum ramosissimum
SQUAW APPLE

Description:

Intricately branched shrubs to 6 feet tall; leaves ¾ to 2 inches long; petals ¼ to ⅜ inch long, pale pink in color; fruit a little apple ⅜ to ⅝ inch wide, yellowish-golden to reddish-brown in color when ripe.

Dry hills and valleys. Colorado west to the Pacific coast. In our area found in western Colorado and Utah, but since it grows within a few miles of northern New Mexico and northern Arizona it should be expected in those two states.

Use:

The fruits are rather sour when unripe, but some of us have learned to enjoy nibbling on them. As they ripen the flavor changes to "bitter," and when fully ripened they take on a sweetish taste, but with a still bitter aftertaste. The ones that are almost dry on the plants are sweetish and best, but for some reason are usually few in number. Our conclusion is that these fruits are not likely to be very popular when eaten raw.

The fruits were used to make a jelly of good consistency and a lovely amber color. It had a distinctive taste not altogether pleasing to some people. We have also used a recipe of half currant juice and half squaw-apple juice, following the Sure-Jell recipe. This jelly has a milder flavor as one would expect.

The squaw-apples can be spiced following any standard recipe for crab apples, and in the process the bitter taste seems to be lost. We found them good.

There is almost always a good crop of fruit, they are easy to pick and are reasonably large in size. We include them here mostly because they do not seem to be as widely utilized as they, well might be.

Related Species:
None.

References (to numbers in the bibliography):
56.

Physalis spp.
Ground-cherry, Husk-tomato

Description:

Annual or perennial plants, sometimes with creeping root-stocks; stems leafy; flowers rather large, usually between ½ to 1 inch wide, usually light yellow in color but in one species purple; fruit a berry, usually yellow in color when ripe, enclosed in a characteristic, inflated, thin-walled covering.

Plants characteristic of open ground, prairies, plains and roadsides, sometimes acting as weeds. Widely distributed over the United States.

Use:

The fruits of ground-cherries are relished by many people who seem to like their distinctive taste. Several of our native species have been selected by plant breeders and now appear in cultivation. The Indians used the berries raw or mashed them up along with other products such as chili and raw onions. Colyer (56) reported that seeds of *Physalis* were found in almost every fecal sample of the ancient Mesa Verde Indians, and she postulates that the plants may have been cultivated or at least encouraged to grow in their fields. The berries were often dried and stored for future use, sometimes they were ground into meal for bread.

The berries can be eaten raw, cooked into sauces, made into preserves or jams, and are said to make excellent pies. Gibbons (92) gave some recipes for making these items, but any standard fruit recipe could easily be adapted to ground-cherries. Muenscher (167) reported that animals have been poisoned by eating large quantities of the tops and the unripe berries, especially in periods of drought. It would be wise to avoid these unripe berries, however, since these probably would have an objectionable taste. Children are often warned that the fruits of wild ground-cherries are deadly poisonous, but we have no actual record of this poisoning ever happening.

They appear to be a good emergency source of food for the plants often occur in some abundance, the fruits in their outer covering store for fairly long periods, and they can be eaten raw.

Related Species:

Any of the species, especially those with yellowish flowers, would

Fr.1
x2

Fr.2
x2

F1
x1.5

x1

F2
x6

y. Matsumura

5CM

GROUND-CHERRY *(Physalis lanceolata)*

be worth a trial. *Physalis heterophylla, P. subglabrata, P. lanceo-lata, P. longifolia* and *P. pubescens* are mentioned particularly in the literature.

References (to numbers in the bibliography):

13, 18, 43, 56, 84, 92, 93, 95, 96, 97, 99, 117, 138, 158, 162, 163, 167, 192, 194, 195, 204, 218, 219, 220, 240, 242, 249, 254, 256, 259.

Prunus americana (P. ignota)
AMERICAN PLUM, WILD PLUM

Description:

Tall shrubs or small trees to 16 feet tall, frequently growing in thickets; leaves 2½ to 4 inches long; petals white or sometimes pink, each ¼ to ½ inch long, the whole flower about ¾ to 1 inch wide; fruit a plum, nearly round to oval, varying in size, but sometimes over 1 inch long.

Along streams in valleys. From the eastern states west to New Mexico and northern Utah. Rather irregularly scattered in the Rocky Mountain area, usually at lower elevations.

Use:

Wild plums are well known and used wherever the plant grows. They were utilized extensively by the Indians who often dried them for winter use. This was done by cutting them open, removing the central stones and spreading them out in the sun. The fresh fruits can be eaten raw, cooked into a sauce or made into a jam or jelly, following any recipe for cultivated plums. Here are two we have tried.

WILD PLUM JAM

Pit fruit. To every 2 cups raw fruit add ½ cup water. Boil this about 15 minutes or until the skins are tender. Measure ¾ cup sugar for each cup of fruit pulp. Mix and cook to jelly stage stirring constantly. Pour into sterilized jars and seal at once.
The jam is good but rather tart in general, like that of cultivated plums.

WILD PLUM JELLY

Put the whole fruit into boiling water and boil for about 15 to 25 minutes. Strain material through a piece of cloth. Measure the juice. Measure a cup of sugar for each cup of juice and set the sugar aside. Boil the juice carefully for about 25 minutes and add the sugar. Boil and stir for about a minute. Pour into sterilized jars and seal.

AMERICAN PLUM *(Prunus americana)*

Wild plums vary in size and flavor from tree to tree, and children usually have their favorite trees spotted. The fruit is subject to attack by insects and diseases, so that we seldom see a prime crop produced in any abundance in this area. Whenever this does occur the fruit should be utilized, especially in an emergency. In the latter event it is worth noting that the green fruit can be eaten when cooked with sugar. We have also been told that in fall after the fruit has fallen and the pulp has decayed away, the stones of the fruit can be cracked off and the kernel inside eaten raw (Meserve, 162).

Related Species:

No other wild plum is present in our area.

References (to numbers in the bibliography):

26, 29, 43, 57, 63, 83, 84, 96, 98, 103, 115, 117, 145, 158, 162, 182, 219, 240, 242, 243, 254, 258.

Prunus virginiana (P. melanocarpa, P. demissa)
CHOKECHERRY

Description:

Shrubs or small trees, in this area seldom over 15 feet tall; leaves 1½ to 4 inches long; flowers small (for a cherry), the petals ⅛ to ¼ inch long, white in color; fruit a rather small cherry, usually dark purple or black in color, but reddish or orange-colored fruits are sometimes present.

Hills, valleys and riverbanks. Widespread in the United States and the Rocky Mountain area.

Use:

The chokecherry is often very abundant, and fortunately the fruit is remarkably free from insect or disease damage. The bitter, astringent taste is too well known to need comment; if you haven't tried eating the fresh fruits, your outdoor education has been sadly neglected. Different races or varieties, perhaps even individual plants, do seem to vary in the amount of the substance that very aptly gives the name "chokecherry" to the species. The fruits were very popular with the Indians who sometimes managed to eat them raw. They also dried the fruits whole and stored them for winter. These were then soaked in water and eaten like fresh fruit.

We have found these dried fruits nice to nibble on; they seemed to have lost some of their biting quality and to have taken on an added sweetness.

The ripe fruits were often ground up, stones and all, then dried in the sun into cakes which could be stored for later use. They could be soaked up in water when needed, mixed with flour, sugar and water, then used to make a sauce. We have tried this procedure and found the taste very good, except that the hulls of the seeds are not ground fine enough to be completely ignored in chewing. These pieces of hulls do not seem to bother the Indians, for the Navajos in whose area the chokecherry is scarce, pay a rather high price to the Utes for these patties (in 1962 it was fifty cents per cake according to Colyer, 56). The kernels of the fruits are said to contain some prussic acid but this probably is diluted in the mixture. Children have been reported to have been poisoned by eating too many of the fruits, so it might be well to take it a bit easy at first. The danger probably can't be too great considering the very wide use of the fruit.

The Indians would often mix this dried fruit with dried meat and fat to manufacture the "pemmican" so famous as a concentrated food, especially in the North.

Chokecherry fruits are popular in making jelly and have even been on sale for that purpose in our local grocery stores. We have many recipes for jelly on file, most of which we have tried, but lack of space forbids giving them here. In general it is advised that you follow any of your recipes for sour cherry jelly, the one on the package of pectin will do. Some of us feel that a mixture of half chokecherry and half apple juice makes a better tasting product. In any case, some added pectin is advisable as this is lacking or very low in chokecherries.

Mrs. John May made a delightful chokecherry syrup which has been for sale at certain local markets for several years. She obtained the proper consistency by using just ½ the pectin used for jelly. This syrup goes nicely with pancakes, but we like it especially as topping for ice cream.

Chokecherries are famous for making wine. We have several interesting recipes but the following one is a good one.

CHOKECHERRY WINE (Contributed by William May of Steam-
boat Springs, Colo.)

Heat 16 quarts of chokecherries and 6 gallons of water to the boiling point. Simmer for 10 minutes and strain off the juice, pressing
the fruit to extract it.

Place this liquid in a stone crock or wine keg and add 3 pounds
of granulated sugar to each gallon of juice, mix and cool to
lukewarm.

Add ½ cake of compressed yeast and ½ pound of chopped seedless
raisins to each gallon of juice. Mix well, cover the container and
allow the mixture to ferment for about 5 days or until bubbling
has ceased. Stir well and add 1 pint of good brandy. Keep
covered for 3 months, then filter and bottle the wine. (Note: You
do not need to add the brandy to get good wine.)

The wine has a nice wine color and tastes very good.

Other recipes often omit the raisins and yeast.

The juice from fresh chokecherries can be obtained by mashing
the fruit, draining off the juice, and by adding water and sugar
to it a drink can be obtained that is unusual and refreshing (Bagdonas, 11A). It is no wonder that the fruit of this plant has been
so popular down through the years in spite of its astringent taste
in its fresh condition.

The bark has even been used to make a kind of substitute for
tea. This has not appealed to us since at least the leaves often
contain poisonous amounts of prussic acid and have caused severe
losses of livestock grazing upon them.

Related Species:

Another species of cherry often known as "Pin-cherry" *(Prunus
pennsylvanica)* grows in our area and produces fruit used particularly for jelly (Gillespie, 93; Hedrick, 117; Fernald & Kinsey, 84;
Medsger, 158; Morrell, 163; Yeager, Latzke & Berrigan, 258; Leslie,
145; Palmer, 181; Smith, 208). We also have a small plant called
"Bush cherry," *(P. besseyi),* the fruit of which is edible (Yeager,
Latzke & Berrigan, 258; Budrow, 36; Leslie, 145).

5 C M

CHOKECHERRY *(Prunus virginiana)*

References (to numbers in the bibliography):

11A, 12, 18, 26, 29, 40, 43, 49, 52, 56, 57, 58, 65, 68A, 74, 75, 83, 84, 93, 94, 96, 98, 99, 103, 107, 112, 117, 132, 138, 141, 158, 162, 163, 167, 182, 190, 195, 218, 219, 227, 235, 240, 242, 243, 254, 258.

Squawbush *(Rhus trilobata)*

Rhus trilobata (R. oxycanthoides, Schmaltzia trilobata)
Squawbush, Skunkbush, Skunkbush Sumac

Description:

   Shrubs 2 to 6 feet tall; leaf divisions (leaflets) usually 3, occasionally only 1 to a leaf, each about ⅜ to 1½ inches long; flowers not very conspicuous, the yellowish petals about ⅛ inch long;

fruit a rather dry berry about 1/4 inch long, red or orange-red in color, covered with both short and long hairs. As two of the common names suggest, the whole plant has a characteristic odor not very pleasant to most of us.

Hills, canyons, valleys and plains. Canada south to Iowa, Mexico and California. In our area it may grow up to at least 9000 feet elevation.

Use:

The berries were commonly used by several tribes of Indians. They ate both the green and ripe fruits, either raw or cooked. Sometimes they would grind up the berries and make the material into cakes, which could then be dried in the sun for future use. The whole fruits were sometimes dried and stored for the winter. They would also use the fruits fresh to make a kind of drink like our lemonade. The leaves were sometimes used as an adulterant or as a substitute for tobacco in smoking. The bark from the woody stems was used to make baskets. As a Navajo boy told us once, "This has been a very useful plant to us."

We have found that the best time of year to collect the berries is in September, just after they ripen and before they dry. However, they can be used all winter just as they have dried on the bushes. The best berries are often found on plants growing close to moist ground. We start by washing the berries and cleaning out the stems and leaves. One handful makes approximately one quart of a fairly good beverage. The berries are tied in a porous cloth and boiled for 10 to 15 minutes, the fruit occasionally being crushed. Then sugar is added to the individual taste and the orange-colored liquid used hot or cooled. The taste reminds one of lemonade with a somewhat "fuzzy" aftertaste, but most of us considered it quite good. A Navajo girl told one of us (Colyer, 56) that she liked a pudding made from ripe sumac berries. The berries were ground, seeds and all, sweetened with sugar and eaten uncooked.

Young (259) gave a typical Navajo recipe.

STEWED DRIED SUMAC BERRIES

3 cups dried berries   2 1/2 cups boiling water
4 tablespoons flour   1/3 cup sugar.

Grind berries. Mix the flour with the ground berries. Gradually stir this into boiling water and boil 10 minutes. Add sugar and serve.

As mentioned before, the odor of squawbush is objectionable to some people. We include it here because its use by the Indians indicates that it is an excellent survival food source. The plant is widely distributed, the fruits are often abundant and can be eaten raw, they are usable over a long period when dried, either stored or when they have dried on the bushes. In such cases the berries often protrude above an ordinary snow cover in winter, and may be the only food source available.

Related Species:
Rhus aromatica of the eastern United States is a related plant that should be tried.

References (to numbers in the bibliography):
12, 15, 17, 18, 26, 43, 45, 50, 56, 57, 74, 83, 85, 98, 103, 125, 138, 157, 173, 183, 216, 218, 227, 239, 240, 242, 248, 254, 259.

Ribes spp. *(Grossularia* spp., *Limnobotrya* spp.)
GOOSEBERRY, GOOSEBERRY CURRANT, PRICKLY CURRANT

Description:
Shrubs up to about 4 or sometimes 5 feet tall; twigs covered with spines or stiff bristles; fruit a berry, red, wine-colored or black when ripe, either smooth or covered with hairs or prickles.

Use:
The currants, those without bristles or spines on the twigs, and the gooseberries or gooseberry currants, those bearing spines or stiff bristles, all produce edible berries that have been used in various ways: fresh, canned, for pies, for jams or for jellies. Some kinds, of course, will be found on trial to be better than others. The following is a more or less standard recipe for jelly that we have used:

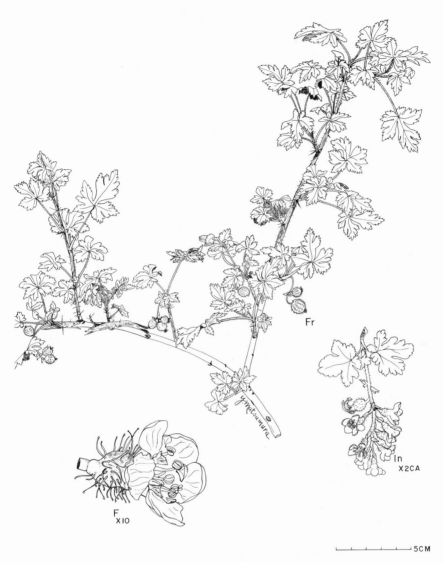

Fr

In
X2CA

F
X10

⊢━━━━━━━┥5CM

GOOSEBERRY *(Ribes montigenum)*

GOOSEBERRY CURRANT JELLY

3½ cups gooseberry currant or gooseberry juice
¼ cup lemon juice
1 package pectin
5 cups sugar

Prepare the juice by grinding fruit through a food chopper. It takes about 5 to 6 cups of berries to make 3½ cups of juice. Then add ½ cup of water to the ground berries and boil for 5 minutes. Pour in a jelly bag and strain out the juice. Mix juices and pectin. Bring to a boil and add sugar. Boil until jelly sheets off a spoon. Skim and pour into sterilized glasses and seal with paraffin.

We have also tried mixing gooseberry or currant juice with equal parts of commercially canned apricot or apple juice. The color and taste were found to be excellent. Jam made from gooseberry fruit *(Ribes inerme)* was rather tart but still very good.

The fresh fruits of gooseberries and gooseberry currants can provide nourishment when eaten raw in an emergency, although they may be rather tart and should be used in moderation. Stevens (219) told about a game played by the Indian children of the Omaha tribe. They would choose sides and then eat the unripe fruit of the Missouri Gooseberry *(R. missouriense)*. The side won with the most members who could eat the berries without making faces.

Related Species:

Some of the species that are recorded as eaten are: *R. lacustre, R. montigenum* (the one illustrated), *R. missouriense, R. inerme, R. setosum, R. hirtellum.*

References (to numbers in the bibliography):

6, 11A, 18, 43, 73, 74, 77A, 100, 138, 146, 162, 182, 219, 240, 254, 258.

Ribes aureum (R. longiflorum, Chrysobotrya aurea) WAX CURRANT, SQUAW CURRANT

Description:

Shrubs 3 to 8 feet tall; leaves up to 2 inches wide; flowers ¼ to ½ inch long, bright yellow, with a fragrant odor; fruit globe-shaped, ¼ to ⅜ inch wide, black or sometimes red, yellow or orange in color, smooth.

Plains, hills and valleys. Canada south to western South Dakota,

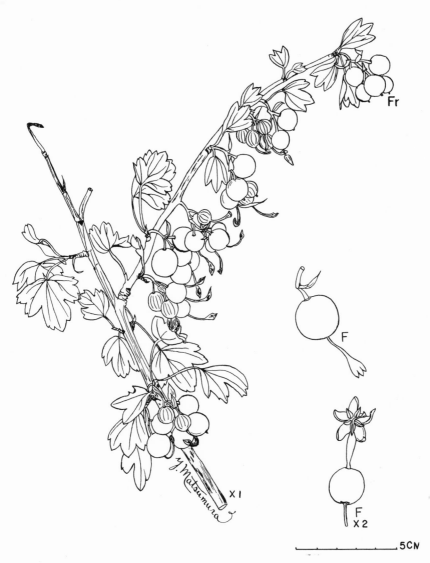

Fr

F

F
X2

X1

5CN

WAX CURRANT *(Ribes aureum)*

New Mexico, Arizona and California. Widespread in the Rocky Mountain area.

Use:

The fruits of this currant are relatively large and flavorful, so much so that the plant is often cultivated in our area for that reason alone. In addition, the flowers are very attractive: a shrub covered with a bright yellow blanket of blossoms is quite an attractive sight. We have transplanted this plant from the wild into cultivated ground many times without a single failure; it seems to be particularly adapted to exposed rather dry sites. The berries of this currant were often used by the Indians, particularly in making pemmican. The fruit was dried, then mixed with dried buffalo meat and the whole pounded together. Then fat or tallow was added to form the pemmican into loaves or cakes.

We have made jelly from the fruit using the following recipe:

WAX CURRANT JELLY

Wash fruit, add ½ as much water as fruit. Boil over low heat until fruits are soft and pop. Drip through jelly bag. Add one cup sugar to each cup of juice and cook to jelly stage. Pour into sterilized glasses and seal with paraffin.

We thought the jelly was very good, sweet but not tart, very flavorful and nice tasting. Some folks like the juice mixed with equal parts of apple juice. A jam made of equal parts of currant, rhubarb and apple, or currants and blackberries together, has been recommended by some.

Few people would object to a wild currant pie. Any good recipe will do; we have tried the following:

WILD CURRANT PIE

2 cups ripe currants	1 tablespoon flour
2 egg yolks	1 tablespoon water
1 cup sugar	1 recipe for pie pastry
½ teaspoon salt	

Wash currants and stem them. Beat egg yolks slightly, add sugar, salt, flour, water and currants. Line pie pan with pastry and pour in filling. Bake in a moderate oven (350 degrees F.) for about 35 minutes or until filling is firm.

For variation you might try the following recipe:

WILD CURRANT ICE CREAM SAUCE

Cook 1 cup washed and stemmed currants in ½ cup water for 10 minutes. Add ⅓ cup sugar or honey and boil gently for 5 more minutes. Serve hot or chilled over vanilla ice cream.

The flowers of this currant, along with some related ones, contain an abundance of nectar, so much so that when the bush is shaken at the proper stage the drops actually rain down onto the ground. Some of us consider that eating the raw flowers in the blooming season is a real treat, like "finding sugar on a bush." Although some of the other currants may have better-tasting flowers than this one, probably none have more delicious fruit.

The wild currants are readily recognized from their resemblance to cultivated plants; the fruit can be eaten raw or can be readily dried for future use. All these points make currants a prime emergency food source.

Related Species:

A closely related currant of the eastern part of the United States has been called "buffalo currant" *(Ribes odoratum)* and has been used in a fashion similar to ours (Vestal & Schultes, 242; Stevens, 219). Some of the other wild currants of our area are discussed under *R. cereum.*

References (to numbers in the bibliography):

6, 11A, 18, 36, 49, 50, 56, 65, 74, 84, 98, 103, 117, 138, 158, 182, 240, 243, 258.

Ribes cereum (R. inebrians, R. pumilum) WAX CURRANT, SQUAW CURRANT

Description:

Shrubs 1½ to 6½ feet tall; leaves ⅜ to 1½ inches wide; flowers ¼ to ½ inch long, pink to whitish in color; berry ¼ to almost ½ inch in diameter, globe-shaped, red in color, usually smooth.

Hills, ridges, slopes and sides of valleys. Canada south to New

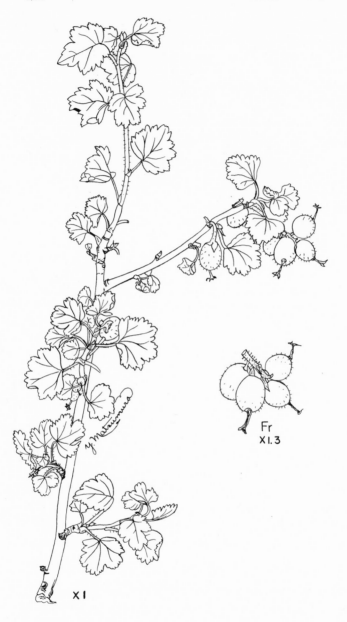

Fr
XI.3

XI

5CM

WAX CURRANT *(Ribes cereum)*

Mexico and California. Widespread and rather common in the Rocky Mountain area, usually not over 9000 feet.

Use:

All the currants and gooseberries of the area produce edible berries, although some kinds are much superior to others. The Indians often used this currant but in telling about it they added the caution that eating too much of the fruit may cause illness. They ate the berries fresh, or preserved them by drying. The young leaves in the spring were sometimes eaten (probably cooked in water), with uncooked mutton or deer fat.

This currant has a sticky feeling and an aromatic odor that is not pleasing to us. We have never found anyone that really liked the taste of the fresh berries much, and the jelly we made from them was not at all good. We include the plant here because it is so common, and recommend it only as an emergency food, even then to be used with caution at first. We have actually found that the nectar bearing flowers were better eating than the berries.

Related Species:

The currants have no spines on the twigs as do the related gooseberries. Many kinds of wild currants have been used (See *Ribes aureum*), including *R. viscosissimum, R. bracteosum, R. americanum, R. triste, R. glandulosum* and *R. nigrum*. (See also *Ribes* spp).

References (to numbers in the bibliography):

6, 11A, 18, 43, 56, 65, 74, 77A, 83, 84, 85, 100, 102, 138, 173, 182, 195, 220, 243, 249.

Rosa spp.
ROSE

Description:

Shrubs with upright or sprawling stems, these bearing prickles and sometimes bristles also; leaves always of 3 or more divisions (leaflets); flowers large and showy, our native species colored some shade of rose, but this often fading to whitish; fruit rather fleshy, somewhat like an apple, the fruit often called a "hip," red or orange-red in color, made up of a vase-shaped, fleshy covering, this lined on the inside with several to many bony, seedlike structures.

Woods, plains, thickets and hills. Widespread over North America. In our Rocky Mountain area usually found below 10,000 feet.

Use:

The rose species are difficult for botanists to classify, and certainly the fruits are very variable. Sometimes they will be large, up to 1 inch or more wide, with a relatively thick pulpy layer; sometimes they are small and less fleshy; often both kinds are present in different areas on what the botanists call plants of the same species. The bony, seedlike structures in the center are more or less hairy and these hairs are rather a nuisance. We have found a good deal of variation in the flavor of rose hips collected at different places and at different elevations. When you locate a desirable fruit-producing area, it is wise to remember it and go back to it the next year.

Various parts of the rose plant are used in many ways by people all over the world, but the fleshy fruits are the most widely utilized. Makino, in his *Illustrated Flora of Japan,* mentioned that *Rosa rugosa* hips are rather fleshy and are used as food in Japan, particularly by children. Rose fruits are listed as high in vitamins A and C, particularly the latter, and are noted for their antiscorbutic effects. In World War II they were collected in quantity in Europe, particularly in England and the Scandinavian countries. Hill (122) mentioned that in 1943 about five hundred tons of rose hips were collected in Great Britain and made into a syrup called National Rose Hip Syrup. We have recently purchased rose-hip powder in a local grocery store. It had been processed and packaged in Sweden and exported to this country to be used for flavoring and for soups, according to the label. Pills made from the fruits have been offered for sale as a source of vitamin C.

The fruits should be taken when ripe, some say after frost. We have found that a bright red color does not necessarily indicate that the fruit is really ripe. If the fruits are of any size at all, they

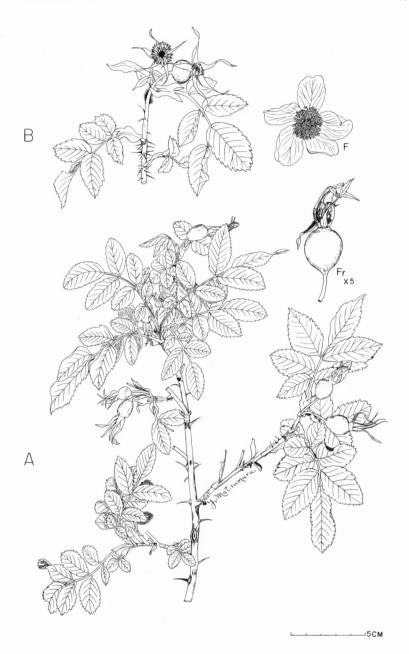

ROSE *(Rosa* spp.)

can be split longitudinally and the inner seedlike structures removed. This gets rid of the hairs that are attached to them. The
blossom end is usually removed and the pulp can be eaten raw
or stewed, or can be used to make wine, jam or jelly. We used the
"mayhaw" recipe given in the Sure-Jell directions and no trouble
was experienced in getting the juice to jell. The color was a dark,
rich red and the taste was very good, not too strong but not too
bland. The only drawback we found was the time and labor ex-
pended in securing and processing a large amount of the fruits.
A blend of rose juice with that of other more easily secured fruits
like apple, should be tried. We made a puree following the recipe
given by Angier (6):

Rose Hip Puree

Grind 4 cups of rose hips. Add 2½ cups of water and boil 20 minutes in a covered, enameled saucepan. Then rub through a sieve.
This can be bottled in small glass containers and heated for 20
minutes in boiling water. Angier suggested using it to flavor soups
or mixed with tapioca pudding. We have used the puree with
stewed meats, with vegetables such as Zucchini squash, green beans,
and in soups, adding it just before serving so as not to cook out the
vitamins. We did not care for it alone but found it quite acceptable as a flavor.

The rose hips can be dried and kept for long periods. These
dried fruits can be ground into a powder, even leaving the seedlike structures in if the fruits are small. This powder can be used
to flavor various kinds of other foods and drinks. We added it to
pancakes, concluding that it blended in well but did not add much
to the flavor.

Even the green fruits, when peeled and cooked, have been utilized as food. The young shoots in the spring are said to make an
acceptable potherb. The leaves have been used to make a tea. The
rose petals can be eaten raw, in salads, candied, used in making
syrup, or dried and made into a beverage like tea. The rose roots
were used likewise by certain of the Indians for tea making, and
the inner bark was sometimes smoked like tobacco. The petals
are often dried and placed in jars to be used as a perfume or have

actually been used to give an odor and flavor to butter. For other uses of roses, see Gordon (99A).

Rose hips dry on the twigs and can be used for at least the early part of the winter. They may protrude above the snow and furnish the only readily available nourishment for hungry wayfarers. We have often collected a handful of these dried fruits and let them soak in the mouth, after which they can be chewed on with some satisfaction. We consider rose hips an excellent emergency food, both raw and cooked, as well as a fairly good source of general food. How strange that so many of our parents have warned us as children that these red fruits are poisonous. Even the Indians had some such mistaken idea for several members of the Ute Tribe told us that if we should touch rose hips we would itch all over, the information apparently handed down by their parents, not from personal experience.

Related Species:
Any species of rose produces edible products.

References (to numbers in the bibliography):
2, 5, 6, 8, 11A, 13, 26, 29, 43, 50, 56, 57, 58, 65, 77A, 82, 83, 84, 93, 95, 99, 102, 107, 112, 115, 117, 119, 121, 122, 130, 132, 134, 145, 146, 158, 162, 164, 181, 182, 206, 212A, 216, 219, 228, 239, 240, 243, 249, 256.

Rubus parviflorus (Bossekia parviflora, Rubacer parviflorum)
JAPANESE RASPBERRY, THIMBLE-BERRY, SALMONBERRY

Description:
Stems woody, at least at base, 3 to 6 feet tall, lacking prickles or bristles; leaves large, usually over 4 inches long; flowers rather large, each petal about 5⁄8 to 1 1⁄4 inches long, white in color; fruit a typical raspberry, about 3⁄8 to 3⁄4 inch wide, red in color when ripe.

Open woods and open slopes. Canada south to Michigan, Mexico and California. Widespread through the Rocky Mountain area at medium to high elevations, at least up to 10,000 feet.

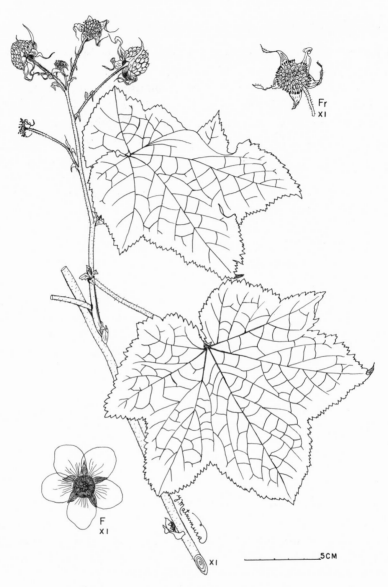

JAPANESE RASPBERRY *(Rubus parviflorus)*

Use:

This plant produces a fruit resembling that of the garden raspberry; it is sweet and has a delicious tart flavor. Some folks describe it as being "insipid and uninteresting," but we have never
found it so. The seeds are smaller than those of our red raspberry

and the fruit is inclined to be more mushy, especially when really ripe; it may not be quite as flavorful, but it compares favorably with it (See *Rubus strigosus*). We often take glass jars along and pick the fruit directly into them. This prevents the packing and settling damage you get by using a pail for picking. The fruits can then be eaten fresh, or they can be canned or frozen, without moving them from the jars. They make good jam and excellent jelly. We followed the recipe for sour cherries or raspberries as printed on the package of pectin (Sure-Jell or Certo). The flavor was rather high and delicious, something like that of garden raspberries.

The Indians ate the fruits fresh, or managed to dry them for storage. They often ate them in the Northwest with half-dried salmon eggs (hence the common name salmonberry). The leaves are sometimes used to make a tea by boiling them twenty to thirty minutes in water. The young shoots in the spring are said to make a good potherb like asparagus or spinach.

This plant fruits over a period of about ten days to two weeks, and hence would be available as emergency food over a reasonably long period. We have seldom found it in large quantities, partly because it seems to bear the most fruit in almost inaccessible places. If you have help in picking, especially from children, you had better supervise the operation very closely or more may end up in their mouths than in the pails.

Related Species:

A similar species with a larger flower, but with a smaller, drier fruit is found at lower elevations. It is often called "boulder raspberry," and a botanist, through not being acquainted with the fruit and probably because it resembled the Japanese raspberry, or else in fine sarcasm, named it *Rubus deliciosus*. The seeds are large, and the fleshy pulp very thin indeed; probably you could eat the fruit in case of necessity, but you wouldn't call it "delicious." *Rubus spectabilis* is another similar plant in general appearance and type of fruit, but is not present in our area.

References (to numbers in the bibliography):
52, 56, 74, 77A, 107, 119, 157A, 182, 217, 227, 243, 254.

Rubus strigosus (R. melanolasius, R. idaeus variety *strigosus)*
Red Raspberry

Description:

Stems woody, armed with stiff bristles (not really stiff enough to be called prickles); leaf divisions (leaflets) usually 3 but sometimes 5, each 1 to 3 inches long, the color white to gray below, green above; flowers medium in size, each petal about $\frac{1}{4}$ inch long, white in color; fruit a typical raspberry about $\frac{1}{2}$ inch wide, red in color.

Slopes and open places, often in dry locations. This plant is widespread over most of Canada and the United States. In our area mostly in the mountains up to timberline, often on talus slopes and canyon bottoms.

Use:

The fruit of this plant, as in all the raspberries, is composed of many fleshy round bodies clustered together; when ripe these separate from the hemispherical structure to which they were attached. The blackberry fruit is similar, but the fleshy bodies, instead of falling away from their attachment structure, come away with it. The recipes and suggestions given for raspberries will apply equally well for blackberries. The red raspberry produces a favorite fruit wherever it is found in any abundance, and is preferred by many of us to the various cultivated forms. It has a high tart flavor that is considered delicious by practically everyone; usually it is used to make jam, jelly and pies. We have made the berries into jam following a standard recipe for raspberries, but found the seeds were rather bothersome. The product, however, was delicious, with a pleasing color, taste and odor. We recommend that they be made into jelly instead, using the recipe on the jar or box of pectin. If the fruit is somewhat unripe you may be able to get the product to jell without this pectin, but it is better to play safe. Wild raspberry jelly is justly famous the country over. Another use is to mix the washed unsweetened fruit into

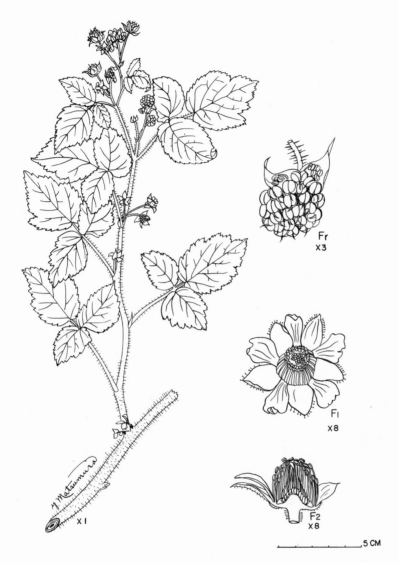

RED RASPBERRY *(Rubus strigosus)*

vanilla or butterscotch instant pudding. This can be poured into a pie shell for an excellent quick raspberry cream pie.

In fact, any of your recipes for cultivated raspberries can be used for the wild fruit. Many people of the area cultivate this plant in their gardens because they prefer it to the horticultural forms, but the plant is not everbearing and has but one main crop a year. The Indians ground up the fruit, dried it in the sun and were able to store it for later use, sometimes using it mixed with cornmeal. The young, tender, peeled shoots are edible, both raw and cooked like asparagus or spinach. A substitute for tea can be made from the leaves or the twigs, but it would be wise to take it slowly at first as some species may cause physiological trouble (Cheney, 51). Such "tea" appears for sale in a few of our local grocery stores. Boorman (29) gave recipes for making soup and wine from raspberries that sound worth trying out.

This is a widespread, very useful plant under any conditions. The fruits become available over a period of several weeks, but in a good season a reasonable quantity can often be gathered at one time. We once directed a group of boys who were collecting seeds for a reseeding project. It was remarkable how few red raspberry fruits found their way into the collecting sack, all of which suggests that the fruit tastes excellent raw. It is available during its season as an emergency food.

Related Species:

At least two other raspberry species are used in this area. Black Raspberry *(Rubus occidentalis)* is a favorite (Uphof, 240; Hedrick, 117; Coon, 58; Yeager, Latzke & Berrigan, 258; Gibbons, 92; Gillespie, 93; Fernald & Kinsey, 84; Cheney, 51). The dwarf raspberry *(R. triflorus)* has been utilized (Hedrick, 117; Yeager, Latzke & Berrigan, 258). The various species of blackberries are used (Palmer, 182; Littlebee, 146; Jaeger, 132; Coon, 58; Fernald & Kinsey, 84). In fact, the fruits of any of our raspberries or blackberries are readily recognizable and almost invariably delightful to eat.

References (to numbers in the bibliography):

6, 11A, 18, 26, 29, 51, 56, 57, 75, 77A, 83, 84, 93, 95, 98, 117, 132, 138, 145, 146, 158, 182, 216, 239, 240, 243, 254, 258.

Sambucus spp.
ELDER, ELDERBERRY

Description:

Shrubs or possibly small trees up to 15 feet tall; twigs rather coarse, with very large pith in the center, this white to brownish-red; leaf division (leaflets) 5 to 11; flowers in flat-topped or umbrella-shaped clusters, these 2 to 8 inches across; each flower white, rather small; fruit a round, fleshy berry containing 3 to 5 seeds, the berries up to 1/4 inch in diameter, black, purple or some shade of red in color.

Damp places, often in valleys, along streams and bases of cliffs. The various species are widespread in Canada and the United States and to be expected anywhere in our area.

Use:

The berries of the elder are extensively used wherever the various species grow. The fruits of the black or blue-purple kinds are the ones generally eaten by the white people of our area; in fact, the statement is often made that the red-berried kind is poisonous. However, many Indian tribes used the red fruits without ill effects, and sometimes seemed to prefer them to the others (Palmer, 183). It is possible that the red-berried elder (called by botanists either *Sambucus pubens, S. racemosa* or *S. microbotrys*) varies in the quality of its fruit in different areas. We know of people who have suffered severe intestinal upsets by eating red elderberries before frost, but we have repeatedly tried rather small quantities both before and after frost without any ill effects. The raw berries have an unpleasant bitterness about them which seems to be merely intensified by cooking. One of our acquaintances used small quantities of the red fruit mixed with large amounts of apple juice to make jelly, but to us the product still had a bitter tang. It is possible some people might like this taste, but on the basis of our own experience we cannot recommend the red-berried elder fruit for general use. The black or purple fruit gives us a different story altogether.

The elderberry plants often bear relatively large quantities of these blackish or bluish-purple fruits; one cluster has been found

Fr
x 3

Y. Matsumura

F
X13CA

⌐_____5CM

ELDER *(Sambucus melanocarpa)*

that weighed several pounds. The fruits can be eaten raw, or they can be dried for storage as the Indians did. Some people think that the drying actually improves their flavor. We used them for jelly making, following the recipe for elderberry jelly as given on the Sure-Jell package. When the elderberry juice is used half and half with apple juice the jelly is delicious; some people consider it the very best of all. Elderberry jelly can be purchased in many grocery stores, and those we have tried have a pleasant, brisk and tart flavor.

Another popular use of elder fruit is in making wine. We have many such recipes in our files but here is a simple one as given by Gibbons (92):

ELDERBERRY WINE

Take 20 lbs. of berries, mash them in a 5 gallon crock and add 5 quarts of boiling water. Cover the crock and let them stand 3 days. Then strain the juice, return it to the crock and add 10 cups of sugar. Let this stand in the crock until fermentation is over, then remove the scum. Strain the wine, pour into bottles and cap them. Let stand for a year.

Other recipes call for the addition of raisins, cinnamon, ginger, cloves, allspice, yeast or brandy. Even the flowers can be used to prepare a wine called "Elder Blow Wine" with raisins and yeast being used to assist the process. Jam or pies can be made from elder fruit, often with the addition of other fruits such as rhubarb and apple. The flowers can be stripped from the plant and added to batter, to make an interesting tasting batch of pancakes. The entire flower cluster can be cut off, the large stems removed and the whole dipped in batter. This when fried in deep fat gives a kind of "fritter." A palatable beverage can be prepared by crushing the raw berries in water and adding sugar.

Certainly the elder is a plant that can be used in a great many ways. Some writers claim the young shoots can be used as a potherb (Morton, 166; Gillespie, 93), but the roots, bark and mature leaves are listed as poisonous to livestock (Durrell, Jensen & Klinger, 79; Muenscher, 167). For that reason we have used only the fruits and flowers. The flowers have also been used to make a tea, but this we have not tried, although we have seen it for sale in this area. The large central pith has long been used in biological laboratories to assist in cutting thin sections of fragile material. The object is supported between pieces of the pith and this is sliced with a sharp blade. According to Coville (65) the Snake Indians punched out the pith of the elder twigs and used the cavity to store crickets as food for winter.

In cases of emergency the dark-colored fruits of the elder can be used both raw or cooked. It would be wise to use them in rather limited amounts at least at first. The red-colored ones should be avoided altogether.

Related Species:

(Black or purple-blue fruited ones only): The eastern *Sambucus canadensis* comes into the eastern edge of our area. The western *S. coerulea (S. glauca)* is in the western part of the Rocky Mountain region, while *S. melanocarpa* is scattered throughout the area.

References (to numbers in the bibliography for all species of *Sambucus*):

13, 18, 25, 26, 29, 43, 49, 56, 57, 58, 59, 65, 68A, 73, 74, 77A, 79, 84, 92, 93, 98, 99, 102, 107, 112, 117, 119, 121, 122, 132, 138, 146, 158, 162, 164, 167, 174, 179, 181, 183, 192, 216, 217, 227, 228, 240, 241, 242, 243.

Shepherdia argentea (Lepargyraea argentea)
Silver Buffaloberry

Description:

Shrubs or small trees to 20 feet tall, usually with thorny, silvery-scaly twigs; leaves silvery-scaly on both sides, ¾ to 2 inches long; flowers small and inconspicuous; fruit a roundish, one-seeded berry about ⅛ to ¼ inch wide, scarlet to golden in color.

River banks, valleys, plains or low meadows. Canada south to Kansas, New Mexico and California. Widespread in the Rocky Mountain area.

Use:

Only part of the trees in a buffaloberry stand produce fruits, since some individuals bear pollen only. But the fruiting trees may produce astonishingly large quantities of the red berries, which the Indians gathered by hand picking, or by spreading a thin

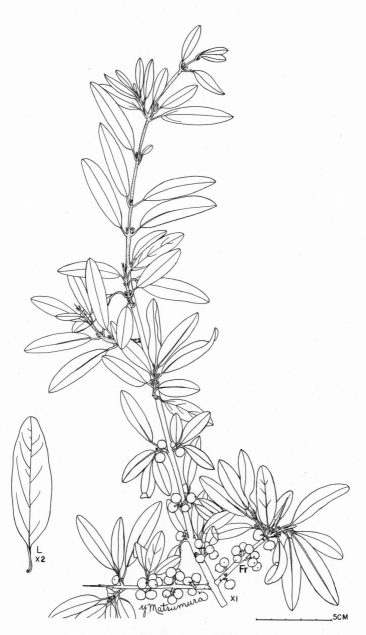

L
x2

Fr

x1

5CM

SILVER BUFFALOBERRY *(Shepherdia argentea)*

cover on the ground and beating off the fruits upon it. These
fruits were sometimes eaten raw, often cooked into a sauce which
was used to flavor buffalo meat (hence the common name), or
they were dried for winter use. The raw fruits are thought by some
people to be sweeter and less acid after frost, but we have often

eaten them in late summer, and found them tart but very pleasant to the taste. The seeds are fairly large, but they do chew up readily with the rest.

The buffaloberry is now most popular in making jelly and at one time appeared for sale on some local markets (Blankinship, 26). We have used them in this manner well before frost, and found that adding pectin was not necessary.

Buffaloberry Jelly

Wash and crush berries and add ½ cup water to every 2 quarts of fruit. Boil slowly for 10 minutes, stirring frequently to prevent scorching. Put into a jelly bag and drain off juice. To each cup of juice add 1 cup sugar. Bring to a boil and boil until it jells by the standard "jelly test."

This makes a clear jelly, with the color of golden honey or pale apricot. It has a pleasant "bright" or nearly "tart" taste, something like currant jelly. If you want to be sure that it will set, especially when the fruit is very ripe after frost, use commerical pectin, following the recipe for currant jelly on the package. The juice may have a milky appearance at first, but it soon clears in the cooking process.

We have also made a preserve that was somewhat different using 6 cups berries, 6 cups sugar and 2 cups water. Olive Truelsen of Dolores, Colorado, makes her jelly with 2 cups of buffalo berry juice and 1 cup of crabapple juice to 2½ cups sugar, with the pectin from the apples augmenting that in the buffaloberry fruit.

We have seen the Ute Indians grind up the fruits, seeds and all, then shape them into patties which were dried in the sun. These dried berries can be used to make a beverage. Just add a cup of these fruits to a pint of cold water and mash them thoroughly. Sugar can be added. Yeager, Latzke & Berrigan (258) gave a recipe contributed by C. A. Bar of Smithwick, South Dakota.

Buffaloberry Beverage

Put ½ pint of berries in a quart jar, add ½ pint of sugar. Fill with boiling water and seal.

A dessert can be made from buffaloberries according to Vliet (243) as follows: Wash berries, place in a container and mash them thoroughly. Then beat the mixture into the consistency of whipped cream.

The buffaloberry fruit is a good emergency food either raw or dried. In the areas where it grows it certainly provides a source of tart-tasting, fresh fruits. The only drawback is that the individual fruits are small and some people may consider them tedious to gather. However, they may be borne very abundantly on some trees in favorable seasons, and we have never found it difficult to secure a reasonable amount in a rather short time.

Related Species:

We have another species widespread in the Rocky Mountain area *(Shepherdia canadensis)* that goes by such common names as "bitter buffaloberry, russet buffaloberry or soapberry." It is a spineless shrub usually growing in partial shade, with leaves more or less brownish-dotted below; it does bear attractive looking reddish berries. These have been variously described as being at once sweet, bitter, acidic and aromatic. The Indians are reported to have used them extensively, either fresh or dried. The berries contain a rather high percentage of "saponin" (Havard, 115, said 0.74%), this substance not only gives them the bitter taste but also allows them to be whipped like thick cream into a frothy mass that was used as a kind of dessert.

Perhaps one can acquire a liking for their bitter taste, but we have often tried these bitter buffaloberries both raw and cooked, and cannot recommend them very highly. The best we can say is that we have never become actually ill from eating small quantities of them.

References (to numbers in the bibliography for both species of *Shepherdia*):

5, 26, 49, 50, 56, 57, 74, 77A, 84, 95, 98, 100, 103, 107, 115, 117, 119, 130, 138, 145, 158, 162, 174, 182, 183, 204, 217, 228, 234, 240, 243, 244, 252, 254, 256, 258.

Solanum nigrum (S. interius)
NIGHTSHADE, BLACK NIGHTSHADE, COMMON NIGHTSHADE, GARDEN NIGHTSHADE

Description:

Annual plants; stems 4 inches to over 2 feet tall, branched; leaves about 1 to 3 inches long, often with many small insect holes when mature; flowers ¼ to ½ inch wide, white; berry globe-shaped, about ¼ inch to nearly ½ inch wide, black at maturity.

Waste ground and fields, often acting as a weed. This plant was probably introduced from Europe, and is now spread through the cultivated places in the United States. Usually found below 7000 feet in the Rocky Mountain area.

Use:

This plant provides a kind of paradox and one wonders whether to place it in one of the edible plant chapters or in the one on poisonous plants. Some writers flatly stated that this plant contains a serious toxic substance in all of its parts, while others definitely recommended it as a food plant. The Indians certainly ate the plant, and many of our acquaintances eagerly gather the ripe berries for pies, jams, preserves and puddings. Furthermore, a husky, large-fruited form of this species is fairly common in cultivation under the name of "wonderberry, sunberry, garden huckleberry or Morelle." Many people eat these fruits without harm and learn to relish the musky flavor, but even this garden form has been reported to have occasionally caused illness. It is possible that the toxic content of the wild form varies from plant to plant, perhaps because of geographic or soil differences. What is more likely, cases of poisoning may have occurred when the green, unripe fruits are consumed, often by children trying them out while at play. As far as our own experience and observation goes, the ripe black fruits of either the wild or cultivated form can be eaten with safety. Nevertheless, we advise that you go slow until you are sure that you suffer no serious ill effects from this plant. You may be extra sensitive to it.

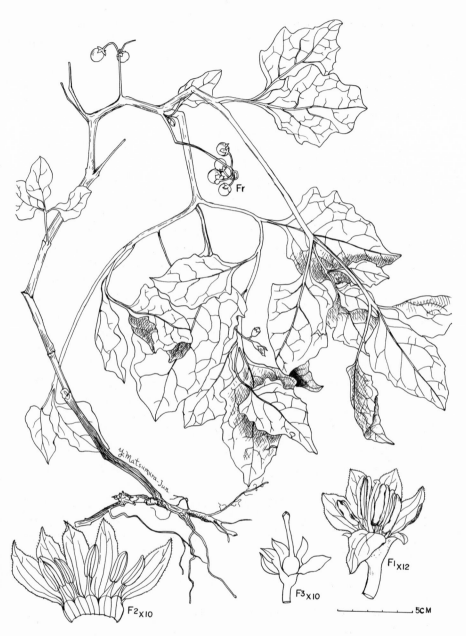

NIGHTSHADE *(Solanum nigrum)*

We have often eaten the berries made into pie and always enjoyed the pleasant musky taste. A good recipe for courageous people who would like to try the plant is as follows:

Mrs. Blehm's Nightshade Pie

2 cups nightshade berries   2/3 cup sugar
½ tablespoon lemon juice (optional)
Flour or tapioca to thicken (about 2 tablespoons)

Although the foliage has been reported to poison livestock, the young, cooked shoots are widely used over the world as a pot-herb, prepared like spinach. It is possible that heating destroys any toxic material that might be present in the fresh plant.

This nightshade would be a reasonably good plant to use in times of food scarcity. If the berries were eaten raw they should be taken in limited quantities until you are sure they do not affect you. The same could be said for the cooked fruits, or the young shoots. When one is lost and hungry it is no time to risk sickness. However, they are worth a cautious trial under any conditions.

Related Species:

A very closely related species, *Solanum americanum,* may be in our area and probably would be about like the common one. A plant with more deeply lobed leaves and fruit green at maturity, *S. triflorum* is in the area and has likewise been reported to be both edible and poisonous (Muenscher, 167; Stevenson, 220; Castetter, 43; Uphof, 240). We have never tried these berries largely because of their green color.

A sister species, *S. elaeagnifolium,* commonly called "white horsenettle" because of the silvery leaves, grows in this area. Its berries were used by the Indians to curdle milk and Young (259) gave a recipe for the process.

Navajo Cottage Cheese

2 white horsenettle berries (fresh or dried)
1 quart goat's milk
Crumble the berries into the milk. Boil 5 minutes or more. Drain and season. Eat at once.

Other references for white horsenettle (Muenscher, 167; Hedrick, 117; Curtin, 66; Wooton & Standley, 254; Kearney & Peebles, 138; Stevenson, 220; Steggerda & Eckardt, 218; Castetter, 43).

A climbing species with arrow-shaped leaves, purple flowers and bright red fruits is to be expected in this area. It should be avoided as being possibly poisonous.

References (to numbers in the bibliography):

5, 16, 52, 59, 69, 79, 84, 93, 117, 134, 138, 141, 151, 160, 165, 167, 216, 219, 230, 240.

Vaccinium spp.
WHORTLEBERRY, BLUEBERRY, GROUSEBERRY, BILBERRY, HUCKLEBERRY

Description:

Our plants are low shrubs rarely over 1 foot tall; leaves always with small teeth on the margins; flowers white to rose, rather small, not over ¼ inch long, vase-shaped; fruit rather small, not over ⅜ inch across, a red, black or blue berry which is crowned at the apex with the small withered remnants of the flower.

Mountain slopes. Canada and the United States, especially the northern part and in the mountains. The species scattered in the Rocky Mountain area, usually at medium to high elevations in the mountains.

Use:

This is a popular wild fruit, and in some areas where the larger fruited kinds grow the berries are gathered commercially. Our kinds produce small berries, and at least in the southern half of the Rocky Mountains are usually stingy producers. One old-timer told us that they used to be much more abundant, but grazing sheep had thinned down the stands. We have had no trouble finding plenty of plants, but the berries were usually few and far between.

The sweet, flavorful berries can be used in a variety of ways, eaten raw with sugar and cream, cooked into a sauce, or made into

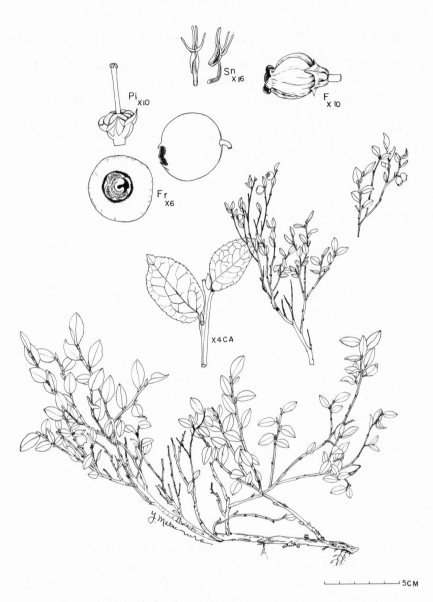

Pi x10

Sn x16

F x10

Fr x6

X4CA

5CM

WHORTLEBERRY *(Vaccinium scoparium)*

a pie. They are also favorite fruits to mix with various kinds of
dough to make muffins, breads or pancakes; in fact, one can pur-
chase these various mixes in the stores where whortleberries are
included in the package under the name of blueberries or huckle-
berries. They can be home canned, or the canned product can be

bought at your grocery. Canned pie mixes are for sale, also a syrup made from this popular berry.

Whortleberries are famous for making jams and jellies, and are often mixed with other fruits like peaches or apples. We have used the following recipe.

WHORTLEBERRY JAM

4 cups crushed berries	1 package powdered pectin (such as Sure-Jell)
2 tablespoons lemon juice	5 cups sugar

Mix berries, lemon juice, and pectin. Place over high heat and stir until it comes to a hard boil. Then add sugar and boil hard one minute. Remove from heat and alternately stir and skim for 5 minutes. Pour in scalded jelly glasses and seal with paraffin. It should make about 9 glasses. The black- or blue-fruited species in our area make a very good tasting jam with a brisk, pleasant flavor.

Pancakes made with these berries are usually available at any restaurant specializing in pancakes. If you make your own, then use any recipe mix for pancakes and stir in a cup of whortleberries. Boorman (29), gave an interesting recipe which he called:

CANOE-TRIP PANCAKES

1 cup pancake or biscuit mix	Powdered milk (in proportion
1 powdered egg	to water)
1½ cups water	1 cup of whortleberries

Stir the pancake mix, the powdered milk and powdered egg together in a pan. Add water beating to a thin batter. Add berries. Makes about 12 small pancakes.

The Indians used to gather the berries and dry them in the sun or over the campfire. They were stored, and used later in various ways much as we do raisins. They used them to flavor other foods like meat, to thicken soup, or to work into their famous "pemmican" product. The berries dry fairly nicely, especially when finished off in an oven. It has been suggested that if the fresh fruit is sealed in a jar and placed in an ice box or refrigerator it will keep as long as a month. We have never tried this, probably because we never had the will power to keep such delicious fruit on hand for so long.

The leaves of whortleberry can be used fresh or dried to make a kind of tea. Our experience has been that some kinds make a pleasant tasting beverage, others not so good. *(Vaccinium myrtillus* is our favorite and appears for sale at one of our local grocery stores). We have also been told that a wine can be made from the fruit.

This is a very valuable group of fruit-producing plants. It is too bad that the fruits are so small and so scarce in our area. The red-fruited whortleberry appears to us to be stronger in flavor than the others, but we try to gather any kind we encounter.

Related Species:

We have at least 3 species in this area. The black or blackish-fruited one is *Vaccinium myrtillus,* which is found over the whole Rocky Mountain area. The blue-fruited *V. caespitosum* and the red-fruited *V. scoparium* are in the northern part of the area.

References (to numbers in the bibliography):

2, 8, 29, 56, 57, 58, 65, 74, 77A, 84, 93, 100, 102, 117, 162, 216, 240, 243, 254.

Viburnum edule (V. pauciflorum)
Squashberry, Mooseberry, Viburnum, Arrowhead

Description:

Woody shrubs 3 to 6 feet tall; leaves 1½ to 4 inches long; flowers in clusters, these clusters ½ to 1½ inches broad, each flower milky-white in color; fruit a red or orange-red berry with one large, flat seed.

Woods and thickets. From Canada, south in the northern parts of United States. In the Rocky Mountain area it extends south to central Colorado.

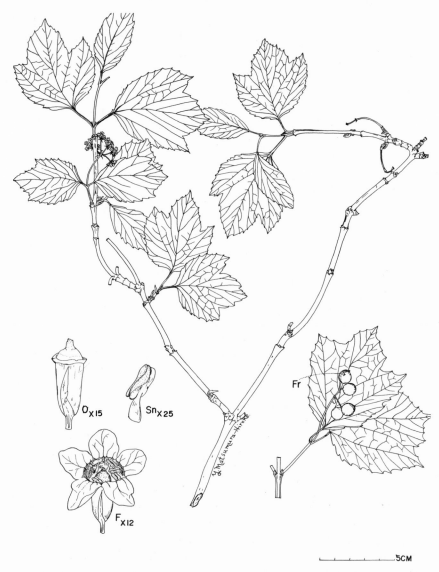

O×15 Sn×25 Fr F×12

5CM

SQUASHBERRY *(Viburnum edule)*

Use:

The berries have a characteristic musty odor, a rather tart taste, especially when young (a taste that reminds one of cranberries), a tough skin and relatively large seeds. We consider it desirable to remove the skins and seeds before using the pulp. These fruits can be eaten raw, and we consider them quite palatable. When ripe, they become soft and almost transparent. They persist on the twigs well through the winter, but are considered to be best when gathered just after ripening, but before the first frost. The Indians preserved them for winter use, probably by drying them in the sun, but also in oil obtained from seals and other animals. The commonest use for the berries is to make a sauce or a jelly.

Squashberry Sauce

5 cups fully ripe fruit   1 envelope unflavored gelatin
¼ cup water   1 cup sugar (or more if desired)
Wash and crush berries. Add water, heat to boiling and simmer 10 minutes. Cool and press through a colander until only seeds and skin remain; these are discarded. Moisten gelatin with ½ cup of the squashberry juice. Add to remainder of pulp and heat. Add sugar and stir until dissolved, then cool. The sauce should be thick, but not jelled. If a thicker product is desired use 2 packages of gelatin. We found this sauce delicious, especially with lamb.

Squashberry Jelly

4 cups squashberry juice   6 cups sugar
1 package powdered pectin (like Sure-Jell)
Crush about 2 quarts of fully ripe squashberries. Add ½ cup water. Heat to boiling and simmer 10 minutes. Strain through a jelly bag to obtain the juice. Mix pectin with juice. Place over high heat and stir until mixture comes to a hard boil. Add sugar. Bring to a full rolling boil and boil hard for one minute, stirring constantly. Skim and pour into scalded jelly glasses and seal immediately with paraffin. This should yield about 9 glasses of jelly. The product we made was of a dark red color with a very pleasant, rather tart or tangy taste.

Related Species:
Several species of *Viburnum* from the eastern part of the United

States produce edible fruit. These include *V. trilobum (V. opulus americanum)*, *V. lentago* and *V. prunifolium*. (Gilmore, 95; Hedrick, 117; Fernald & Kinsey, 84; Gordon, 99; Angier, 8).

References (to numbers in the bibliography):
75, 77A, 84, 100, 107, 119, 214, 228, 240.

Vitis spp.
GRAPE, WILD GRAPE

Description:

Woody vines, scrambling or climbing by tendrils; leaves always broad and more or less lobed; flowers small, greenish in color, in pyramid-like clusters; fruit a juicy berry (grape), seldom as much as ½ inch wide, blackish in color, but often with a whitish waxy cover that rubs away readily, borne in characteristic "grape" clusters.

Banks, roadsides, thickets, streambanks, valleys and edges of woods. The various species are rather widespread in the United States. In the Rocky Mountain area we have *Vitis vulpina* and *V. longii* coming into the eastern part while *V. arizonica* is limited to New Mexico, Arizona and southern Utah.

Use:

Wild grapes are so commonly used in areas where they grow that little need be said about them. In general, they can be used in most of the various ways that their cultivated counterparts are utilized. The fruits are smaller of course, and may be more tart to the taste, but still they are "grapes." Their commonest use is to make grape juice, wine or jelly.

Start by washing the grapes, leaving on a few stems if you wish. Add just enough water to keep them from sticking (try 1 cup to 10 lbs. grapes). If you mash the fruit you will probably get a cloudy looking product. The free running juice can presently be strained through a jelly bag overnight. The liquid can be used to make grape juice, wine or jelly. Grape juice should be pasteurized by placing it in large jars or jugs, these are then put in

Fr

GRAPE *(Vitis vulpina)*

a hot water bath (at about 165 degrees F. for 40 minutes). The liquid can then be poured into smaller bottles, and pasteurized again for 20 minutes before sealing.

The simplest way to make jelly is to follow the directions for making cultivated grape jelly as given on the pectin package (such as Sure-Jell). Immature grapes may jell without pectin, but it is safer to use it, or at least mix them with apples. We know people who use ¾ cup of sugar to every cup of grape juice. Of course the seeds can be removed and the unstrained pulp can be used to make grape jam.

The wild grape fruits were eaten raw by the Indians, but were often dried in the sun for future use. These "raisins" were often ground, seeds and all, and used to thicken or flavor other foods. Castetter (43) suggested that wild grapes were actually cultivated by some of the Indian tribes. Wild grapes have been used to make various foods such as dumplings, while grape pie is justly famous. The young tendrils make fairly good food when eaten raw. The leaves are sometimes used to wrap around other foods, such as rice or ground meat, which is then baked or roasted. In such cases, recipes usually call for boiling the leaves for a few minutes before using them (Sopher, 212A).

The fresh, wild grape leaves are commonly chewed by some people to allay thirst. The Air Force Manual (2) suggested obtaining drinking water from the vines. These are cut off near the ground and placed in a container. Then a slantwise cut is made in the vine about six feet up, which allows the water to run through the inner tubes of the stem down into the container. Additional cuts lower down may provide an additional flow of water.

Related Species:
Any of the available species of *Vitis* should be utilized. Our species seldom fruit prolifically in the Rocky Mountain area.

References (to numbers in the bibliography for all species of *Vitis*):
2, 18, 26, 29, 43, 58, 83, 84, 92, 93, 99, 112, 117, 132, 138, 145, 146, 158, 182, 183, 212A, 216, 219, 240, 258.

CHAPTER VIII: NONFLESHY FRUITS AND SEEDS
(like Wheat)

The dry fruits and seeds of native edible plants are of special value as food, since they are relatively high in nutritive value as compared with most other plant parts. It must be admitted that many of them are very small. This creates a problem in gathering them in quantities, but, on the other hand, they are often borne in large numbers on one individual. If you secure a mature plant when these structures are about ready to be shed naturally, and then shake or beat the plant over a cloth or flat rock surface, you will probably be surprised by the amount of your harvest. Many of us have learned to collect those parts bearing the fruits or seeds just before they are ready to shed, and then stow them away in large cloth or paper sacks to dry out. Later on these sacks can be shaken or beaten and the harvest collected in the bottom. The leaf pieces and dry bracts can be removed by winnowing in the breeze, or by using a sieve.

Dry seeds and fruits are better if ground up, especially if they are very small. If you are under primitive conditions a couple of stones of proper shape (mano and metate) can be used. Such cracked or ground material can be utilized in many ways. In many cases the enclosing bracts and coverings can be ground up right along with the contents. If the seeds or fruits are ground fine enough a kind of flour can be secured.

Of course, plants with these parts infected with disease (such as ergot or smut) should be avoided, but these blackish malformations can be readily recognized. Seeds and dry fruits store for long periods of time, and are fairly easily carried around from place to place. This may be necessary under certain types of emergency conditions. Fortunately, very few of our native plants produce poisonous seeds or dry fruits, but of course it would be wise to avoid those from known poisonous species. If you have the patience you can secure a large amount of food material from the dry fruits and seeds of native plants, and many of them will provide you with new, agreeable taste sensations.

Plants with non fleshy fruits and seeds but illustrated or described in another chapter.

Agave utahensis IV.
Amaranthus graecizans III.
Amaranthus retroflexus III.
Asclepias speciosa IV.
Atriplex patula III.
Brassica nigra III.
Calochortus spp. VI.
Cannabis sativa II.
Capsella bursa-pastoris III.
Chenopodium berlandieri III.
Cirsium spp. VI.
Cleome serrulata III.
Ephedra spp. IX.

Malva neglecta VIII.
Monolepis nuttalliana III.
Nuphar polysepalum VI.
Portulaca oleracea III.
Rumex crispus III.
Salsola kali III.
Scirpus acutus VI.
Sisymbrium spp. III.
Taraxacum officinale III.
Thlaspi arvense III.
Triglochin maritima II.
Typha latifolia VI.

Agropyron repens
QUACKGRASS, WHEATGRASS

Description:

Perennial grasses with long, vigorous, straw-colored rootstocks; stems 1 to 3½ feet tall, usually rather erect; leaf blades flat, usually dark green in color, ⅛ to ⅜ inch wide, bearing at their bases small forward projecting appendages called "auricles" (see drawing); flowers and grains borne 3 to 7 together, accompanied by scalelike bracts, the unit called a spikelet, these units borne on a narrow, elongated central stalk, the whole rather resembling the head of wheat or rye.

This grass is often weedy in habit, but sometimes appears in meadows and pastures well away from habitations. It is widely distributed throughout the United States, and can be expected

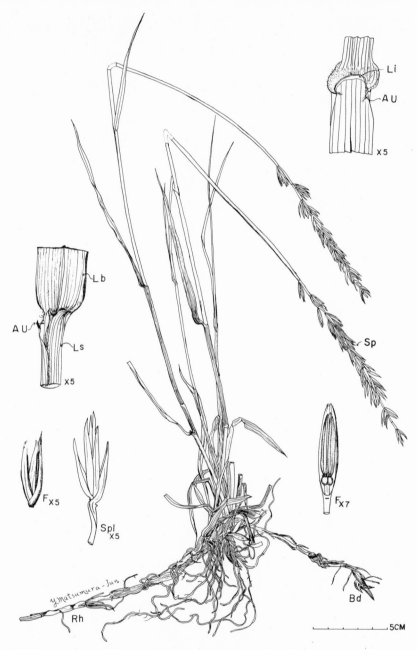

QUACKGRASS (*Agropyron repens*)

anywhere in our Rocky Mountains, especially below 9500 feet elevation.

Use:

The long rootstocks have often been dug up, dried, ground into flour and used for breadmaking, especially in time of famine. They have also been roasted, ground and used as a substitute for coffee. The Gosiute Indians are reported to have used the grain as food (Chamberlin, 49), but it would be rather tedious to gather since the grain does not fall free from the surrounding bracts. *The Range Plant Handbook* (Dayton et al., 74), pointed out that the grains of this plant are often infected with the poisonous fungus "ergot." In such cases a black mass of spores replaces the grain and, when eaten, causes severe illness or death, both in livestock and human beings. However, it should not be difficult to avoid these spore masses when using wheatgrass as food. The writer has not tried this grass and at present considers it an emergency food only.

Related Species:

Any species of *Agropyron* could surely be utilized, particularly western wheatgrass *(A. smithii)*, which is a common native grass. In fact, any grass grain of any size at all, and not affected by ergot or smut, could be used as emergency food. The grains might be tedious to gather, but ground or crushed they could be utilized as a flour or porridge.

References (to numbers in the bibliography)*:*
   49, 74, 84, 117, 228, 240.

Astragalus succulentus (A. mexicanus, Geoprumnon succulentum)
MILKVETCH, GROUND PLUM, BUFFALO PEA

Description:

The stems are sprawling, about 4 inches to 1½ feet long; ultimate leaflets ¼ to ¾ inch long; flowers in rather short clusters;

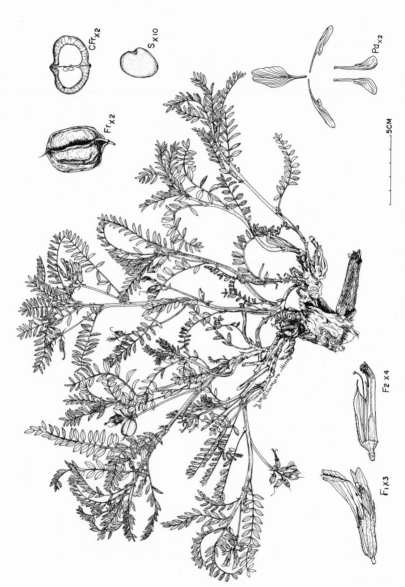

MILKVETCH (*Astragalus succulentus*)

flowers 3/4 to 1 inch long, white or yellow-white, the center (keel) deep purple-tipped, the whole sweetpea-shaped; pod up to 1 inch long, nearly round, very fleshy and somewhat resembling a plum when young.

This plant grows on prairies and plains in the eastern part of the Rocky Mountain area, east to Nebraska.

Use:

The fleshy, immature pods are highly esteemed by those of us who have tried them, and were often used by the Indians. They can be eaten raw, boiled, or made into spiced pickles. Medsger (158) suggested cooking and preparing them like garden sugar peas, the ones where the entire pods are eaten. The fruits should be picked young, but even after they toughen up a bit they can still be cooked, and the seeds hulled out like peas to provide a little food. In fact, this can be a good emergency food, but ought not to be mistaken for the poisonous relatives. (See *Astragalus bisulcatus* and *Oxytropis* spp. in Chapter II). Fortunately, none of the latter have this green, fleshy, round or oval pod, which has been compared in general appearance to a green-gage plum.

Related Species:

Several species resemble the above described one, they differ in color of the flowers and the shape of the leaflets, but all have the fleshy, edible, plumlike pod. They include *Astragalus crassicarpus* and *A. plattensis (A. caryocarpus).*

Several other species with pods more like the poisonous kinds were used by the Indians, sometimes the pods, often the roots (Castetter, 43; Hough, 128; Kearney & Peebles, 138; Whiting, 249), but since identification is difficult in these plants, even for botanists, we recommend that you leave them alone.

References (to numbers in the bibliography):
26, 84, 96, 117, 127, 138, 140, 158, 162, 219, 240.

Avena fatua
WILD OAT

Description:

The wild oat resembles the cultivated oat, but has longer awns that are definitely twisted at their bases. The stems are about 1 to 3 feet tall; the seeds are borne 2 or 3 together, in units that hang from an open cluster. The so-called "seed" is the one-seeded grass fruit which falls enclosed in 2 narrow bracts, one of which bears an awn from the back.

Wild oats are common around cultivated fields, in disturbed ground in general, and perhaps because of the use of horses in wilderness areas, may even be found well away from any human habitation. In the Rocky Mountain area these plants are seldom found above 7500 feet elevation.

Use:

Wild oats were often used by the Indians. They shattered them into baskets, then singed off the long hairs on the bracts by putting in some live coals and shaking the mixture. This got rid of the hairs, and incidently parched the grains to some extent. Then the grains could be ground into a meal or crushed to form a kind of rolled oats, in fact, used in the same way as we use cultivated oats. The real grain is enclosed in chaffy bracts which can be ground up in the process, or perhaps winnowed out in a breeze. We have never had occasion to try wild oats as a food, but there seems no reason why it shouldn't be a good emergency food. The wild oat grain is relatively large in comparison with that of most of our wild grasses, and this is an advantage.

References (to numbers in the bibliography):
52, 57, 74, 117, 151, 158, 240.

Corylus cornuta (C. rostrata)
BEAKED HAZELNUT, BEAKED FILBERT

Description:

Shrubs 3¼ to 6 feet tall; leaves 1½ to 5 inches long; flowers

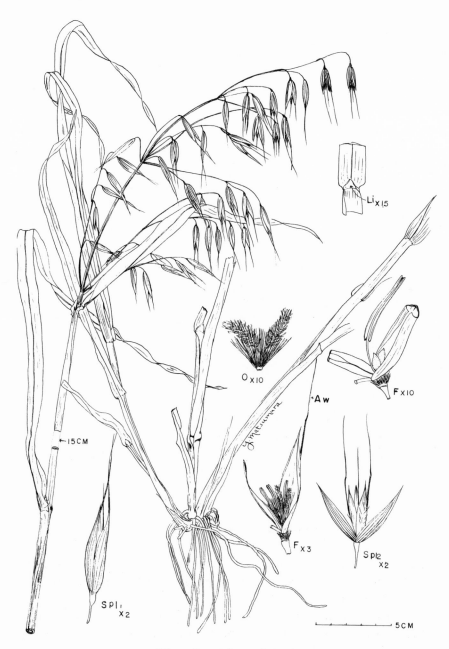

WILD OAT *(Avena fatua)*

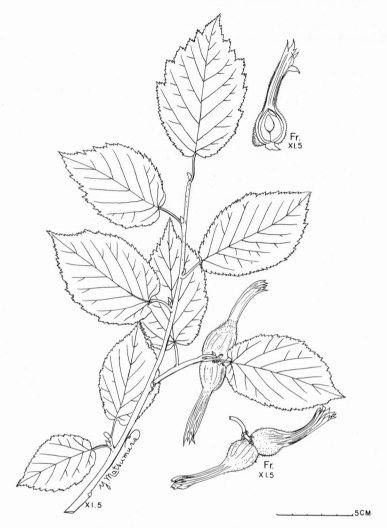

BEAKED HAZELNUT (*Corylus cornuta*)

rather inconspicuous; nut ⅜ to ⅝ inch long, encased in a husk that narrows at the apex to a long tubular beak, this beak usually over 1 inch long.

Thickets, slopes and valleys, from the Atlantic Ocean west to the Black Hills of South Dakota, and to the eastern mountain slopes of Colorado, usually well below 8000 feet elevation.

Use:

This is a famous nut producing shrub. The nuts crack easily, the kernel is reasonably large, and everyone surely knows how good they taste. The Indians often gathered the nuts for winter use. The kernels can be dried for long storage, and can be ground into a flour or meal. Several good modern recipes call for this hazelnut flour, these can be found in many cookbooks. Coon (58) gave the following interesting recipe: "One pound of hazelnuts should be finely chopped or ground in a mill. A mixture of 4 ounces of granulated sugar and 4 tablespoons of water is boiled along with a small quantity of candied orange peel for not over 3 minutes. The nuts can then be stirred into this mixture and the whole set aside to cool. This flavorful mixture can be used for turnovers, mince pies and so forth." Of course nuts from the beaked hazel can be used in cakes, puddings, candies, etc., in any recipe calling for nuts in general.

These nuts ripen in the autumn, are easy to find and one can easily crack out the kernel, which is tasty and nutritious when eaten raw. For these reasons it is an ideal survival food; it is too bad that the plant is limited to the eastern part of the Rocky Mountains. Unfortunately, according to our observation, it is rather stingy in setting fruit in the extreme western part of its range. Even for these few you have to run a race with the squirrels.

Related Species:

The eastern United States species, *C. americana,* produces a similar nut, but not in a beaked husk. It too is a favorite nut producer.

References (to numbers in the bibliography):
    2, 58, 84, 93, 95, 117, 146, 158, 162, 198, 208, 240.

Descurainia spp. *(Sophia* spp.)
TANSY MUSTARD, FLIXWEED

The species of this genus resemble each other closely and all of them can probably be used in the same way as food. They unite in sharing the following characteristics.

Description:

Annual or at most biennial plants usually with an aromatic but rank odor; stems commonly branching, usually not over 2½ feet tall; leaves filmy and fern-like, bearing very tiny clusters of hairs (use lens); flowers rather small, of 4 whitish to yellow petals; pods varying in length from ⅛ to 1 inch long but always narrow in shape.

Hillsides, plains, valleys; in open ground, often as a weed in fields and waste places. The species are widely distributed, mostly from the Rocky Mountains westward.

Use:

These plants have been used, particularly by the Indians, as a source of seed for making "pinole." They pounded the dry pods in various ways, and the accumulated seeds were then parched and ground into a meal. This was cooked into a mush, made into bread, or used to thicken soup. It may be rather tedious to gather a sufficient quantity of these seeds, but since the species is so abundant in certain local areas it may well be used as a means of obtaining nourishment in an emergency.

The Indians used the young tender growth as a potherb, often baking it in a firepit lined with stones. By piling alternating layers of the greens and hot stones, then covering over the top, they were able to secure a kind of fireless cooker. They let the plants steam for about 30 minutes and used them at once, or let them dry out for future use. This method was thought to produce a better product than could be obtained by boiling. We have never tried this Indian method, but have tasted them raw, and the odor and bitter taste were not at all pleasing to us. The fresh plants were also boiled for 3 or 4 minutes, with 2 changes of water. Some of the objectionable odor and taste was removed by this treatment, but there was still a lingering, bitter aftertaste. As one of our collaborators remarked, "In my opinion, a taste must be acquired for tansy mustard." It has been reported that in Utah, cattle grazed heavily on these plants had general health difficulties. We are including them here as an emergency food, largely because of their abundance.

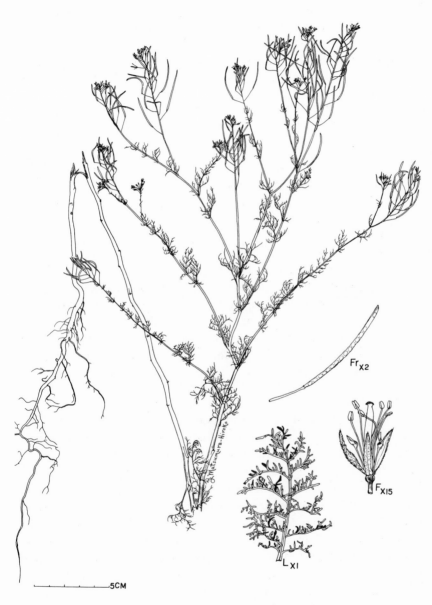

Fr X2

L X1

F X15

TANSY MUSTARD *(Descurainia sophia)*

Related Species:

D. pinnata ochroleuca, a winter annual in New Mexico has been reported and proved fatal to cattle grazing exclusively on this species on sparse ranges.

All other species of this genus can be utilized, but it is possible some are better tasting than others.

References (to numbers in the bibliography):

12, 14, 18, 41, 43, 66, 138, 173, 183, 195, 206, 227, 240, 249.

Echinochloa crusgalli (Panicum crusgalli)
BARNYARD GRASS, COCKSPUR, WATERGRASS

Description:

Annual grasses; stems 8 inches to 3½ feet tall, erect or sprawling; leaves very unusual in lacking any form of a little collar-like structure (ligule) at the junction of the sheath and the blade; inflorescence 4 to 8 inches long; ultimate units of flowers and scales (spikelets) about ⅛ inch long, not counting the awns.

Moist, rich soils along ditches, yards, lakes, etc. Widely distributed in the United States, and in the Rocky Mountain area, especially at lower elevations.

Use:

This grass is locally very abundant, has fairly large seeds, and was often used as food by the Indians. The seeds were dried or parched, then ground into a meal or flour. This was mixed with water or milk and baked into cakes, or made into a mush; in any form it was said to be of good flavor and nutritious (Kephart, 140). As far as we know, any grass will produce edible seeds, providing they are not affected by a fungus infection such as ergot. The ergot forms a black, cylindrical or cigar-shaped body that replaces the grass seed. This mass is poisonous, but fortunately it is rather conspicuous. In an emergency we would not hesitate to select any grass that is abundant in the area, and has reasonably large seeds. These we would parch and try to eat them whole, or attempt to grind them into a meal or flour between rocks. Barn-

L

In_{X5}

Spl
$X10$

$F3$
$X10 CA$

y. matsumura

Spl
$X10$

5CM

BARNYARD GRASS (*Echinochloa crusgalli*)

yard grass would certainly be worth your trial. We have ground the seeds, chaff and all, and made cakes with the flour. They were surprisingly delicious.

Related Species:

A related species (or by some botanists considered merely a variety of the above) is *Echinochloa frumentacea,* often called "Japanese millet." It is cultivated in Japan and the East Indies and used as a cereal.

References (to numbers in the bibliography):
   11A, 14, 84, 93, 138, 140, 240.

Helianthus annuus (H. aridus, H. lenticularis)
SUNFLOWER, COMMON SUNFLOWER, KANSAS
   SUNFLOWER

Description:

Annual plants; stems usually branched, from 1 to 6 feet tall; leaves to 8 inches long; flowers of 2 kinds, these both clustered in the same head, the marginal, strap-shaped ones yellow, the central, tubular ones tinged with reddish-purple or brownish red at their ends; heads terminating the branches. The cultivated sunflower with the taller, thicker stem bearing a single large head has been called a variety of this species *(H. annuus* var. *macrocarpus).*

This plant grows on open plains and valleys, often on arid ground, from the Mississippi River westward, but is established or cultivated in the eastern part of the United States.

Use:

The seeds (achenes) of the cultivated variety are now sold in almost every grocery store, but of course are larger than those of the wild type. The sunflower has always been a favorite food source of the Indians, probably from prehistoric times, and was apparently cultivated by some of the tribes. One of our colleagues, Professor Jenkins, brought us a bottle of sunflower seeds a few

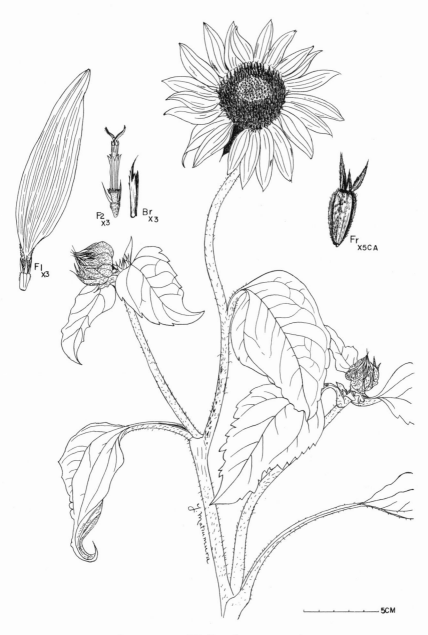

SUNFLOWER *(Helianthus annuus)*

years ago which had been stored in a pot by the early inhabitants of the area and were exposed by plowing up a field in southwestern Colorado. They must have been at least several hundred years old. These seeds were gathered by the Indians, parched and some-times eaten whole. This we have tried and found the thin hulls could be readily eaten along with the kernel. Of course, the seeds can be ground and the hulls removed. Gibbons (92) suggested an interesting method. If you have a food grinder available run the seed through a plate just large enough to crack the hulls. Dump the mixture in a bowl of water and the hulls will float to the top where they can be skimmed off. Then drain off the water and dry the kernels, using heat if necessary. Perhaps the hulls can be winnowed out in a breeze, or will come to the top on shaking the mixture. The kernels can be ground and the meal or flour used alone, or it can be mixed with cornmeal to make soup, mush, gruel or bread.

According to one report, the entire "seeds" can be roasted and ground as a substitute for coffee. Also, the ground seeds can be boiled until the oil, which is said to be about 20% of the contents, rises to the surface. This can be skimmed off and used as a cooking oil. The Hopi Indians still use this oil for greasing a hot flat rock on which they cook their blue cornmeal paper bread (Colyer, 56). The sunflower seeds appear to be worth trying under any condition, but appear to be particularly valuable as an emergency food. They occur in great abundance; we have all seen entire fields showing an almost solid sheet of yellow from the heads. The yellow marginal flowers are sometimes chewed as emergency food by boy scouts. In addition to the above mentioned uses of the plant, the young heads are reported to be edible when boiled in water and eaten like Brussels sprouts. This would be worth trying, but the plant contains a sticky, unpleasant smelling resin that we suspect may affect the taste. Perhaps the water will remove it. This species of sunflower is the state flower of Kansas.

Related Species:

Another common annual sunflower is *Helianthus petiolaris*. It has narrower leaves and smaller heads than the common sunflower; it may even be more abundant in certain localities. It can be used in similar fashion. Apparently the seeds of all the species of sunflower are edible in the same way. There are a few perennial ones that produce thickenings on the roots that resemble tubers.

The most famous one is *Helianthus tuberosus,* usually called "Jerusalem artichoke." These tubers were extensively used by the Indians who boiled, baked or fried them like potatoes. The early pioneers learned their value and they were taken back to the Old World where they were cultivated. These tubers are reported to sometimes grow to be over two inches in diameter, and are said to be nutritious and flavorful. They seem to lack starch and therefore may be eaten by persons who are suffering from ailments precluding that substance in their diet. The tubers are said to contain a mucilaginous substance that may remain in the water after boiling, and can be used to thicken soup.

This plant should be a good survival food since the tubers can be dug up and eaten any time during the fall, winter or spring. The only reason we have not formally and separately included the species here is that it does not appear to be very abundant in the Rocky Mountain area according to our observations. (Some references for Jerusalem artichoke—Yanovsky & Kingsbury, 257; Verrill, 241; Newberry, 174; Gibbons, 92; Barrett, 16; Uphof, 240; Palmer, 182; Rusby, 198; Rexford, 194; Holmes, 125; Harris, 112; Oswold, 179; Hoffman, 124; Georgeson, 91; Gilmore, 94; Gilmore, 96; Gilmore, 95; Bale, 13; Stevens, 219; Hedrick, 117; Kephart, 140; Whiting, 249; Gillespie, 93; Coon, 58; Jaeger, 132; Medsger, 158; Gordon, 99; Grieve, 102; Fernald & Kinsey, 84; Havard, 115.)

References (to numbers in the bibliography for species of *Helianthus*):

11A, 18, 26, 30, 41, 43, 45, 49, 56, 57, 66, 83, 84, 92, 93, 97, 112, 115, 117, 118, 130, 132, 138, 140, 158, 174, 181, 182, 183, 204, 213, 218, 219, 223, 227, 239, 240, 243, 249, 259.

Malva neglecta (M. rotundifolia)
MALLOW, CHEESE WEED

Description:

Annual plants (or appearing to live 2 years) from rather thickened roots; stems prostrate, 4 inches to over a foot long in favorable places; flowers ¼ to ⅜ inch long, white to pale blue in

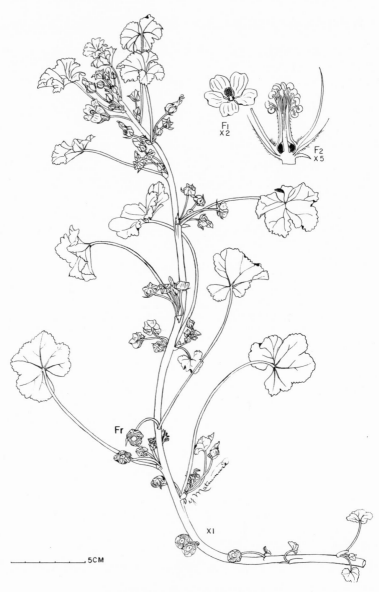

F1
X2

F2
X5

Fr

X1

5CM

MALLOW *(Malva neglecta)*

color; fruit round, but flattened from top to bottom, much like some kinds of cheeses.

Naturalized from the Old World into most of the United States where it acts as a weed. In the Rocky Mountain area it is found around cultivated ground or habitations, usually at lower elevations.

Use:

This plant is used in many countries as a potherb. Very young tender shoots and leaves should be used, prepared in the usual way. They are said to be mild tasting, with a mucilaginous juice, and should be especially good for making soup. The Indians have used the plant in this fashion. Some people think the species makes a good salad when eaten raw.

The green immature fruits are favorite nibbles of many people, especially children, who usually call them "cheeses." These are borne thick enough on many plants so that they can be stripped off in reasonable quantities. The green whorl of the outer parts of the flower (sepals) can be removed if desired, but we found this unnecessary. The fruits can be eaten raw and have a crisp, slightly sweet, pleasant taste when used in a salad or on a relish dish. They can also be pickled in brine and vinegar. We have often used them by cooking them about fifteen minutes in soup, such as tomato or chicken noodle. These fruits can even be utilized when they have begun to turn somewhat brown.

If you pull up a young plant and hang it upside down in a shady place until the leaves are crisp and dry, you will find it can be used as a substitute for tea. A few polite guests have even said they liked it better than the commercial product. A commercial product called "Malva Leaves" is on the market as a "tea," probably made from this mallow.

This plant is often abundant and worth experimenting with in additional ways. Because of its habitat around cultivated areas it may not always be available in times of emergency. Chewing the fruits has been thought by some people to keep the mouth from drying out in times of water shortage.

Related Species:

M. parviflora and *M. verticillata,* (Curtin, 66; Medsger, 158) and probably several other species have been used in similar fashion.

References (to numbers in the bibliography):

11A, 56, 57, 84, 93, 102, 112, 117, 138, 158, 181, 219, 225.

Martynia louisianica (Proboscoidea louisianica)
DEVILSCLAW, UNICORN PLANT

Description:

Annual plants; stems with the longer branches sprawling, up to
3½ feet long; leaves large, often up to a foot wide; flowers large,
up to 2 inches long, cream-colored or yellowish, spotted with
purple or violet; fruit a long, beaked pod covered with hairs, the
seed-producing part about 3½ to 4 inches long, the curved beak
even longer than the body.

Waste places, fields and gardens, to be expected as a coarse weed
anywhere in the United States.

Use:

The pods of this plant are large and curiously shaped (see drawing). The long hooked beak splits with the pod, and may become
entangled in the wool of sheep, or it may even fasten itself for
a time just above the hoof of an animal. This gives the fruit a
chance to scatter its seeds, but since the beak is sharp at the end
it can't be comfortable to the animal. A friend related to us that
he once had one of these sharp-pointed fruits fasten around his
ankle in rattlesnake infested country, just as he was making his
way through a barbed-wire fence. He claimed he left most of his
clothes on the fence.

The Indians used the pods of this and related species to make
baskets, by peeling off the outer coat into strips (Castetter & Bell,
47). The young, still fairly tender pods have been sometimes used
as a substitute for garden pickles, in fact, it is said that the plant
has been cultivated for that purpose. We used the following recipe:

DEVILSCLAW PICKLES

4 quarts sliced pods	1½ teaspoons turmeric
6 medium sized onions	1½ teaspoons celery seed
2 green peppers	2 tablespoons mustard seed
⅓ cup salt	3 cups vinegar
5 cups sugar	

Fr
X1/5

F1
X1

F2
X1

Pe

Pe

Pe

Pe

Pe

Fs

X1/2

5CM

DEVILSCLAW *(Martynia louisianica)*

Mix sliced pods, onions, peppers and salt, cover with cracked ice and let stand 3 hours, then drain. Combine other ingredients and pour over the drained pickle mixture. Heat to boiling point, seal in sterilized jars.

The taste of the devilsclaw pickles was acceptable but not really excellent as compared with garden pickles. The fruit is covered with so called "glandular" hairs, that is, coarse hairs with sticky drops of liquid at the ends, and these not only give an unpleasant, sticky-syrupy feeling to the touch, but apparently impart a rather unpleasant taste and odor to the food product. We suggest that you boil the fruits for a few minutes before pickling to try to get rid of this slightly displeasing taste. We would also like to try the young pods in soup like okra.

Related Species:

They have several related devilsclaws in the states south of our Rocky Mountain area, and the pods of at least some of them were used as food by the Indians.

References (to numbers in the bibliography):

16, 47, 84, 93, 117, 138, 140, 158, 162, 182, 219, 240, 241.

Oryzopsis hymenoides (Eriocoma hymenoides, E. cuspidata)
INDIAN RICEGRASS, INDIAN MILLET, INDIAN MOUNTAIN-RICE

Description:

Perennial bunchgrass; stems erect or nearly so, 8 to 24 inches tall; seed-bearing units (spikelets) $\frac{1}{4}$ to $\frac{3}{8}$ inch long.

Plains, valleys and slopes, often in dry rocky or sandy ground. Canada, south to Texas, Mexico and California. Widespread throughout the Rocky Mountain area but seldom above 9500 feet.

Use:

The seeds of these plants are rather large when compared with those of native grasses in general. For that reason they have been

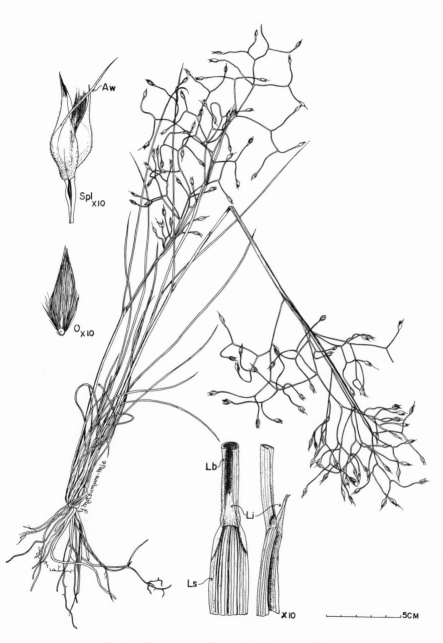

INDIAN RICEGRASS (*Oryzopsis hymenoides*)

used as food by the Indians since prehistoric times, and were often important in their economy as the common names suggest. The so-called "seed" is rather plump and invested with two close-fitting outer scales, these are covered with fine white hairs. The Indians got rid of these hairs by holding a bunch of the stems with the heads extending close to a fire. Apparently the hairs were burned off, and the seeds dropped into a pan or rock below. These seeds can also be gathered in a pan and several small live coals placed in among them. By shaking the mixture, the seeds will not only have the hairs burned off but they will be parched at the same time.

In any event, they were often ground to form a meal that was used in various ways, as a mush or gruel, to thicken soup or to make cakes. Yanovsky, Nelson & Kingsbury (257), analyzed the seeds of this grass and found about 18-20% starch in one sample, with about 6% of sugars. Compared with our cultivated grains this is not a very high percentage of food, but the plant is reported to have a pleasing taste and would certainly make an excellent emergency food. Grasses in general are easy to recognize and any of them with reasonably large seeds should be edible. Of course one must avoid seeds infected with fungi such as smuts or ergot.

It might be advisable to try winnowing out the ground-up chaff from the meal, but Colyer (56) thinks this would not be necessary, in any case it sounds rather impractical. We have not tried this plant ourselves, but it is often available in quantities in just the areas where it might be desperately needed as survival food.

Related Species:

Oryzopsis asperifolia (mountain ricegrass) is an eastern species coming into the eastern part of our area. It has a seed about twice as long as common ricegrass, with fewer, shorter hairs covering it. It has been reported to be very good as a food source (Fernald & Kinsey, 84; Gillespie, 93; Hedrick, 117), and should be equal or superior to our common one. However, we have never found it in any abundance in our area.

References (to numbers in the bibliography):

12, 18, 26, 37, 41, 43, 49, 56, 74, 83, 117, 137, 138, 157, 158, 173, 182, 204, 218, 240, 249, 254, 256, 259.

Pinus edulis (Caryopitys edulis)
COLORADO PIÑON PINE

Description:

A tree becoming 15 to 20 feet tall; needles ¾ to 2 inches long, usually borne 2 together, but rarely 3 or 1; cones ¾ to 2 inches long; seeds wingless, brown in color, often up to ½ inch long.

Foothills, mesas, canyon walls and rocky slopes. Western Wyoming to western Texas and west to the Pacific.

A related species with similar fruits but with needles always borne solitary, is found in Utah, Arizona and westward. Some botanists consider it a mere variant of our piñon pine. Since the seeds are about the same, the two are discussed together below.

Use:

The seeds of piñon pine were at one time an important food source to the Indians, and are still gathered and sold by various groups. One sees the nuts for sale in many grocery stores of the area, and they are often exported to other localities where they are utilized in various ways, often in making candy. New York City used to take the bulk of the export nuts according to Campa (39). Some years we have a small crop and the surest way to secure the seeds is to gather the unopened cones, put them in a safe place to dry, and then gather the shattered nuts later on from the dried cones. The Indians expected a bumper crop every seven years, which was followed, they thought, by an epidemic of smallpox. This could well be the case as during such a harvest there naturally would be an intermingling of various groups, apparently even of enemy factions, which could aid in spreading possible infection.

The nuts were harvested in the fall or possibly in the early winter when the cones were opening and the seeds were about ready to fall. Canvas was spread on the ground and the tree was shaken to bring down the seeds. Apparently some tribes had a kind of superstition against this last procedure, for one of our colleagues, Professor Klinger, told us that when the United States Soil Conservation Service was interested in securing seeds for planting in New Mexico, the Navajo workers refused to shake the trees, and gathered only those that had fallen to the ground. The cones on

COLORADO PIÑON PINE *(Pinus edulis)*

the trees were often collected in bags by climbers. If the cones were not open they were roasted until the scales separated. Rat's nests were often raided. These were found in rock crevices, in hollow logs or under heaps of twigs, one nest often yielding up to 30 lbs. of seed.

Some of the seeds are aborted, with only an empty shell remaining. The flotation method is sometimes used to separate the good ones from the bad. However, from our own experience we have found that some good seeds will float on water. The seeds can be eaten raw at once, or stored for the winter. They have a pleasant oily-nutty taste, and apparently are high in nutritive value. Kephart (140) and Vliet (243) listed the analysis as follows: Protein 14.6%; Fat 61.9% Carbohydrates 17.3%; Ash 2.8%, with a fuel value per pound of 3,205 calories.

The raw seeds become rancid after a time, the Indians say after one year, so they were usually roasted before storing. In any event, this roasting cracked or weakened the seed coat. They were then cracked between rocks, and the hulls winnowed out if this was considered necessary. Apparently at least a few hulls were considered by some tribes to improve the final flavor. In any event, the contents were ground into a meal, and used in gruel, to thicken soup, to make cakes, or in various other ways. The meal was also used to make a kind of pudding, often mixed with pulp of yucca fruits, or used as a substitute for peanut butter. Often it was mixed with cornmeal or meal from sunflower seeds.

Cracking the shells of raw or roasted piñon nuts between the teeth, separating out the kernels with the tongue and enjoying their sweet nutty flavor is an experience everyone should have. It isn't over right away; a bag of piñon nuts lasts a long while. You can even get them from vending machines as you would salted peanuts in many local areas. A nickel buys a fair sized handful.

The needles of this pine can yield a satisfactory tea by boiling them. This has to be done carefully to control the strength desired. All pines probably make an acceptable beverage, but according to Bagdonas (11A) the Boy Scouts of his acquaintance seem to prefer tea made from ponderosa pine *(Pinus ponderosa)*.

The inner bark of piñon pine and also other species was used as a starvation food by the Indians and early white people. The south side of the trunk was usually used, and the outer bark removed in the spring. Then the more tender, fleshy, mucilaginous layer between the bark and the wood was scraped or peeled off. According to report, some people even enjoy the taste of this raw. We tried it from ponderosa pine *(Pinus ponderosa)* in May and voted it flat, resinous tasting, slightly fibrous, and rather leathery. This inner bark can be cooked or dried for storage, later to be cooked or ground into a meal. We doubt if it will be a popular item except in emergencies.

Related Species:

Apparently the seeds of all pines are edible, but many are too small to be practical under ordinary conditions.

References (to numbers in the bibliography):
    A. For *Pinus edulis* and *Pinus monophylla.*
        8, 12, 17, 18, 37, 39, 43, 45, 49, 56, 57, 80, 83, 98, 115, 132,
        138, 140, 158, 173, 174, 182, 183, 192, 195, 215, 216, 218, 220,
        227, 240, 243, 249, 254, 256, 259.
    B. For other species of *Pinus.*
        5, 8, 11A, 12, 14, 26, 43, 45, 57, 58, 65, 67, 84, 100, 107, 120,
        164, 174, 182, 198, 206, 212A, 215, 216, 217, 227, 228, 254,
        256.

Prosopis juliflora (P. glandulosa, P. chilensis) HONEY MESQUITE

Description:

A shrub or small tree to 25 feet high; smallest leaf divisions (leaflets) ⅜ to 1¼ inches long; flower spike 1¾ to 2½ inches long; flowers small, greenish-yellow in color; pods 2 to 8 inches long, straight or somewhat curved, flat, often several in a cluster, not opening when ripe to let the seeds out.

Plains, washes and bottom lands along streams. From Texas and southern Kansas to California and Mexico. In the Rocky Mountain area, north to western Oklahoma, northern New Mexico and northern Arizona.

Use:

The honey mesquite at one time was an important food producer for the Indians of the Southwest, and the fruits are still used by them. The ripe pods contain numerous seeds, between which is a considerable quantity of yellowish, mealy substance that is sweet and agreeable to the taste. These pods were pounded or ground into a kind of meal, some of the seeds and coarse parts of the pods were picked out, and the resulting product used as food in various ways. For example, it might be mixed with water and eaten at once, or allowed to ferment for a time, eventually even producing a kind of beer. The meal was often moistened, made

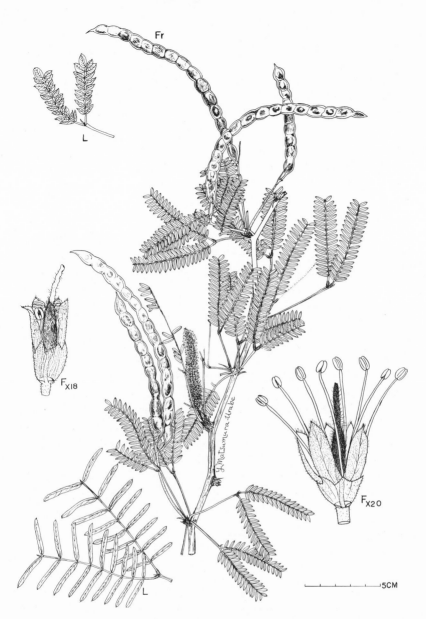

Fr

L

F
X18

J. Matsumura-Drabe

F
X20

5CM

HONEY MESQUITE *(Prosopis juliflora)*

into cakes which were baked in the sun, and stored for future use.

The dry pods could be stored in baskets or granaries of various kinds, sometimes in pits rimmed with circular stones. These ancient structures can still be seen in various parts of the Southwest (Durrell, 78). The fruits were ground as needed, and were said to keep in good condition until the next year's crop.

The isolated seeds were also pulverized into a meal, or cooked with other food products. They are said to have a pleasant lemon flavor. The pods and seeds consist of about ⅓ sugar and the meal from them is thought to be highly nutritious.

Hungry travelers can chew on the ripe, raw pods and secure at least some nutrition. The mingled acidity and sweetness may also help to quench the thirst. The macerated pods would certainly constitute a good emergency food. For example, the ground up mixture can be soaked in water or cooked in water, the liquid can then be drunk with as much of the solid material as possible. One drawback is that the pods and seeds are commonly infected by a weevil and one might find oneself consuming a mixed animal and vegetable diet. This did not seem to bother the Indians much and probably wouldn't make much difference to any starving person.

The flowers have been eaten, stripping the flowers from their central stalk by drawing them between the teeth; they are reported to be sweet to the taste. As the name suggests honey mesquite flowers are well known as a source of nectar for bees, and the plant is considered by some people to be the most important honey producing supply in the areas where it is abundant. A resinous secretion often appears from the bark which contains sugar, and this is sometimes used for candy making. Certainly, this plant has been one of the areas most important food producing source, and could be very valuable in an emergency.

Related Species:

The "screw bean" *(Prosopis pubescens)* is a related plant, but differs in the fruit characters. These fruits, instead of being straight or merely curved, are twisted into a spiral, much like a corkscrew. These pods are used in much the same way as are those of honey mesquite (Medsger, 158; Uphof, 240; Barrows, 17; Holmes, 125; Palmer, 181; Saunders, 204; Palmer, 182; Balls, 14).

References (to numbers in the bibliography):

14, 17, 18, 23, 25, 30, 43, 66, 73, 74, 77, 87, 98, 115, 116, 117, 120, 125, 132, 138, 141, 158, 164, 172, 174, 181, 182, 183, 199, 204, 216, 224, 227, 240, 242, 244, 253, 254, 256.

Quercus spp.
OAK

Description:

Shrubs or trees, but usually small trees in our area; leaves usually toothed or lobed on the margins; pollen producing flowers (staminate) in drooping catkins; fruit an acorn, nutlike, borne in a basal cup.

The various species of oaks are widespread in the United States, are very diverse in general appearance, but all of them bear the characteristic "acorn." The oaks are often abundant, especially in the southern part of the Rocky Mountain area.

Use:

The oak species of the Rocky Mountain area are variable, inclined to intergrade, and are not very well understood by botanists. They are often divided into two groups, the white oaks and the black oaks (including red oaks). These differ in several respects, but the black oaks characteristically have at least some of the leaf veins protruding from the margins as short weak bristles while this is not the case in the white oaks. We have been designating our most abundant oak as *Quercus gambelii*, commonly called "gambel oak." In general the white-oak acorns are preferred as food because they are less bitter tasting and it is fortunate that our common oaks belong to this group.

Acorns have often been used all over the world where oaks grow, and in many places furnished the main source of nourishment for certain Indian tribes. The bitter astringent taste is thought to be caused at least in part by tannin, but fortunately this can be readily removed. The Indians gathered the acorns and cracked off the outer shell, sometimes boiling or roasting the nuts first to facilitate this operation. The kernels were often ground into a meal, and could then be leached with water in various ways to remove any possible bitter taste. The simplest method was to place the meal in a very fine mesh basket or bag, and immerse it in a stream for several hours to several days. This meal was used alone to make mush, thicken soup, make bread or pancakes, or in combination with cornmeal. Sometimes wood ashes were used

5CM

OAK *(Quercus gambelii)*

to provide a kind of lye and this was used in the leaching process. This leaching often took place in holes made in sand or gravel along a stream. The dough contaminated with sand was often used in making soup; the sand grains were supposed to sink to the bottom of the container. The ground up acorns, or possibly the shells only, were often roasted, ground and used in making a beverage that was used as a substitute for coffee. The ground up kernels were sometimes boiled in water and the oil allowed to rise to the surface. This oil was skimmed off and used in various ways. Merriam (159) analyzed acorn meal and found about 20-25% fat present. The protein was about 4.5 to 5.5% and the carbohydrates around 60%. It would accordingly appear that acorn meal is a reasonably nourishing food product. The leaching process did not seem to remove very much of the essential food elements.

Gambel's oak is the only one in the area that we have tried ourselves. The different kinds of oaks not only vary a good deal in bitterness, but different individual plants differ somewhat in this respect. We have collected acorns that could be eaten raw, but even these had a faint suggestion of a bitter aftertaste. We have boiled the whole or broken kernels in water for forty-five minutes, changing the water several times. The discarded water turned yellow in color and apparently carried away the tannin, because the finished kernels were pleasant tasting. These kernels were than ground into a meal. However, the raw kernels can also be ground into a similar meal if you do not mind a slight suggestion of bitterness. Maybe this will actually taste good to you. To us, the flour was excellent, gave breads a crunchy texture and an added flavor. A mixture of half acorn flour and half wheat flour made very acceptable pancakes. Young (259) gave a recipe that sounds practical for making bread, using 2 cups of acorn meal combined with 2 cups cornmeal and 8 cups of wheat flour. Cracked acorn kernels can also be used as nuts to flavor cookies and cakes; to us they taste much like other nuts.

Some years the acorn crop is scarce and only certain clumps of oaks produce much of a yield. Since you have to run a race with birds and animals they may best be collected just as they ripen. They should be shelled at once, as many are infected with a wormlike larvae that can spoil your stored material. The kernels can be dried raw or first leached in the ways described, and then dried, in which form they keep at least for several months. We have found these dried kernels can be placed in the mouth, allowed to soak up for several minutes, and when chewed provide a palatable mouthful. This could be of value in certain emergency situations.

The acorn, when properly used, provides what we have voted to be one of the most palatable wild foods. It is often produced in abundance, is easily harvested, the individual kernel is large and easily processed. The astringent taste of many kinds is somewhat of a drawback, but this can be overcome as indicated by repeated boilings or leaching in cold water. The Indians used their common method of mixing certain clay soil with the meal to hide this taste. Fernald & Kinsey (84) suggested a nicer sounding method; they added a small amount of powdered gelatine to the acorn meal which helped to remove the bitter taste.

The oaks in our area sometimes cause poisoning to livestock which have grazed the foliage (Dayton et al., 74; Muenscher, 167; Durrell, Jensen & Klinger, 79), but there is no suggestion that the poisonous substance is in the acorn. We know of no record of human beings being poisoned by eating the fruit of oaks.

Related Species:

Any plant producing the well-known oak acorn can probably be used as food if it is properly prepared.

References (to numbers in the bibliography):

2, 3, 12, 14, 17, 18, 30, 32, 41, 43, 45, 46, 49, 52, 56, 57, 74, 75, 83, 84, 92, 93, 94, 97, 98, 112, 115, 117, 120, 132, 135, 138, 158, 159, 164, 174, 182, 183, 189, 192, 195, 198, 208, 209, 210, 211, 216, 218, 227, 240, 243, 253, 254, 259.

Yucca baccata
Yucca, Datil Yucca, Spanish Bayonet, Soapweed

Description:

Plants with short thick stems; leaves densely clustered, 16 to 30 inches long and about 2 inches wide, rigid, with a few coarse fibers on the margin as shown, and very sharp-pointed at the ends; flower cluster arising from the center of the leaves, the whole cluster 1½ to 3 feet long; flowers large, each 2 to 6 inches long, white or cream-colored; fruit about 5 to 8 inches long, be-

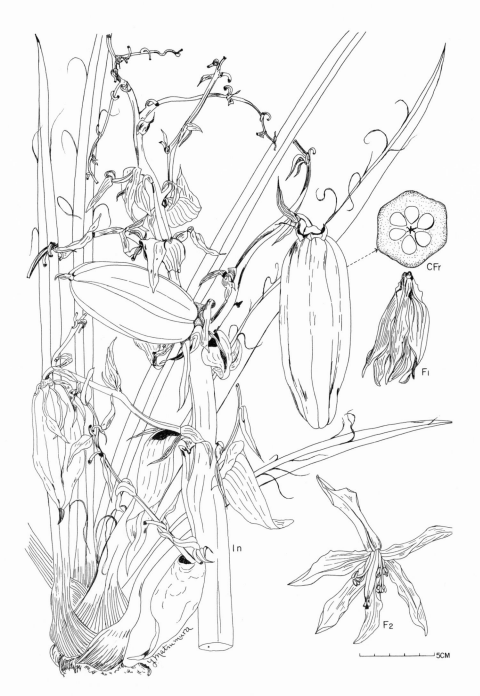

CFr

Fi

In

F2

5CM

YUCCA *(Yucca baccata)*

coming fleshy at maturity and turning purplish or yellow, resembling a short banana.

Dry plains and slopes. California east to southwestern Colorado, south to Texas and Arizona. This plant is in the southern part of our Rocky Mountain area, north to southern Utah and Colorado.

Use:

This was an important economic plant to the Indians of the Southwest, who found it useful in several ways. The species of *Yucca* in general can be separated into two groups based on the characters of the fruit. In one group the fruits are dry when ripe, separating into sections and allowing the seeds to fall out. In the second group the fruits become fleshy, somewhat on the order of an apple or a banana; in such a case the seeds do not fall out in any definite fashion, but are freed when the pulp decays away. The fruits of the datil yucca are fleshy at maturity, and have often provided a source of a sweet, palatable, succulent food in an area where other such fruits may be few and far between.

The Indians split the fruits open, then the seeds and fibers were scraped out. Sometimes they were roasted or boiled before opening, sometimes the outer peels were removed but often they were left on. The fleshy pulp was used in various ways, for example, as a filling for a pie. The Indians dried this pulp for later use by cutting it in strips and hanging it out in the sun. Sometimes the fruit was baked, the skins and seeds removed, and the fleshy part boiled down to a paste. This was molded into cakes and dried. Often the cakes were perforated by a sharp stick to facilitate rapid drying. These cakes could be later boiled and used in such things as gruel, dumplings, bread, conserve, etc.

The flowers of the datil yucca are usually abundant every year, but abundant fruit may not develop each season. The pollination system is almost unbelievable, involving a small white yucca moth that often stays throughout the day in the closed flowers. In the night time the moth carries pollen from flower to flower, forcing it on the proper receptacle (stigma) in a most deliberate looking fashion. In any event, the system apparently does not operate very effectively every year. The fruits are reported to be cathartic to some degree, particularly to those not accustomed to them, so it would be best to be somewhat moderate in eating them—at least at first. The large black seeds were roasted by the Indians and eaten whole, or were ground into a kind of meal. Partly mature fruit can be used, or these can be ripened after picking, like bananas. In fact, the Indians often gathered them before ripening in order to circumvent the animals and birds who also appreciated this desert delicacy.

The flowers of all the yuccas we have encountered are edible but the datil yucca does not rate very high in this respect according to reports and our own experience. We have boiled them and found them rather bitter and "soapy" tasting. Perhaps a change or two of water in the process would help. The Indians reported that the older flowers were the best. The young tender flower stalks can be cut out just as they are emerging from their cluster of leaves and prepared like mescal or agave (See *Agave utahensis*).

In addition, the fibers in the leaves or the actual leaves themselves were much used by the Indians for such things as sandals, leggings, mats, cord, rope, baskets, etc. To obtain the fibers they would soak the leaves in water until they became soft, then pound out the fibers with a mallet. Finally, the roots can be crushed to provide a fairly good substitute for soap. Simply mash the root portions in water and agitate the liquid to a lather. We know of several people who have used this datil yucca as soap and consider it especially good for washing the hair (See *Yucca glauca*.) Rose (197), said that yucca soap made from this plant was on the market before 1899, made by a soap company in Illinois. Certainly this is a valuable plant for general use and especially useful in an emergency.

Related Species:
Several fleshy fruited species of *Yucca* are found in the Southwest, and some have been used as food, but none come into our specific area.

References (to numbers in the bibliography):
12, 14, 18, 23, 25, 30, 43, 45, 56, 57, 67, 83, 98, 115, 117, 132, 138, 158, 164, 171, 173, 182, 183, 192, 195, 197, 199, 203, 204, 215, 218, 220, 227, 239, 240, 243, 248, 249, 254, 256.

Yucca glauca
Yucca, Small Soapweed, Spanish Bayonet

Description:

Plants perennial with short, woody stems; leaves crowded on the short stem, stiff and sharp-pointed, about ¼ to ½ inch wide, margins with fibers as shown; flower cluster 1 to as much as 5 feet long; flowers white or greenish-white in color, each 1¼ to 2 inches long; fruit about 1 to 1½ inches long and sometimes longer, becoming dry at maturity, finally splitting and letting the large, black seeds fall out.

Dry plains and slopes. Kansas and Texas, west to New Mexico and Colorado. In the Rocky Mountain area found in Colorado and New Mexico east of the Continental Divide. In the western part of the area the closely related *Yucca angustissima, Y. standleyi* and *Y. harrimaniae* take over.

Use:

There are two main classes of yucca depending on the type of mature fruit. One kind has fleshy fruits (see *Yucca baccata*), the other group has fruits dry at maturity as in the above mentioned one. However, the immature or partly developed fruit of these latter types are edible, and were once very popular with the Indians. We boiled them for 15 to 25 minutes, then sliced them and served them with butter, salt and pepper. The taste reminded us of summer squash, slightly sweet, but with a lingering background of bitterness. We have found that the most of this bitter taste can be removed by peeling the fruit before cooking. We have also baked the young fruits for 20 minutes at 300° F. wrapped in aluminum foil. They were then sliced, buttered and seasoned. The taste was somewhat bitter, but not obnoxiously so. The Indians used to bake them in the ashes of a fire; this method would be worth remembering, especially in an emergency. The pods can be sliced raw or after cooking, then dried in the sun for future use, the way the Indians did it. If the fruits are past their prime you may have to remove the seeds before you eat them, but the young pods can be eaten seeds and all. The Indian method of digging a fireless cooker (see *Agave utahensis*), can be used to prepare the fruit and also the young flower stalk. The latter is cut off just as it emerges from the leaf cluster, then cooked, and the whitish inner portion eaten.

The flowers of this and related species of yucca are eaten raw as a salad or boiled to make a potherb. Standley (216) said that in 1920 it was common to find yucca flowers for sale in the food markets of Mexico. We boiled the flowers for about 15-25 minutes, serving them with seasoning, vinegar or butter. They were very pleasant tasting to us, and certainly could be prepared in various special ways as you would spinach or asparagus.

The yucca leaves can be tied into bundles to make a primitive kind of broom, or used to make sandals, matting, etc. The leaves can be soaked in water until soft and the fibers can then be beaten out with a wooden mallet. These fibers can then be woven into cord or rope.

Finally, the roots of this yucca can be used like the other species as a substitute for soap. We dug out pieces of the root, scraped them in a basin in warm water and agitated them to form a lather; this was not very copious, but still moderately so. We would say on the basis of our experience that it was about the quality of rather poor soap, of course much cheaper and sometimes more available. Yucca soap has been marketed at various times in the past, but has never become very popular although some people like it to wash the hair. If you try this soap from yucca roots, perhaps you will agree with the Indians, as reported by Gilmore (96), who claimed "It makes the hair grow."

It can be seen that the dry-fruited yuccas may be useful in several ways, both generally and in time of emergency. It should be pointed out that the yucca leaves contain salicylic acid and the roots saponin, according to Durrell, Jensen & Klinger (79), and should never be eaten. In fact, it would be wise to eat any part of this yucca with some moderation until you are sure it has no bad effect on you; although we have never noticed any of this on ourselves. If the flowers or the young fruits are used as food they should be looked over carefully for insect adults or larvae, especi-

SPANISH BAYONET (*Yucca glauca*)

ally if you are one of those people who prefer to keep animal and vegetable foods separate on your plate.

Related Species:

We believe that any of the yuccas that have fruits which are dry and split at maturity can be used in the same way as the small soapweed. Some of these in our area are listed following the description above.

References (to numbers in the bibliography for this and related species):

12, 23, 43, 79, 83, 84, 96, 98, 117, 132, 158, 173, 195, 215, 216, 220, 240, 242, 254.

Chapter IX: MISCELLANEOUS—BEVERAGES, FLAVORS, SMOKING, NIBBLES, ETC.
(like Tea)

This chapter concerns itself with certain native plants that have been used in various ways connected (at least in some degree) with the general subject of edibility, but which have not been covered elsewhere. Perhaps you may wonder how tobacco substitutes got into the chapter. The reason is that some people under survival conditions may actually find these plants more useful in ministering to their bodily needs than those providing food. We suggest that smokers try to work in such substitutes as a mixture with the tobacco they have on hand, before their supply is completely exhausted. This will gradually accustom them to the taste of the new plant; some do take a lot of getting used to before they are really appreciated.

The use of native plant flavors is largely a matter of personal preference. Some of the ones highly recommended to us by others have proved to be too strong, even to the point of tasting objectionable. We suggest that you give them a fair trial over a rather extended period of time; you may finally learn to like them. In any event, they will certainly provide a unique flavor you may not have experienced before.

Many more plants can be used as a substitute for tea than are mentioned here. It is surprising the number of species that have been used to brew beverages; you may wish to experiment a bit yourself. Avoid known poisonous plants, of course. The part used should be dried quickly in the shade, and then stored in tight containers for future use. The young leaves or fresh flowers should be selected, if these are to be the parts to be used. The general rule for making "tea" is to use $\frac{1}{2}$ to 1 teaspoon of the dried material to a cup of boiling water. If fresh material is used it will take about twice as much. Otherwise, use about the same procedure as you would in brewing commercial tea. Some of us enjoy mixing the product of several plants, often adding a little of commercial tea. These substitutes make a more or less agreeable hot drink, but it must be admitted that they may lack, for you, the stimulating quality of the original tea. Some grocery stores take pride in stocking a wide variety of unusual tea substitutes; we know of several of them in this area. The teas we noticed for sale here were packaged by the Select Dietary Products Co., P. O. Box 71648, Los Angeles, California, but surely other companies have had the same idea.

Many trees besides the famous sugar maple produce a sap that can be collected in the early spring and boiled down to form a reasonably palatable syrup. The sap itself may contain a relatively small amount of sugar, but many believe that a gallon concentrates down to contain about the nourishment required for a small meal. Besides the maple *(Acer* spp.) and the boxelder *(Acer negundo),* you might try collecting the sap of various species of ash *(Fraxinus)* and birch *(Betula).* This sap in the early spring may prove of value in times of food shortage, at least under favorable conditions.

By "nibbles" we mean certain portions of the plant that can be picked along the way and nibbled for flavor or tang. Plants producing chewing gum and those having thirst-quenching properties may also find a place in this chapter. The number of possible plants we could mention is legion, and it is too bad that so few can be included here. The use of such plants is usually more casual than critical, so the real, important food-producing ones have to take precedent.

This chapter includes plants producing the following: chewing gum, fibers, smoking, tealike, flavors, nibbles, thirst quenchers, down, paint, tonic, bark, soap, flowers, cord, sugar, etc.

Plants with some of the uses described here but illustrated or described in another chapter.

Agave utahensis IV. *Plantago major* III.
Apocynum cannabinum II. *Prunus virginiana* VII.

Arctium minus VI.
Asclepias speciosa IV.
Asparagus officinalis IV.
Brassica nigra III.
Cannabis sativa II.
Capsella bursa-pastoris III.
Cirsium spp. VI.
Cleome serrulata III.
Epilobium angustifolium III.
Equisetum arvense IV.
Fragaria spp. VII.
Gaultheria humifusa VII.
Juniperus scopulorum VII.
Perideridia gairdneri VI.
Pinus edulis VIII.

Rhus trilobata VII.
Rosa spp. VII.
Rubus parviflorus VII.
Rubus strigosus VII.
Rumex acetosella V.
Rumex crispus III.
Sambucus spp. VII.
Taraxacum officinale III.
Typha latifolia VI.
Urtica dioica III.
Vaccinium spp. VII.
Viola spp. V.
Vitis spp. VII.
Yucca baccata VIII.
Yucca glauca VIII.

Acer negundo (A. nuttallii, A. negundo var. *violaceum, A. interius, A. negundo* var. *interius, Negundo interius, N. nuttallii, N. kingii, Rulac negundo)* BOXELDER

Description:

Trees with trunks and bark usually gnarled and irregular; leaves compound with 3 to 5 leaflets arranged on a central stalk (pinnately compound), the leaflets about 2 to 4 inches long; fruit double, each part with a membranous wing up to 2 inches long.

These trees are widely distributed over the United States and in the Rocky Mountains, often along streams in valleys and canyons.

Use:

Several different kinds of trees were used by the Indians as a source of syrup and sugar, but the various species of maple were probably the general favorites. The early white settlers learned the procedure and the maple-syrup industry developed, particularly in New England, using for the most part *Acer saccharum*

In x4
♂

Fr

In x4
♀

5CM

BOXELDER *(Acer negundo)*

(sugar maple). The boxelder tree has also been extensively used for this purpose, especially in areas out of the range of the sugar maple. (Uphof, 240; Blankinship, 26; Hedrick, 117; Vestal & Schultes, 242; Gilmore, 95; Medsger, 158; Vliet, 243; Confar, 57.)

Bore a hole on the sunny side of the trunk into the sapwood, about three feet from the ground, using an auger if this is available, then insert a wooden peg with a groove in the upper side. A can or pail may be hung or set under the spigot to collect the sap. The trees can be tapped anytime from New Years Day until the leaves appear, but the sap flows best on warm sunny days following frosty nights. This sap can be boiled down, using only moderate heat in order not to scorch it. The Indians placed the sap in bark or wooden vessels, and boiled it down by adding hot stones, or allowed the sap to freeze overnight and in the morning threw off the frozen water leaving the syrup at the bottom (Fernald & Kinsey, 84). It takes patience to carry out the boiling process, as several hours may be required and the shrinkage is alarming, often 30 to 1. However, the resulting syrup is well worth the trouble, and additional boiling at higher temperatures forms an acceptable sugar. Many mouth watering recipes for sauces, puddings and candies are in print (See Gibbons, 92; Coon, 58), as well as some for making maple beer (Gibbons, 92; Fernald & Kinsey, 84).

Related Species:
Any species of maple would be worth trying in this connection. For example, *Acer grandidentatum* is in our range. It might be worth experimenting with birch and ash trees, which have been utilized to some extent in syrup production. The bark of the maples and boxelder has been used as emergency food, and the young shoots of *Acer glabrum* have been used like asparagus. This latter is the common mountain maple in the Rocky Mountains and the shoots and inner bark have often been used in emergencies (Confar, 57; Vliet, 243). However, it is usually shrubby in habit, and the trunks would probably be too small to tap for the sap.

References (to numbers in the bibliography):
18, 58, 84, 92, 93, 98, 138, 140.

Allium cernuum (A. recurvatum, A. neomexicanum) ONION, NODDING ONION

Description:

Plants with characteristic "onion" or "garlic" odor, growing from underground bulbs of varying size, these usually around 1/2 to 3/4 inch in diameter; stems from 6 inches up to 2 feet tall; leaves flat to nearly round; flowers in clusters, with each individual flower stalk meeting at a common point (umbel), the cluster nodding as shown; individual flowers whitish to rose in color, about 1/8 to 1/4 inch long.

This onion is widely distributed throughout the United States and in the Rocky Mountains. It grows on plains, hills and mountains, usually on open ground below 10,000 feet elevation.

Allium geyeri (A. funiculosum, A. dictyotum, A. pikeanum) ONION, GEYER ONION

This onion looks (and smells) much like the preceding one, except the flower cluster (umbel) does not nod but is nearly or quite upright on the main stalk. It is more likely to be restricted to the Rocky Mountain area, where it may be locally common.

Use:

The wild onions can always be told by the flower cluster (umbel), the underground bulb and the characteristic "onion" odor. This latter varies in strength and desirable quality among different species. Some observers, including the author, have noticed a fetid smell in some species which to us is definitely objectionable. This may partially disappear in the cooking process, and in our area wild onion species are definitely worth a trial by anyone. The Air Force Manual (2) stated that wild onions are never poisonous. However, cultivated onions sometimes cause poisoning to livestock (Durrell, Jensen & Klinger, 79) and any onion when grazed by milk cows may impart an "onion" or "garlic" flavor to the milk.

The bulbs or leaves of wild onions can be used as a flavoring to soups, stews and meats. The tops and bulbs can also be boiled

ONION *(Allium cernuum & Allium geyeri)*

or fried as the main food ingredient of the meal. Bourke (30), reminded us that General George Crook, on his "Starvation March"
down the Yellowstone in 1876, said that wild onions formed a
welcome addition to the food supply. Hedrick (117) stated that

nodding onion *(A. cernuum)*, and the eastern wild garlic *(A. cana-dense)*, formed almost the entire food source of Marquette and his party on their journey from Green Bay, Wisconsin to the present site of Chicago in the fall of 1674. The juice of wild onions can be boiled down to a thick syrup, and has been used as a cure for colds and throat irritations.

Wild onions can be used in place of their cultivated relatives in cooking, and for the same general purposes. Various recipes have been published for using them in salads, for frying them, for making soups, and for pickling the bulbs (Gibbons, 92; Little-bee, 146), but anyone who uses the cultivated varieties much will have their own favorite methods of preparation for onions.

The Indians used wild onions extensively and apparently still do in many areas. They constitute both a readily identifiable and available emergency food. The bulbs can be dried and stored for future use should this be necessary. We have seen people out collecting wild onions and blithely gathering up death camas with them! (See *Zygadenus*.) Such a mistake could be fatal (11A).

Related Species:
Any wild onion would be worth a trial, but you may find certain species or varieties are particularly desirable.

References (to numbers in the bibliography):
2, 5, 11A, 18, 26, 30, 43, 49, 56, 57, 58, 67, 79, 83, 84, 92, 93, 94, 97, 99, 107, 115, 117, 119, 138, 146, 148, 158, 162, 167, 173, 195, 198, 206, 217, 218, 228, 239, 240, 243, 249.

Arctostaphylos uva-ursi
BEARBERRY, KINNIKINNICK, MANZANITA

Description:
The plant has woody prostrate main stems; leaves are evergreen, without hairs and rather shining above, $3/8$ to 1 inch long; flowers about $1/6$ or $1/5$ inch long, white to pink, shaped like a narrow mouthed vase or urn (not shown in drawing); fruit bright red, round, $1/4$ to $2/5$ inch wide.

BEARBERRY *(Arctostaphylos uva-ursi)*

This plant grows in shade or at the edge of forests. Widely distributed in North America, especially in the mountains and the northern part of the United States. It is rather common in the Rocky Mountain area and has recently been found in northeastern Arizona.

Use:

The very attractive fruits are much used for decorations around fall or Christmas. A piece of the twig, with the bright red berries contrasting with the shining green of the evergreen leaves, makes an attractive table decoration. This fruit has been eaten by the Indians and white settlers, but the seeds are rather large and the pulp is mealy and dry. It can be eaten raw as an emergency food, especially in late fall or winter when little else may be available. It is better cooked, and jelly has been made from it. Colyer (56), reported making something resembling cranberry sauce by boiling the fruit for 15 minutes and adding sugar. It probably would be better if the seeds were strained out and it was cooked longer.

This was served hot with meat and added to the general flavor of the meal. All in all, this fruit cannot be considered very desirable as food, and it does seem a shame to use such lovely objects in quantities.

The evergreen leaves have long been utilized as a substitute for tobacco, often used mixed with it. The leaves are somewhat bitter tasting when fresh and have been chewed in moderation by some people to prevent thirst, since they seem to cause the saliva to flow (Sears, 206). Reagan (190, 191, 193), mentioned that several Indian tribes smoked the leaves and the general effect was an intoxication due to the narcotic content. Kephart (140), stated that the leaves were milder in summer than in winter. A smoker deprived of his favorite "weed" could gather the leaves, dry and toast them, and could surely use them at least in moderation for smoking. Bearberry-leaf tea is on the market and it is probably from this or a related species.

Related Species:

The Rocky Mountain area has several more upright species of *Arctostaphylos* which could be tried in the same way as our more common prostrate plant.

References (to numbers in the bibliography):

5, 14, 18, 32, 56, 57, 74, 75, 79, 84, 95, 98, 103, 107, 117, 119, 125, 140, 158, 164, 181, 182, 187, 190, 191, 193, 194, 206, 214, 217, 228, 240, 243, 256.

Ceanothus spp.
NEW JERSY TEA, TOBACCO BRUSH, SNOWBRUSH

(Several species occur in the Rocky Mountain area and since they are rather similar in appearance and use they are discussed together here.)

Description:

Shrubs about 1 to 9 feet tall; branches spiny or spineless; leaves with margins smooth or toothed, up to 3 inches long, but often much shorter, varying from rather narrow to broad, as shown in

350

F
×10

5CM

NEW JERSY TEA *(Ceanothus velutinus)*

the drawing; flowers in clusters, the petals narrow at base and white in color; fruit a dry pod (capsule). All the species have rather characteristic leaf veins and the flowers have the stamens (which bear the pollen) coming out directly in front of (opposite to) the narrow petals.

Species of this genus are widespread in the United States, usually growing on slopes and mountainsides, often in partial shade.

Use:

All the species of this group (Genus) are famous as substitutes for tea, and some kinds were widely used during the American Revolution, such as the two species, *Ceanothus americanus* and *C. ovatus*. The latter species comes into the eastern part of the Rocky Mountain area and we have often tried it as a beverage. We gathered the leaves and flowers at any time during the growing season (but some recommend collecting them when young), and allowed them to dry out. The leaves were stripped from the branches by pulling the shoot through the closed hand. The leaves and flowers were steeped in boiling water for about five minutes. The liquid was yellowish in color and tasted similar to tea, but seemed to us to be milder and sweeter. *C. ovatus* certainly makes a very pleasant tasting drink. We have also tried the leaves of the spiny *C. fendleri,* but did not like the resulting beverage as well. The species pictured, *C. velutinus,* has leaves covered with a shiny resinous coat and probably would be better as a substitute for tobacco than tea.

Related Species:

C. velutinus, C. fendleri and *C. ovatus* are fairly common in

the Rocky Mountain area.

References (to numbers in the bibliography) :

43, 56, 57, 58, 74, 84, 92, 95, 99, 127, 132, 138, 158, 216, 219.

Cichorium intybus
CHICORY, SUCCORY

Description:

Perennial plants with deep taproots; stems 1 to 3 feet tall; leaves both basal and on the stems, 2 to 6 inches long; flowers in heads like a dandelion, but blue in color.

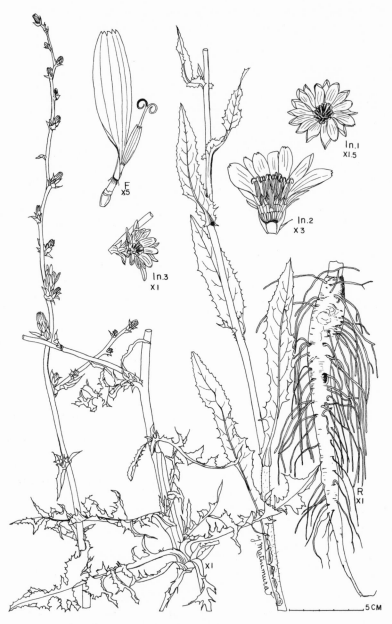

CHICORY *(Cichorium intybus)*

Naturalized from Europe and now a common weed in Canada and the United States. Sometimes it is very abundant in the Rocky Mountain area, particularly at lower elevations.

Use:

This is a plant of many uses and has been cultivated in various parts of the world, particularly in Europe and in the state of Michigan in this country. It is famous as an adulterant or even as a substitute for coffee. The thick taproots can be dug at any time (some say they are better just after the flowering period is over or in the fall), and then scrubbed thoroughly or the outer layer peeled off. They can then be sliced, roasted in an oven, and ground into a coarse powder. This powder is supposed to give a desirable bitterish taste when mixed with coffee, at least according to some people. This mixture is much used in some areas, particularly in the southern part of the United States, and often appears for sale in the markets. We have tried the blend and found it very acceptable. Ground chicory can be purchased (try coffee or tea companies in any fair sized city), and added to coffee in any desired proportion. It can also be used to season other food, such as stews and gravies. Heinr. Franck Sons, Port Huron, Mich., a company who raise and package chicory, issued a booklet "Forty-five Tested Recipes," available for five cents at this writing. In some parts of the world the young roots are boiled and eaten like carrots or parsnips.

The young leaves and shoots are used raw as a salad, especially after blanching the plant. This can be done with heaped up earth, straw, or by covering the very young plants with canvas or baskets. The yellowish shoots that develop in the absence of light will be more tender and lack much of the bitter taste so characteristic of the green plant. Roots can be dug in the fall and brought in and planted in earth in the cellar. When well watered these roots may produce sprouts during the winter that can be used as a welcome addition to the table. The young leaves and shoots can be used as "greens" like the dandelion plant. It would be wise to change waters two or three times, and cook the material longer than one would spinach, but chicory is justly famous in this respect.

Related Species:

The familiar endive of the markets is either a cultivated variety of common chicory or at least a related species *(Cichorium endivia).* Its piquant rather bitter taste is well known and relished by many of us.

References (to numbers in the bibliography):

2, 13, 18, 38, 42, 53, 58, 62, 79, 84, 92, 93, 99, 102, 107, 112, 117, 124, 129, 132, 134, 138, 140, 151, 158, 168, 181, 194, 196, 212A, 219, 225, 228, 240.

Cornus stolonifera (C. instoloneus, Svida instolonea, S. interior, C. sericea)
REDOSIER DOGWOOD, RED WILLOW

Description:

Woody shrubs up to 12 feet tall (but usually about 3 to 6 feet); branches often prostrate and rooting, the twigs a dull but still an attractive red in color; leaves about 2 to 3½ inches long; flowers white, the petals about ⅛ inch long; fruit white, ¼ to ⅜ inch in diameter.

Found in rather moist ground in valleys, often along streams in the northern part of the United States, but south in the Rocky Mountains to Mexico.

Use:

This was one of the chief substitutes for smoking tobacco used by the Indians and the early pioneers. They used the leaves to some degree, but mostly the inner bark. They selected both the young and the older twigs that still retained the thin red bark. This outer bark was shaved off with a thin knife, discarded, and the soft greenish inner bark scraped away and utilized. Sometimes the inner bark was only partially scraped away and then allowed to hang in shreds. These twigs were toasted before a fire and this inner bark used at once. It was usually mixed with tobacco in various proportions. Kephart (140) says two parts of bark were used to one of tobacco. We have never tried it ourselves, but it is

REDOSIER DOGWOOD *(Cornus stolonifera)*

said to be aromatic and pungent, giving a narcotic effect approaching stupefaction. It certainly should be used in moderation, at least at first.

Related Species:

Cornus canadensis is so unlike the above that one would hardly suspect a relationship. It is a nonwoody plant not over 1 foot tall; the leaves are in a single circle near the apex of the plant. The flowers are in a ball-like head and the fruits are red and fleshy. It is found well scattered over most of the northern part of the United States. The berries are often used raw or cooked, as well as the leaves for smoking. (Hedrick, 117; Reagan, 191; Gillespie, 93; Smith, 208; Fernald & Kinsey, 84; Densmore, 75; Harris, 112.)

References (to numbers in the bibliography):
    26, 49, 95, 103, 117, 140, 216, 240.

Ephedra spp.
Jointfir, Desert Tea, Mexican Tea, Mormon Tea, Brigham Young Tea, Jointpine

Several species grow in the western part of the Rocky Mountains. They are quite similar in general appearance and the following description applies to all of them.

Description:

Branching shrubs, usually about 8 inches to 4 feet tall; twigs green to yellowish green, jointed-looking, rather rigid and wiry; leaves 2 or more at one circle on the stem, very small and inconspicuous, reduced to teeth; flowers not colorful or very conspicuous; seeds up to $\frac{1}{2}$ inch long.

Sandy or rocky plains and canyons from the Rocky Mountains westward to the Pacific.

Use:

As the common names suggest, this plant has been extensively used by both the Indians and white people for making a tea.

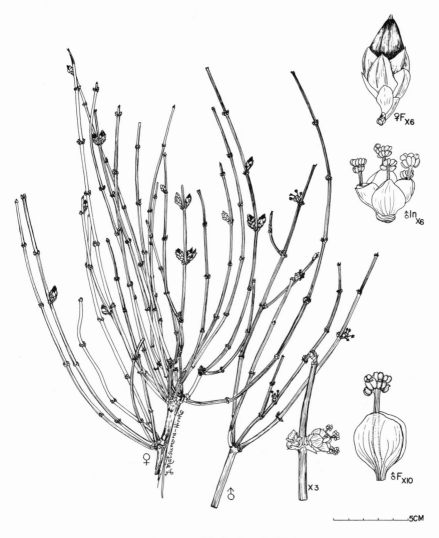

$♀F_{X6}$

$♂In_{X6}$

$♂F_{X10}$

⊢————————⊣5CM

JOINTFIR *(Ephedra viridis)*

Sometimes it was taken as a tonic for its reputed medicinal effects, but many persons used it rather regularly by preference as a beverage. The greenish twigs were gathered, and were either used fresh or allowed to dry for later use. We have tried them both ways and can see little difference in the flavor. These twigs were boiled in water for just a few minutes, and the mixture allowed to steep for 5 to 15 minutes. The liquid took on a yellowish or pinkish color, and had a very acceptable odor and taste. You should experiment with varying amounts to suit your taste, but we suggest you start by using a small cup of broken stems to 6 or 8 cups of water. The taste may take a bit of getting used to, and we have never learned to like it quite as well as we do ordinary tea. But it certainly does make a very acceptable substitute. The Ute Indians often roasted the twigs before using them, and claimed this improved the flavor (Colyer, 56). The plants seem to contain certain alkaloids such as pseudoephedrin and tannin (Kearney & Peebles, 138), but apparently our species does not produce the well-known drug "ephedrin," as does the related *E. sinica* of China. Many people have written to us inquiring about this matter, sometimes they are interested in the possibility of harvesting the plant commercially for the drug, or often they are wondering if prolonged use of the tea might have harmful effects. We know of no immediate or cumulative ill effects from using the tea, but this does not mean it could not occasionally happen.

The Indians roasted the seeds of jointfir and ate them whole, or ground them into a meal or flour. The bread made from this product is said to be bitter tasting. These plants are often abundant in the desert area, just where an emergency food and a stimulating beverage might be desperately needed.

Related Species:

All the species of *Ephedra* should be tried, and though they may vary somewhat in taste of the product, we would expect them all to be good. We have only tried the one species, *E. viridis,* but *E. torreyana, E. nevadensis* and *E. californica* are recorded in the literature as being acceptable.

References (to numbers in the bibliography):

14, 17, 18, 56, 73, 74, 83, 98, 132, 138, 158, 220, 227, 240, 254.

Geum rivale
AVENS, WATER AVENS

Description:

Underground parts brownish and rather creeping; stems 10 inches to 2 feet tall, usually unbranched; flowers 1 to 4 to a stem;

AVENS *(Geum rivale)*

petals ¼ to ⅜ inch long, flesh-colored, or sometimes yellow-tinged with purple veins.

Low open ground in meadows and near swamps. Newfoundland to British Columbia, south to New Jersey, Missouri and New Mexico.

Use:

The fresh or dried reddish-purple or brownish rootstocks of this plant can be used to make a beverage similar to chocolate, at least in color. Cut the dried or fresh root stalk into pieces, boil them as much as needed in water, add sugar, and you have an acceptable beverage. Some folks claim the taste is a bit astringent, but this chocolate-like drink has been very popular with some people. It may be that you will decide that it forms a welcome variation from the "tea" that can be made from so many other wild species.

Related Species:
None.

References (to numbers in the bibliography):
84, 93, 132, 158, 163, 181, 194, 204.

Nicotiana spp.
WILD TOBACCO

Description:

Annual or perennial plants; leaf edges smooth or wavy, surface usually rather sticky-hairy; flowers tubular, but more or less flaring near the ends, sometimes yellow, but more commonly white to greenish-white.

Plains and valleys, common along sandy washes. The various species widespread throughout the United States.

Use:

The leaves of most wild tobacco species contain nicotine, and are reported to cause poisoning to livestock at certain times, although animals usually avoid these plants. The Indians, braver

WILD TOBACCO *(Nicotiana attenuata)*

than the animals, dried the leaves and smoked them in various ways, often as a ritual, this being a part of a ceremony, sometimes as a religious rite, occasionally as an offering of respect to their superiors, or even to cure some disease (Ginter, 97). They either cultivated some kinds of the plant or at least encouraged the plants to grow nearby. The use of cultivated strains of tobacco among white people is too well known to need discussion.

Related Species:

The following species are in the Rocky Mountain area and would be available for smoking, *Nicotiana attenuata, N. trigono-phylla, N. rustica* and possibly others.

References (to numbers in the bibliography):
14, 65, 85, 97, 132, 138, 167, 220, 239, 240, 249.

Osmorhiza spp.
SWEET CICELY, SWEETROOT

(We have several species in our area, but they unite in having the following characteristics.)

Description:

Perennial plants with thickened, often clustered roots, these latter structures, along with the fruits, have a sweet anise-like or licorice-like odor; stems leafy, up to 3½ feet tall; flowers yellowish, greenish-white, in roundish to flat-topped clusters (umbels); fruit narrow, tapering at one or both ends, in most species readily penetrating and clinging to wool, hair or clothing (as in Fr 2 in the illustration).

Shaded or partly shaded areas, often on slopes and in valleys. The various species widespread in the United States.

Use:

The roots have often been used in flavoring other foods because of their sweet licorice or anise flavor. This is certainly less pronounced in some species for we once collected *O. obtusa* in the

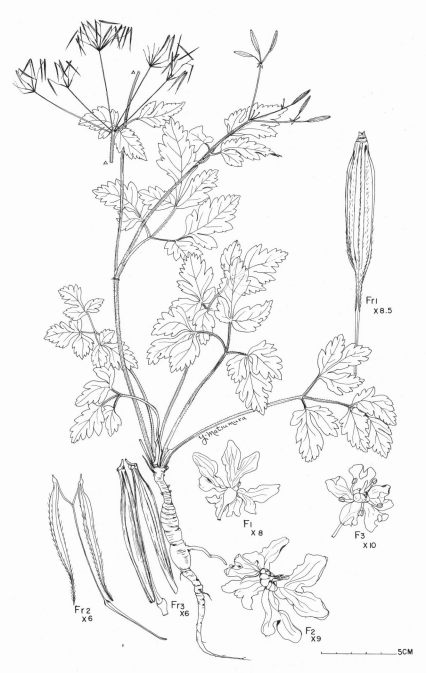

Fr1
x8.5

Fr2
x6

Fr3
x6

F1
x8

F3
x10

F2
x9

y.matsumura

5CM

SWEET CICELY *(Osmorhiza obtusa)*

latter part of June, boiled the roots for 15 minutes, peeled off the rind and ate the contents without being bothered by too strong a flavor. They were starchy, tasted much like parsnips and were very palatable to us. We also tried them in the middle of October and found the flavor more pronounced, but they were still edible, even in the raw state. The roots and fruits were dried and tried as seasoning, but lost most of their characteristic flavor in the process.

On the other hand, *O. occidentalis* had a much stronger odor and taste, probably too strong to allow eating the roots for food. Accordingly, these roots were dried, stored, and later scraped or pulverized into a powder, this to be used as a flavoring. This flavoring can be utilized in various ways. Douglass (77A) suggested the following recipe for cookies:

Sweet Cicely Cookies

Prepare powdered root liquid for the recipe by taking 2 teaspoons of powdered root and adding this to 4½ tablespoons of boiling water. Drain this through a cloth or fine strainer. If a stronger flavor is desired you can use 3 teaspoons of the powder instead.

½ cup shortening	2 cups enriched flour
¾ cup sugar	¼ teaspoon salt
1 egg	½ teaspoon baking powder
2 teaspoons powdered root liquid	4½ teaspoons milk

Thoroughly cream shortening and sugar. Add egg and beat well. Stir in the sweet cicely powdered root liquid. Add sifted dry ingredients alternately with milk; mix thoroughly. Roll dough ⅛ inch thick on a lightly floured surface. Cut into desired size and bake on ungreased cookie sheet in a moderate oven (375 degrees F.) for 12 minutes or until delicately brown. Makes about 1½ dozen large cookies which we thought were delicious.

The sweet cicely root apparently can be gathered for flavoring at any season of the year, including the winter time, providing of course the ground is not frozen.

The seeds (really fruits) of these plants, at least in some species, can be dried and used as seasoning. They are sometimes nibbled raw when they are still fleshy, and are often sweet and flavorful. We do not have too many good native plants for seasoning, and this provides a pleasant taste to most people.

Related Species:

Any species should be tried, but *O. obtusa* and *O. occidentalis* seem to be the favorites.

References (to numbers in the bibliography):

56, 77A, 84, 93, 158.

Rhus glabra (R. cismontana, Schmaltzia glabra) SMOOTH SUMAC

Description:

Shrubs up to 6½ feet tall (usually 1 to 3), often growing in dense patches; leaf divisions (leaflets) 2 to 5 inches long; flowers borne in a large pyramid-like cluster about 4 to 8 inches long; petals very small, whitish to greenish yellow in color; fruits berry-like, but rather dry, each one about ⅛ inch long, roundish, densely covered with short red hairs.

Valley slopes and along streams. This plant is widespread in Canada and the United States, reaching into Mexico. It is to be expected anywhere in the Rocky Mountain area, especially in the foothills or the lower mountains.

Use:

The red velvety berries have long been used to make a beverage something on the order of lemonade; they have an agreeable, acid taste when properly prepared. The red covering of hairs is said to contain this acid principle, and the preparation of the drink is simple. Some authorities suggested putting the fruit cluster in boiling water for a short time. Others advised against this, stating that too much tannin is extracted by the hot water. From our own experience we would agree with this latter advice. We select ripe, insect free clusters, and wash them briefly in water. The fruits can be placed in a cloth bag, but it is simpler to put them in the

5 CM

SMOOTH SUMAC (*Rhus glabra*)

water directly, crushing them somewhat with a spoon. The liquid
can then be strained through a cloth to remove the hairs, etc. A
good proportion to start with would be one cluster to a glass of
water. Add sugar to suit the individual taste, and ice cubes if they

are available. The color is pink to rose and the flavor is agreeable to most of us. It may be wise not to prepare the drink too far in advance as it becomes rather rancid tasting after an hour or more. The Indians were said to dry the berries for winter use. They would then soak them in water, heat the liquid and then enjoy a kind of hot lemonade.

Some claim that the fruits are edible raw, but we have never found them good eating. It is said that some tribes of Indians used the young shoots as a salad (Barkley & Sweet, 15). They also utilized the dried leaves as a tobacco substitute. In any event, smooth sumac can be a rather useful plant.

Related Species:

The staghorn sumac, *Rhus typhina* (also called *R. hirta)*, is a related plant of the eastern United States; its fruits are also used to make a beverage.

References (to numbers in the bibliography):

13, 15, 57, 58, 84, 92, 93, 98, 99, 117, 120, 127, 132, 138, 140, 158, 179, 195, 209, 211, 216, 219, 227, 240, 242.

Thelesperma megapotamicum (T. gracile)
GREENTHREAD, NAVAJO TEA

Description:

Perennial plants from deep roots; stems 1 to 2⅔ feet tall, branched; flowers clustered in heads, yellowish to brownish in color; fruits seedlike, each with 2 barbed awns at the apex, at least when young.

On open plains and slopes. Nebraska west to Wyoming and Utah, south to Texas, Arizona and Mexico, also in South America.

Use:

The Indians used this plant to make a kind of tea. They often tied the plants into small bundles, and dried them in the shade. These bundles could then be stored for the winter, and the tea was prepared by dropping one of them into boiling water. Some

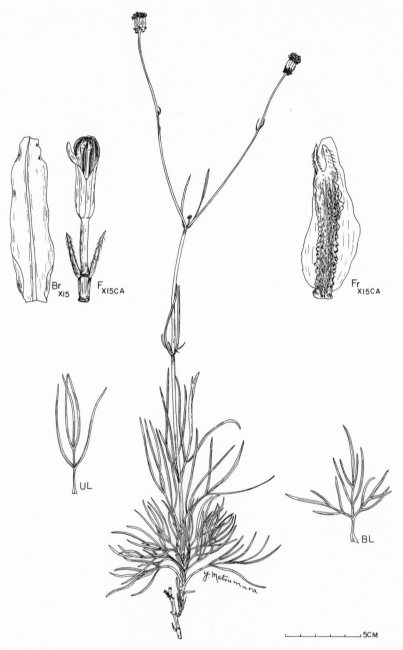

GREENTHREAD (*Thelesperma megapotamicum*)

writers claim the plant was used before flowering, but we have tried it when the heads were mature and found it made an excellent beverage in that stage. The material leaches out rapidly, so a few minutes of boiling will be sufficient. In fact, we have prepared the tea by pouring boiling water on the plant portion and letting it steep for just a few minutes. The color of the tea is greenish-yellow to dark yellow-red, and when properly made it is delicious—we think the best of the native teas. You may discover just a suggestion of "mint" in its aftertaste.

Related Species:

Two other species of the southern part of the Rocky Mountain area are used to make a beverage in this same way as the one described above. They are *Thelesperma subnudum* and *T. longipes,* sometimes also known as "Navajo tea" or as "cota." (Underhill, 239; Kearney & Peebles, 138; Whiting, 249; Wooton & Standley, 254; Elmore, 83; Bartlett, 18).

References (to numbers in the bibliography):

12, 18, 83, 85, 138, 157, 195, 239, 240, 248, 249, 259.

BIBLIOGRAPHY

1. Abrams, L.

An Illustrated Flora of the Pacific States, Washington, Oregon and California, Stanford University Press, 4 Volumes. 1940-1960 (last Vol. by Abrams & Ferris).

2. Air Force, U.S. Department of

Survival, Air Force Manual Number 64-5, Department of the Air Force, Washington 25, D. C., December, 1952.

3. Anderson, E.

"White-oak Acorns as Food," *Missouri Botanical Garden Bulletin,* 12:32-33. 1924.

4. Anderson, J. P.

"Plants Used by the Eskimo of the Northern Bering Sea & Arctic Regions of Alaska," *American Journal of Botany,* 26(9):714-16. 1939.

5. Anderson, J. R.

Trees and Shrubs, Food, Medicinal, and Poisonous Plants of British Columbia, Published by Dept. of Education. Victoria, B. C., 1925.

6. Angier, B.

How to go Live in the Woods for $10.00 a Month, The Stackpole Company, Harrisburg, Pennsylvania, 1959. General Delivery, Cambria, California.

7. Angier, B.

Living off the Country—How to Stay Alive in the Woods, The Stackpole Company, Harrisburg, Pennsylvania, General Delivery, Cambria, California, 1956.

8. Angier, B.

Wilderness Cookery, The Stackpole Company, Harrisburg, Pennsylvania, 1961.

9. *Annual Report of the Board of Regents of The Smithsonian Institution,* Washington, Government Printing Office, 1912.

10. Avery, A. G., S. Satina, J. Rietsema

Blakeslee: The Genus Datura, The Ronald Press Company, New York, 1959.

11. Bacon, A. E.

"An Experiment with the Fruit of Red Baneberry," *Rhodora,* 5:77-79. 1903.

11A. Bagdonas, C. R.

"Observations on Edible Native Plants of Colorado" (Unpublished). 1964.

12. Bailey, F. L.

"Navajo Foods and Cooking Methods," *American Anthropologist*, 42(2):270-290, April-June, 1940.

13. Bale, R. O.
Outdoor Living, Burgess Publishing Co., Minneapolis, Minn., 1961.

14. Balls, E. K.
Early Uses of California Plants, University of California Press, Berkeley & Los Angeles, 1965.

15. Barkley, F. A. and H. R. Sweet
"The Use of the Sumacs by the American Indian," *Missouri Botanical Garden Bulletin*, 25:154-158, 1937.

16. Barrett, O. W.
"The Food Plants of Puerto Rico," *Journal of Department of Agriculture Puerto Rico*, 9(2):61-208, 1925.

17. Barrows, D. P.
The Ethno-botany of the Coahuilla Indians of Southern California, Chicago, University of Chicago Press, 1900, 82 pp.

18. Bartlett, K.
"Edible Wild Plants of Northern Arizona," *Plateau* 16(1):11-17, 1943. Northern Arizona Society of Science and Art Museum of Northern Arizona, Flagstaff.

19. Beath, O. A., C. S. Gilbert, and H. F. Eppson
"The Use of Indicator Plants in Locating Seleniferous Areas in Western United States," I and II. *American Journal of Botany* 26:257-269, 296-315, 1939.

20. Beath, O. A., C. S. Gilbert, and H. F. Eppson
"The Use of Indicator Plants in Locating Seleniferous Areas in Western United States," III Further Studies. *American Journal of Botany*, 27:564-573. July, 1940.

21. Beath, O. A., C. S. Gilbert, H. F. Eppson, & I. Rosenfeld
Poisonous Plants & Livestock Poisoning, University of Wyoming, Wyoming Agricultural Experiment Station, Bul. 324. July, 1953.

22. Bell, W. H., and E. F. Castetter
"The Utilization of Mesquite and Screwbean by the Aborigines in the American Southwest" *Ethnobiological Studies of the American Southwest V*, Biological Series, Vol. 5, No. 2, University of New Mexico Bulletin 314, October 1, 1937.

23. Bell, W. H., and E. F. Castetter
"The Utilization of Yucca, Sotol and Beargrass by the Aborigines in the American Southwest." *Ethnobiological Studies in the American Southwest VII*, University of New Mexico Bulletin, Whole Number 372, Biological Series, Vol. 5, No. 5, December 1, 1941.

24. Bennion, D.
"Ever Eat Sego Lily Roots?" *The Desert News*, Sec. 3, Pt. V, March 23, 1935.

25. Benson, L. and R. A. Darrow
The Trees and Shrubs of the Southwestern Deserts, The University of Arizona Press, Tucson and the University of New Mexico Press, Albuquerque, March 15, 1954.

26. Blankinship, J. W.
Native Economic Plants of Montana, Montana Agricultural College Experiment Station Bulletin 56, Bozeman, Montana, April, 1905.

27. Bohmont, D. W.
Chemical Control of Poisonous Range Plants, Wyoming Agricultural Experiment Station, Bul. 313. April, 1952.

28. Bomhard, M. L.
"Leaf venation as a means of distinguishing Cicuta from Angelica." *Juorn. Wash. Acad. Sc.* 26(3):102-107, 1936.

29. Boorman, S.
Wild Plums in Brandy, McGraw-Hill Company of Canada, Ltd., Toronto, 1962. 176 pp.

30. Bourke, J. G.
"The Folk-foods of the Rio Grand Valley and of Northern Mexico," *Journal of American Folk-Lore* 8:41-71. 1895.

31. Brown, A. P.
Types of Greens or Potherbs Used in Utah Homes, Experiment Station Circular No. 104, 1934.

32. Brown, R.
"On the Vegetable Products Used by the Northwest American Indians, As Food and Medicine, in the Arts, and in Superstitious Rites," *Transcripts of the Botanical Society of Edinburgh* (1866-68) 9:378-396, May, 1868.

33. Brown, W. H.
Wild Food Plants of the Philippines, Minor Products of Philippine Forests Vol. II, Bul. No. 22, Department of Agriculture and Natural Resources. Bureau of Forestry, pp. 225-377. 1921.

34. Bruce, E. A.
"Iris Poisoning of Calves," *Journal of American Veterinary Medicine Association* (N.S. 9) 56:72-73, 1919.

35. Bryan, N. G. and S. Young
Navajo Native Dyes, Their Preparation and Use, Education Division Publication, U.S. Office of Indian Affairs, February, 1940.

36. Budrow, J. T.
Some Useful Native Plants of Colorado, The Courier Printing & Publishing Co., 1895.

37. Burgh, R. F. and C. R. Scoggin
University of Colorado Studies Series in Anthropology No. 2, The Archaeology of Castle Park Dinosaur National Monument, University of Colorado Press, Boulder, Colorado, October, 1948.

38. Cameron, L. C. R.
The Wild Foods of Great Britain. Where to Find Them and How to Cook Them, London, Geo. Routledge and Sons, Ltd., 1917.

39. Campa, A. L.
Piñon as an Economic and Social Factor, N. M. Business Rev. 1(4):144-147. 1932.

40. Campbell, J. B., R. W. Lodge and A. C. Budd
Poisonous Plants of the Canadian Prairies, Pub. 900, Research Branch, Canada Department of Agriculture, June, 1956.

41. Carpenter, T. M. & M. Steggerda
"The Food of the Present-day Navajo Indians of New Mexico and Arizona." *Journ. of Nutrition,* 18(3):297-305. Sept., 1939.

42. Carver, G. W.
Nature's Garden for Victory and Peace, Agricultural Research and Experiment Station, Tuskegee Institute Bull. No. 43, Tuskegee Institute, Alabama, March, 1942.

43. Castetter, E. F.
Uncultivated Native Plants Used as Sources of Food, Ethnobiological Studies in the American Southwest I, University of New Mexico Bulletin No. 266, Biological Series. Vol. 4, No. 1, pp. 1-62, May 15, 1935.

44. Castetter, E. F., W. H. Bell, and A. R. Grove
The Early Utilization and the Distribution of Agave in the American Southwest. Ethnobiological Studies in the American Southwest VI, University of New Mexico Bulletin, Biological Series 5, No. 4, pp. 1-92, Bulletin No. 335, Dec. 1, 1938. Albuquerque, Univ. of New Mexico Press.

45. Castetter, E. F. and M. E. Opler
The Ethnobiology of the Chiricahua and Mescalero Apache. The Use of Plants for Foods, Beverages and Narcotics, University of New Mexico Bulletin, Ethnobiological Studies Bulletin 297, Biological Series 4, No. 5:1-63. Nov. 15, 1936.

46. Castetter, E. F. and R. M. Underhill
The Ethnobiology of the Papago Indians. University of New Mexico Bulletin Ethnobiological Studies in the American Southwest II, Biological Series, Vol. 4, No. 3 Whole Number 275, October, 1935.

47. Castetter, E. F., and W. H. Bell
Pima and Papago Indian Agriculture, University of New Mexico Press, Albuquerque, 1942.

48. Chamberlain, L. S.
"Plants Used by the Indians of Eastern North America," *American Naturalist,* 35:1-10. 1901.

49. Chamberlin, R. V.
"The Ethno-botany of the Gosiute Indians of Utah," *Proceedings of the Academy of Natural Sciences of Philadelphia* 63:24-99, 1911.

50. Chamberlin, R. V.
"Some Plant Names of the Ute Indians," *American Anthropologist* 11:27-40, 1909.

51. Cheney, R. H.
"Tea Substitutes in the United States," *Journal of New York Botanical Garden* Vol. 42 (509):117-124. May, 1942.

52. Chestnut, V. K.
Plants Used by the Indians of Mendocino County, California, Contribution to U.S. Nat. Herbarium, Bul. VII, No. 3, 1902.

53. Clarkson, R. E.
Herbs: Their Culture and Uses, Macmillan Co., 1942.

54. Classen, P. W.
"A Possible New Source of Food Supply (Cat-tail Flour)," *Scientific Monthly* 9:179-185, 1919.

55. Clements, F. E. & E. S. Clements
Rocky Mountain Flowers, The H. W. Wilson Co., New York. 3d Ed. 1945.

56. Colyer, M.
"Observations on the Edible Native Plants of Southwestern Colorado" (Unpublished) 1962, 1963.

57. Confar, B.
Survival in the Nuclear Age, (X-2557) July 14, 1961.

58. Coon, N.
Using Wayside Plants, Hearthside Press Incorporated, New York, Third Revised Edition, 1960.

59. Core, E. L., J. H. Reitz and W. H. Gillespie
The Poisonous Plants of West Virginia, West Virginia Department of Agriculture, Charleston, no date.

60. Correa de Serra, J.
"Notice Respecting Several Vegetables Used as Esculents in North America," LXVII *Trans. Horticulture Society of London,* 4:443-446. 1892.

61. Coulter, J. and A. Nelson
New Manual of Botany of the Central Rocky Mountains (Vascular Plants), American Book Co., 1909.

62. Coville, F. V.
Some Additions to Our Vegetable Dietary, Yearbook of the United States Department of Agriculture 1895. pp. 205-214. Government Printing Office. Washington, D. C., 1896.

63. Coville, F. V.
Wokas, a Primitive Food of the Klamath Indians, U.S. Nat. Museum Report, 1902.

64. Coville, F. V.
Desert Plants as a Source of Drinking Water, Smithsonian Institute Annual Report 1903, pp. 499-505. 1904.

65. Coville, F. V.

"Notes on the Plants Used by the Klamath Indians of Oregon," *Contrib. U.S. National Herbarium,* 5(2):87-110, 1897.

66. Curtin, L. S. M.

By the Prophet of the Earth, Willard Hougland, United States of America, 1949.

67. Cushing, F. H.

Zuni Breadstuff, Indian Notes & Monographs, Vol. 8, N.Y. Museum of the American Indians, Heye Foundation. 1920.

68. Cutler, H. C.

"Exploration for Prehistoric Foods," *Missouri Botanical Garden Bulletin,* 34(8):205-209. October, 1946.

69. Dalgren, B. E. and P. C. Standley

Edible and Poisonous Plants of the Caribbean Region, Bureau of Medicine and Surgery, Navy Department, Government Printing Office, Washington: Superintendent of Documents, Washington, D. C., N 10.2:P 69. NAVMED 127. 1944.

70. Davidson, J.

"Douglas Fir Sugar," *The Canadian Field Naturalist,* 33(1):6-9. April, 1919.

71. Davis, R.

Flora of Idaho, Wm. D. Brown Co., Dubuque, Iowa, 1952. 828 pp.

72. Dawson, J. F.

Place Names in Colorado, J. Frank Dawson Publishing Co., Denver, Colorado, 1954.

73. Dayton, W. A.

Important Western Browse Plants, U.S. Dept. Agriculture Miscellaneous Publication 101, 1931.

74. Dayton, W. A. and others

Range Plant Handbook, United States Forest Service, 1937.

75. Densmore, F.

Uses of Plants by the Chippewa Indians, 44th Annual Report of the American Bureau of Ethnology 1926-27. pp. 275-397. U.S. Government Printing Office, Washington, D. C., 1928.

76. Dodge, J. R. (editor)

Food Products of the North American Indians, Report of the Commissioner of Agriculture for the Year 1870. pp. 404-428. Washington, D. C., Government Printing Office, 1871.

77. Dodge, N. N.

100 Desert Wildflowers in Natural Color, Southwestern Monuments Association, Globe, Arizona, 1963.

77A. Douglass, J. and M. Douglass

"Observations on Edible Native Plants of Colorado (Unpublished) 1961, 1962.

78. Durrell, L. W.

"Trip to Death Valley," Talk to Botany Seminar, Febraury 1, 1961.

79. Durrell, L. W., R. Jensen and B. Klinger
Poisonous and Injurious Plants in Colorado, Colorado Agricultural and Mechanical College, Bulletin 412A, January, 1952.

80. Dutcher, B. H.
"Piñon Gathering Among the Panamint Indians," *The American Anthropologist* 6:377-380. October, 1893.

81. Edwards, E. E. and W. D. Rasmussen
A Bibliography of the Agriculture of the American Indians, United States Department of Agriculture Miscellaneous Publication No. 237. Washington, D. C., January, 1942.

82. Ell, L.
"The Taste of Summer," *Outdoor Nebraska* 40(7):26-27, 32, July, 1962.

83. Elmore, F. H.
Ethnobotany of the Navajo, Albuquerque: University of New Mexico and School of American Research, 1944.

84. Fernald, M. L. and A. C. Kinsey
Revised by Reed C. Rollins
Edible Wild Plants of Eastern North America, 452 pp. Ill., Harper & Brothers, Publishers New York, revised ed. 1958.

85. Fewkes, J. W.
"A Contribution to Ethnobotany," *The American Anthropologist*, 9:14-21, January, 1896.

86. Fohn-Hansen, L.
Alaska Berries, Extension Bulletin F-11, University of Alaska and U.S.D.A., October, 1957 and 9th edition June, 1955.

87. Forde, C. D.
Ethnography of the Yuma Indians, University of California Publications in American Archaeology and Ethnology 28(4):83-278. December 12, 1931.

88. Fremont, J. C.
Memoirs of My Life, Vol. I. Belford, Clarke and Co. 1887.

89. Fremont, J. C. (edited by Allan Nevins)
Narratives of Exploration and Adventure, Longmans, Green & Co. New York, 1956.

90. Gaertner, E. E.
"Freezing, Preservation and Preparation of Some Edible Wild Plants of Ontario," *Economic Botany*, Vol. 16, No. 4, October-December, 1962.

91. Georgeson, C. C.
"The Economic Plants of Japan," *The American Garden*, Vol. XII and XIII, 1891 and 1892, respectively.

92. Gibbons, E.
Stalking the Wild Asparagus, David McKay Company, Inc. New York, 1962.

93. Gillespie, W. H.
A Compilation of the Edible Wild Plants of West Virginia, Press of Scholar's Library, New York, 1959.

94. Gilmore, M. R.
A Study in the Ethnobotany of the Omaha Indians, Collections of the Nebraska State Historical Society, 17:314-357, 1913.

95. Gilmore, M. R.
Uses of Plants by the Indians of the Missouri River Region, Annual Report of Bureau of American Ethnology, 1911-1912. pp. 43-154. Washington, D.C., Government Printing Office, 1919.

96. Gilmore, M. R.
Some Native Nebraska Plants with Their Uses by the Dakota, Coll. of the Nebraska State Historical Society 17:358-370. 1913.

97. Ginter, P. L.
Some Wild Plants Used by the American Indians, Paper delivered at Colorado-Wyoming Academy of Science, November 8, 1941. (Mimeo, Copy from author) Issued by the Forest Service, U.S.D.A. Denver, Nov. 27, 1941.

98. Goodding, L. N.
Notes on Native and Exotic Plants in Region 8 with Special Reference to Their Value in the Soil Conservation Program, U.S. Department of Agriculture, *Soil Conservation Service Bulletin* 247, 1938.

99. Gordon, E. L.
Wild Foods, Cornell Rural School Leaflet Vol. 36, No. 4, March, 1943. The New York State College of Agriculture at Cornell University, Ithaca, New York.

99A. Gordon, J.
Rose Recipes, Red Rose Publications, Woodstock, Vermont. 1959.

100. Gorman, M. W.
"Economic Botany of Southeastern Alaska," *Pittonia* (1896-98) 3:64-85, 1896.

101. Grant, A. L.
A Monograph of the Genus Mimulus, Washington University Doctoral Dissertations, Publications of Washington University Series V, St. Louis, 1924.

102. Grieve, M.
A Modern Herbal, (2 Vols.) Hafner Publishing Co., New York, 1959.

103. Grinnell, G. B.
The Cheyenne Indians: Their History and Ways of Life, Vol. 2 Yale University Press, New Haven, 1923.

104. Gunther, R. T.
The Greek Herbal of Dioscorides, Hafner Publishing Co., New York. 1959.

105. Hagan, W. A.
"Bracken Poisoning in Cattle," *The Cornell Veterinarian* 15(3):326-332, 1927.

106. Hagan, W. A. and A. Zeissig
"Experiment Bracken Poisoning of Cattle," *The Cornell Veterinarian* 17:194-208. 1927.

107. Hardy, G. A.
Fifty Edible Plants of British Columbia, Provincial Museum of Natural

History and Anthropology, Victoria British Columbia (Brit. Col. Prov. Mus.) Handbook, No. 1, 1942.

108. Hare, R. F. & D. Griffiths
The Tuna as Food for Man, Bulletin 64, New Mexico College of Agriculture and Mechanical Arts, April, 1907, Agriculture Experiment Station Bulletin.

109. Harrington, H. D.
Manual of the Plants of Colorado, Sage Books, Denver, Colorado, 1954.

110. Harrington, H. D.
How to Identify Plants, Sage Books, Denver, Colorado, 1957.

111. Harrington, H. D. and L. W. Durrell
Colorado Ferns and Fern Allies, Colorado Agricultural Research Foundation at Colorado Agricultural and Mechanical College, Fort Collins, Colorado, 1950.

112. Harris, B. C.
Eat the Weeds, The author, Worcester, Mass., 1955 (new ed. 1961).

113. Haskin, L. L.
"A Frontier Food, Ipo or Yampa, Sustained the Pioneers," *Nature Magazine* 14:171-172, 1929.

114. Havard, V.
"Drink Plants of the North American Indians," *Torrey Botanical Club Bulletin* 23(2):33-46, 1896.

115. Havard, V.
"Food Plants of the North American Indians," *Torrey Botanical Club Bulletin* 22(3):98-123, 1895.

116. Havard, V.
"The Mesquite," *The American Naturalist* 18(5):451-459. May, 1884.

117. Hedrick, U. P. (editor)
Sturtevant's Notes on Edible Plants, N. Y. Dept. Agri. Annual Report XXVII 2(2), J. B. Lyon, Albany, 1919.

118. Heiser, C. B., Jr.
"The Sunflower Among the North American Indians," *American Philosophical Society*, Vol. 95, No. 4, August, 1951.

119. Heller, C. A.
Edible & Poisonous Plants of Alaska, University of Alaska, 1953.

120. Herter, G. L. & J. P. Herter
Professional Guide's Manual, Herters, Inc. Third edition, Waseca, Minnesota, 1961.

121. Hill, C. C.
Spring Flowers of the Lower Columbia Valley, University of Washington Press, Seattle, 1958.

122. Hill, J.
Wild Foods of Britain, Third ed., 4, 5 & 6 Soho Square, London W. I., A. and C. Black, 1944.

123. Hodge, F. W.
Handbook of the American Indians North of Mexico, Bulletin of Bureau of American Ethnology, Smithsonian Institute Bulletin 30, Washington, D.C., part I, 1907.

124. Hoffman, I. B.
The Book of Herb Cookery, Houghton Mifflin Co., Boston, Mass., 1940.

125. Holmes, G. K.
Aboriginal Agriculture—The American Indians, In Cyclopedia of American Agriculture, edited by L. H. Bailey, 4:24-39. New York, Macmillan Co., 1909.

126. Holmgren, A. H.
Handbook of the Vascular Plants of the Northern Wasatch, Lithotype Process Co., San Francisco, Calif., 2nd edition, 1959.

127. Hopkins, M.
"Wild Plants Used in Cookery," *New York Botanical Garden Journal* 43:71-75, 1942.

128. Hough, W.
"The Hopi in Relation to Their Plant Environment," *The American Anthropologist* 10(2):33-44. February, 1897.

129. Hussey, P. B.
A Taxonomic List of Some Plants of Economic Importance, The Science Press Printing Company, Lancaster, Pennsylvania, 1939.

130. Indian Children
Indians at Work, Special Childrens' Number by Indian Children, Office of Indian Affairs, Washington, D.C.

131. Jacobson, C. A.
Water Hemlock (Cicuta), Nevada Agricultural Experiment Station Technical Bulletin 81, March, 1915.

132. Jaeger, E.
Wildwood Wisdom, Macmillan, 1946.

133. Jencks, Z.
"A Note on the Carbohydrates of the Root of the Cat-tail (Typha latifolia)," *Proceedings of the Society for Experimental Biology and Medicine* 17(2):45-46, November 19, 1919.

134. Johnson, C. P.
The Useful Plants of Great Britain: A treatise upon the principal native vegetables capable of application as food, medicine, or in the arts and manufactures, London, Wm. Kent & Co., Paternoster Row, 1862.

135. Johnson, J. R.
Anyone Can Live Off the Land, Longmans, Green & Co., New York, N.Y., 122 pp., 1961.

136. Jones, V. H.
Appendix in R. F. Burgh and C. R. Scoggin, The Archaeology of Castle Park Dinosaur National Monument, University of Colorado Studies in Anthropology 2, 1948.

137. Jones, V. H.
"An Ancient Food Plant of the Southwest and Plateau Regions," *El Palacio* 44(5&6):41-53. February, 1938.

138. Kearney, T. H. and R. H. Peebles
Arizona Flora, University of California Press, Berkeley and Los Angeles, 1951 (2nd edition with supplement, 1960).

139. Kelsey, H. P. and W. A. Dayton
Standardized Plant Names, second edition. J. Horace McFarland Company Harrisburg, Pa., 1942. For American Joint Committee on Horticultural Nomenclature.

140. Kephart, H.
The Book of Camping and Woodcraft, Chap. XVII "Edible Plants of the Wilderness." New York, The Century Co., 1909 and later eds.

141. Kingsbury, J. M.
Poisonous Plants of the United States and Canada, Prentice-Hall, Inc. Englewood Cliffs, New Jersey, 1964.

142. Klein, W.
Personal letter to author. Sept. 11, 1963.

143. Lampman, B. H.
"Savage Gardens, Nature's Crop for Her Nut-Brown Children," *Nature Magazine* 12:32-34, July, 1928.

144. Lechler, G.
Nutrition of Paleolithic Man, Papers of the Michigan Academy of Science Arts and Letters 30:499-510, 1944.

145. Leslie, W. R.
Native Fruits of Manitoba, South Dakota State Horticulture Society Annual Report, pp. 225-236, 1915.

146. Littlebee, C. (compiled by W. O. Nagel)
Cy Littlebee's Guide to Cooking Fish and Game, Missouri Conservation Commission, 1960.

147. Loudon, D. and H. B. Spencer
Jellies, Jams, Marmalades and Pickles, North Dakota Agricultural College Extension Circular No. 64, pp. 1-19, 1924.

148. Lowman, M. S. and M. Birdseye
Savory Herbs: Culture and Use, Farmers' Bulletin No. 1977 U.S. Department of Agriculture, Washington, D.C., May, 1946.

149. Maiden, J. H.
The Useful Plants of Australia, Turner and Henderson: Sydney, 1889.

150. Maisch, J. M.
"Useful Plants of the Genus *Psoralea,*" *American Pharm. Journal* 61:345-352, 1889.

151. Mal'tsew, A. I.
"The Use of Weeds and Other Wild Plants," *Bulletin of Applied Botany and Plant Breeding* 13(3):85-89, 1922-1923, (In Russian)

152. Marsh, C. D. and A. B. Clawson
The Death Camas species Zygadenus paniculatus and Z. elegans as Poisonous Plants, U.S. Department of Agriculture Bulletin 1012. April 17, 1922.

153. Marsh, C. D. and A. B. Clawson
Meadow Death Camas (Zygadenus venenosus) as a Poisonous Plant, U.S. Department of Agriculture Bulletin 1240, 1940.

154. Marsh, C. D., G. C. Roe and A. B. Clawson
Rayless Goldenrod (Aplopappus heterphyllus) as a Poisonous Plant, U.S. Department of Agricultural Bulletin 1391. 1926.

155. Marsh, C. D., A. B. Clawson and G. C. Roe
Nuttall's Death Camas (Zygadenus nuttallii) as a Poisonous Plant, U.S.D.A. Bulletin No. 1376. Washington, D.C. February, 1926.

156. Matsumura Y. and H. D. Harrington
The True Aquatic Vascular Plants of Colorado, Technical Bulletin 57, Colorado Agricultural Experimental Station, Colorado Agricultural and Mechanical College, Fort Collins, Colorado, 1955.

157. Matthews, W.
"Navaho Names and Uses for Plants," *The American Naturalist* 20(9):767-777, 1886.

157A. May, J.
"Observations on Native Edible Plants of Colorado" (Unpublished), 1963.

158. Medsger, O. P.
Edible Wild Plants, New York, Macmillan Co., 1939. Intro. by Ernest Thompson Seton, 1945.

159. Merriam, C. H.
"The Acorn, a Possibly Neglected Source of Food," *National Geographic Magazine* 34(2):129-137, 1918.

160. Merrill, E. D.
Emergency Food Plants and Poisonous Plants of the Islands of the Pacific, United States War Department Technical Manual TM 10-420. U.S. Government Printing Office, Washington, D.C., 1943, April 15.

161. Merrill, E. D.
Plant Life of the Pacific World, Macmillan Co. New York, 1945.

162. Meserve, M. F.
"Some Edible Wild Plants of Colorado and Nebraska," (Unpublished) January 27, 1961.

163. Morrell, J. M. H.
"Some Maine Plants and Their Uses 'wise and otherwise'," *Rhodora* 3(29):129-132. May, 1901.

164. Morton, J. F.
"Principal Wild Food Plants of the United States," *Economic Botany* 17(4):319-330. Oct.-Dec., 1963.

165. Morton, J. F.
"Spanish Needles (Bidens pilosa L.) as a Wild Food Resource," *Economic Botany* 16(3):173-179. July-September, 1962.

166. Morton, J. F.
Wild Plants for Survival in South Florida, Hurricane House, Miami, Florida, 1963.

167. Muenscher, W. C.
Poisonous Plants of the United States, Macmillan, revised edition, 1961.

168. Muenscher, W. C. & M. A. Rice
Garden Spice & Wild Pot-herbs, Comstock Publishing Associates, a division of Cornell University Press. Ithaca, New York, 1955.

169. MacDougall, W. B.
Plants of the Grand Canyon National Park, Bulletin No. 10, January, Grand Canyon Natural History Association, Grand Canyon, Arizona, 1947.

170. McDougall, W. B. & H. A. Baggley
Plants of Yellowstone National Park, 2nd edition. Yellowstone Interpretive Series No. 8. Yellowstone Library & Museum Association Yellowstone Park, Wyoming, 1956.

171. McKelvey, S. D.
Yuccas of Southwestern United States parts 1 (1938) and 2 (1947), Arnold Arboretum of Harvard University, Jamaica Plain, Mass.

172. Navajo Group Eight
Indian Recipes, no date or citation.

173. Neguatewa, E.
"Some Hopi Recipes for the Preparation of Wild Plant Foods," *Plateau* 16(1):18-20. Flagstaff: Museum of Northern Arizona, 1943.

174. Newberry, J. S.
"Food and Fiber Plants of the North American Indians," *Popular Scientific Monthly* 32:31-46. 1887.

175. Ney, L. F.
Gas Exchange by Plants of the Duckweed Family, Final Report, Stanford Research Institute. April 21, pp. 1-19, 1960.

176. Norton, C.
"Would You Starve?" *Nature Magazine* 35(6):295-297, 1942.

177. Ormond, C.
Complete Book of Outdoor Lore, Outdoor Life—Harper & Row, New York, 1964.

178. Osborne, D.
"Solving the Riddles of Wetherill Mesa," *National Geographic* 125(2):155-195. February, 1964.

179. Oswald, F. W.
The Beginner's Guide to Useful Plants of Eastern Wilds, Anderson Press, 73 Wagaraw Road, Hawthorne, N. J., 1956.

180. Palmer, E. L.
"The Berries of *Rhamnus croceus* as Indian Food," *American Naturalist* 8:247, 1874.

181. Palmer, E. L.
Fieldbook of Natural History, McGraw-Hill Book Company, Inc. New York: Toronto, 1949.

182. Palmer, E.
Food Products of the American Indians, U.S.D.A. Report 1870:404-428. 1871.

183. Palmer, E.
"Plants Used by the Indians of the United States," *American Naturalist* 12:593-606, 646-655. 1878.

184. Penhallow, D. P.
"Note on a few of the Useful Plants of Northern Japan," *American Naturalist,* Vol. XVI, 1882.

185. Perez-Llano, G. A.
Lichens Their Biological and Economic Significance, "Lichens Used as Food by Man," *The Botanical Review,* 10(1):33-36, January, 1944.

186. Pesman, M. W.
Meet the Natives, 5th edition, 372 S. Humboldt St., Denver, Colorado, 1952.

187. Porsild, A. E.
"Edible Plants of the Arctic," *Journal of the Arctic Institute of North America* 6(1):15-34. March, 1953.

188. Porter, C. L.
Contributions Toward a Flora of Wyoming, In numbered leaflets. University of Wyoming, Laramie, Wyoming. (Various dates—unfinished to 1966).

189. Powers, S.
"Aboriginal Botany," *Proceedings of the California Academy of Sciences* 5:373, 1873.

190. Reagan, A. B.
"Plants Used by the Bois Fort Chippewa (Ojibwa) Indians of Minnesota," *The Wisconsin Archaeologist* 7(4):230-248. July, 1928.

191. Reagan, A. B.
"Plants Used by the Hoh and Quileute Indians," *Transactions of the Kansas Academy of Science* 37:55-70. 1934.

192. Reagan, A. B.
"Plants Used by the White Mountain Apache of Arizona," *The Wisconsin Archaeologist* 8(4):143-161. July, 1929.

193. Reagan, A. B.
"Various Uses of Plants by West Coast Indians," *Washington Historical Quarterly* 25:133-137, April, 1934.

194. Rexford, O.
101 Useful Weeds and Wildings, Rexford, 1942.

195. Robbins, W. W., J. P. Harrington and B. Freire-Marreco
"Ethnobotany of the Tewa Indians," *Smithsonian Institute Bureau of American Ethnology* Bulletin 55:1-124, 1916.

196. Robbins, W. W. and F. Ramaley
Plants Useful to Man, P. Blakiston's Son & Co., Inc., Philadelphia. The Maple Press Company, York, Pa., 1933.

197. Rose, J. N.
"Notes on Useful Plants of Mexico," U.S. National Museum, *Contribution to United States National Herbarium* 5:209-259, 1899.

198. Rusby, H. H.
"Wild Foods of the United States," *Country Life.* Garden City, N.Y. April, 1906, pp. 718, 752-754; November, 1906, pp. 82-94; February, 1907, pp. 456-458; March, 1907, pp. 546.

199. Russell, F.
The Pima Indians, 26th Annual Report of the Bureau of American Ethnology, (1908):3-391, Washington, D.C., Government Printing Office, 1908.

200. Rydberg, P. A.
Flora of the Rocky Mountains and Adjacent Plains, Colorado, Utah, Wyoming, Idaho, Montana, Saskatchewan, Alberta & Neighboring Parts of Nebraska, South Dakota, North Dakota & British Columbia. Pub. by the author, New York. 2nd ed. 1922.

201. Rydberg, P. A.
Flora of the Prairies and Plains of Central North America, New York Botanical Garden, New York, 1932.

202. Sargent, F. L.
Plants and Their Uses, Holt, 1913.

203. Saunders, C. F.
"The Yucca and the Indian," *The American Botanist* 17(1):1-3. February, 1911.

204. Saunders, C. F.
Useful Wild Plants of the United States and Canada, New York, Robert M. McBride & Co., 1920 revised edition Jan., 1926, pp. 275.

205. Scott, A. B.
"In These Days of High Prices: Foods that cost us nothing," *The Ladies Home Journal,* p. 44. June, 1917.

206. Sears, W. C.
"Project in Edible Plants," (Unpublished manuscript.) June 8, 1961.

207. Sievers, A. F.
Production of Drug and Condiment Plants, Farmers' Bulletin No. 1999 U.S. Department of Agriculture, Washington, D.C., December, 1948.

208. Smith, H. H.
"Ethnobotany of the Forest Potawatomi Indians," *Bulletin of the Public Museum of the City of Milwaukee* 7(1):1-230. May, 1933.

209. Smith, H. H.
"Ethnobotany of the Meskwaki Indians," *Bulletin of the Public Museum of the City of Milwaukee* 4(2):175-326. 1928.

210. Smith, H. H.
"Ethnobotany of the Menomini Indians," *Bulletin of the Public Museum of the City of Milwaukee* 4(1):1-174. 1923.

211. Smith, H. H.
"Ethnobotany of the Ojibwe Indians," *Bulletin of the Public Museum of the City of Milwaukee.* 4(3):327-525.

212. Snow, C. R.
"Vegetables of the Alaska Wilderness," *The Alaska Sportsman* 1(4):6-8, 28-29. April, 1935.

212A. Sopher, M. (Editor)
Encyclopedia of European Cooking, Spring Books, London. 1962.

213. Spinden, H. J.
"The Nez Perce Indians," *Memoirs of the American Anthropological Association* 2:165-274, 1908.

214. Standley, Paul C.
Edible Plants of the Arctic Region, Bureau of Medicine and Surgery, Dept. of Navy, U.S. Government Printing Office, Washington, D.C., 1943.

215. Standley, Paul C.
Some Useful Plants of New Mexico, Annual Report of the Smithsonian Institute, pp. 447-462, Government Printing Office, Washington, D.C., 1912.

216. Standley, Paul C.
Trees and Shrubs of Mexico, Contribution to the U.S. National Herbarium 23(1920-1926):1-1721.

217. Steedman, E. V. (editor) (based on field notes of J. A. Teit)
Ethnobotany of the Thompson Indians of British Columbia, Forty-fifth Annual Report of the Bureau of American Ethnology to the Secretary of the Smithsonian Institution 1927-1928:441-522. 1930.

218. Steggerda, M. & R. B. Eckardt
"Navajo Foods and Their Preparation," *Journal of the American Dietetic Association* 17(3):217-225. March, 1941.

219. Stevens, W. C.
Kansas Wild Flowers, University of Kansas Press, Lawrence, 1948.

220. Stevenson, M. C.
Ethnobotany of the Zuni Indians, Thirtieth Annual Report of the Bureau of American Ethnology 1908-1909:31-102. 1915.

221. Stone, G. E.
Edible Weeds and Pot Herbs, Mass. State Board of Agriculture Nature Leaflet, No. 19. August 7, 1907.

222. Storer, F. H.
"A Record of Analysis of Several Weeds that are Occasionally Used as Human Food," *Bulletin of the Bussey Institution* 2(2):115-129. 1877.

223. Stout, A. B.
"Gum-jum or Gum-tsoy: A food from the flowers of daylilies," *Journal of the New York Botanical Garden* 34(401):97-100. May, 1933.

224. Stout, A. B.
"Vegetable Foods of the American Indians," *New York Botanical Garden Journal* 15(171):50-60. March, 1914.

225. Stratton, R.
Edible Wild Greens and Salads of Oklahoma, Bulletin of Oklahoma Agricultural and Mechanical College 40(2):1-29. January, 1943. Oklahoma A. & M. College, Stillwater, Oklahoma.

Sturdevant (See Hedrick, U. P.)

226. Survival Training Edition
AF Manual 64-3, Department of the Air Force, Washington, D.C. February, 1956.

227. Sweet, M.
Common Edible and Useful Plants of the West, Naturegraph Company, Healdsburg, California, 1962.

228. Szczawinsky, A. F. and G. A. Hardy
Guide to the Common Edible Plants of British Columbia, British Columbia Provincial Museum, Department of Recreation and Conservation Handbook No. 20. Victoria, B.C., April, 1962.

229. Taylor, G. M.
British Herbs and Vegetables, Collins, London, England, 1947.

230. Thomson, R. B., and H. B. Sifton
A Guide to the Poisonous Plants and Weed Seeds of Canada and the Northern United States, University of Toronto Press. 1922.

231. Thorpe, F., Jr., A. W. Deem, H. D. Harrington, and J. W. Tobiska
Suckleya suckleyana, a Poisonous Plant, Colorado Agricultural Experiment Station Technical Bulletin No. 22, 1937.

232. Tidestrom, I.
Flora of Utah and Nevada, Contr. U.S. Herbarium, Government Printing Office, Washington, D.C., Vol. 25, 1925.

233. Tidestrom, I. and Sister T. Kittell
A Flora of Arizona and New Mexico, The Catholic University of America Press, Washington, D.C. 1941.

234. Trimble, H.
"Some Indian Food Plants," *The American Journal of Pharmacy* 60:593-595; 61:4-6, 556-558; 62:281-282, 598-600; 63:525-527. 1888-1891.

235. Thwaites, R. G.
Early Western Travels, Arthur H. Clark Co., Cleveland, Ohio 1905 Vol. XV. Part II of James account of S. H. Long's Expedition. 1819, 1820.

236. Turney-High, H.
"Cooking Camass and Bitterroot," *Scientific Monthly* 36:262-263. 1933.

237. Underhill, R.
Indians of the Pacific Northwest, U.S. Department of the Interior Bureau of Indian Affairs. Branch of Education, Washington, D.C. 1944.

238. Underhill, R.
Workaday Life of the Pueblos, U.S. Indian Service, Department of the Interior. Indian Life & Customs—4. May, 1946.

239. Underhill, R.
Here Come the Navajo! Indian Life and Customs, United States Indian Service. No date.

240. Uphof, J. C. T.
Dictionary of Economic Plants, Published by H. R. Engelman (J. Cramer) New York Hafner Publishing Co., 1959.

241. Verrill, A. H.
Foods America Gave the World, Boston, L. C. Page & Co., 1937.

242. Vestal, P. A. and R. E. Schultes
The Economic Botany of the Kiowa Indians, Botanical Museum, Cambridge, Mass., 1939.

243. Vliet, R.
A Manual of Woodslore Survival as Developed at Philmont or "How to Eat Weeds and Like Em," Tribune Press, Springer, New Mexico (no date).

244. Ward, A.
The Encyclopedia of Food, The Baker and Taylor Company, New York, 1929.

245. Waugh, F. A.
Salad Plants and Plant Salads, Vermont Agriculture Experiment Station Bulletin 54, 1896.

246. Weber, W. A.
Handbook of Plants of the Colorado Front Range, University of Colorado Press, Boulder, Colorado (revised 2nd printing, Feb. 1961).

247. Wherry, E. T.
"Go Slow on Eating Fern Fiddleheads," *American Fern Journal* 32(3):108-109. 1942.

248. White, L. A.
"Notes on the Ethnobotany of the Keres," *Papers of the Michigan Academy of Science Arts and Letters* 30:557-568. 1944.

249. Whiting, A. F.
Ethnobotany of the Hopi, Museum of Northern Arizona Bulletin 15, 1939.

250. Wilks, S. S.
Preliminary Report on the Photosynthetic Gas Exchange Potentialities of the Family Lemnaceae (Duckweed), Biologistics for Space Systems Symposium AMRL-TDR-62-116. 6570th Aerospace Medical Research Laboratories, Wright-Patterson AFB, Ohio, October, 1962. pp. 256-278.

251. Williams, L. O.
Drug and Condiment Plants, Agricultural Handbook No. 172, Agricultural Research Service, U.S. Department of Agriculture, Washington, D.C., April, 1960.

252. Wilson, T.

"The Use of Wild Plants as Food by Indians," *The Ottawa Naturalist* 30(2):17-21. May, 1916.

253. Wittrock, M. A. and G. L. Wittrock

"Food Plants of the Indians," *New York Botanical Garden Journal* 43(507):57-71. March, 1942.

254. Wooton, E. O. and P. C. Standley

Flora of New Mexico, Contr. from the U.S. National Herbarium 19, Smithsonian Institute, 1915.

255. Yanovsky, E.

Food Plants of the North American Indians, U.S.D.A. Misc. Publication 237:1-83. 1936.

256. Yanovsky, E. and R. M. Kingsbury

"Analyses of Some Indian Food Plants," *Journal of the Association of Official Agricultural Chemists* 21(4):648-655. Contribution 138 from the Carbohydrate Research Division, Bureau of Chemistry and Soils, U.S. Department of Agriculture. Nov., 1938.

257. Yanovsky, E., E. K. Nelson and R. M. Kingsbury

"Berries Rich in Calcium," *Science* n.s. 75:565-566, May 27, 1932.

258. Yaeger, A. F., E. Latzke and D. Berrigan

The Native Fruits of North Dakota and Their Use, Agricultural Exp. Station, North Dakota Agricultural College, Fargo, North Dakota, Bulletin 281, April, 1935.

259. Young, S.

Native Plants Used by the Navajo, Mimeographed copy, Home Economics Department, Wingate Vocational High School, Fort Wingate, New Mexico U.S. Department of Interior, Office of Indian Affairs, 1938.

INDEX

Index to Scientific Names

Index to Common Names